## DATE DUE

BRODART, CO.                    Cat. No. 23-221

# Reason in Philosophy

# Reason in Philosophy

*Animating Ideas*

Robert B. Brandom

The Belknap Press of Harvard University Press

Cambridge, Massachusetts · London, England

2009

*Library of Congress Cataloging-in-Publication Data*

Brandom, Robert, 1950–
Reason in philosophy : animating ideas / Robert B. Brandom.
p.   cm.
Includes bibliographical references and index.
ISBN 978-0-674-03449-5 (alk. paper)
1. Rationalism.   2. Reason.   3. Philosophy, Modern.   I. Title.

B833.B65 2009
149′.7—dc22        2008052244

*This one is for Barbara.*

*Thirty-six years of loving marriage make a fine beginning.*

# Contents

# Acknowledgments

The work reported in these pages was generously supported by the Andrew W. Mellon Foundation, through a Distinguished Achievement in the Humanities Award. Chapter Four was originally published in *What Is Philosophy?*, ed. C. P. Ragland and Sarah Heidt (New Haven: Yale University Press, 2001), 74–95. Chapter Seven was originally published in *New Directions in Artificial Intelligence*, vol. 2, ed. Eero Hyvönen, Jouko Seppänen, and Markku Syrjänen, STeP-92 Tekoälyn uudet suunat, Publications of the Finnish Artificial Intelligence Society (FAIS), 1992. Reprinted in *Mind and Cognition: Philosophical Perspectives into Cognitive Science and AI*, ed. Leila Haaparanta and Sara Heinämaa, *Acta Philosophica Fennica* 58 (1995): 16–35.

# Introduction

This book belongs to a venerable tradition that distinguishes *us* as rational animals, and *philosophy* by its concern to understand, articulate, and explain the notion of *reason* that is thereby cast in that crucial demarcating role. We may call this line of thought "philosophical rationalism." Rationalism of this stripe was not much in favor in Anglophone circles during the last century or so. The predominant tendency in analytic philosophy has been strongly empiricist, at least since Ayer and Carnap. The American pragmatism of James and Dewey defined itself by opposition to a pernicious rationalistic intellectualism. Both those movements, and their heirs in the second half of the twentieth century, were properly recoiling from Cartesian non-naturalism about human minds, knowledge, and agency.

The rationalism that is articulated, motivated, and explored in these pages looks back to Kant and Hegel as its forebears, and to Descartes, Spinoza, and Leibniz only as their deepest lessons came to be understood within that German Idealist tradition. Of course all the figures I invoked in the previous paragraph were reacting against what they understood of that German Idealist tradition, too. (If anything was worse than rationalism, it had to be idealism.) But I think Kant and Hegel showed us a way forward for a rationalism that is not objectionably Cartesian, intellectual-

*1*

ist, or anti- (or super-)naturalist. (Nor need it treat the "light of reason" as unacquired or innate.) Recovering the possibility of such a progressive rationalism requires reappropriating central thoughts of Kant and Hegel, disentangling them from the adventitious accretions and subsequent folklore that have grown up so thick around them as almost totally to obscure them. The aim of this book is to make a start on that enterprise, on sketching the sort of rationalism about mind and meaning that emerges from doing so, and on doing that in a way that makes evident its promise and utility for addressing a variety of important philosophical issues that matter to us today.

One of the master ideas pursued here is that <u>rationality</u> is a *normative* concept. In one sense, this is not at all a surprising claim. One can be more or less rational. And other things being equal, more is better. One might object that 'reasonable' and 'rational' are not synonyms in English. Being relentlessly, excessively, or inappropriately rational can be a way of being *un*reasonable. (Just ask anyone who lives with a philosopher!) Perhaps it is better to be more reasonable than to be more rational. But even so, and even though these are different dimensions of normative appraisal, judgments of how rational a belief, commitment, action, or person is do nonetheless have normative consequences. They are relevant to assessments of whether things are as they ought to be, and of what ought or ought not to have been done. (The fact that nonnormative descriptions may provide sufficient reasons for distinguishing more from less rational conduct does not speak against the normative significance of such discrimination. Calling something a "good knife" may be wholly warranted by its satisfying such descriptions as "sharp," "durable," and "firmly grippable." It is still a normative characterization.)

This evaluative or comparative normative dimension of rationality rests on a conceptually prior constitutive one. The constitutive issue concerns whether one is a rational creature at all (something that does not come in degrees), rather than whether one is better or worse, more or less reliable, at doing what rational beings as such do. To be a rational being in this sense is to be subject to a distinctive kind of normative appraisal:

assessment of the *reasons* for what one does—in the sense of "doing" that is marked off by its liability to just that sort of appraisal. Rational beings are ones that *ought* to have reasons for what they do, and *ought* to act as they have reason to. They are subjects of rational obligations, prohibitions, and permissions.

It is only creatures that are in the space of reasons in this sense—ones for whom the question of what attitudes they have reason to adopt and what they have reason to do arises, or to whom demands for reasons are appropriately addressed—that are then further assessable as to how *sensitive* they are in fact to their reasons, how good they are at actually doing what they have the best reason to do. Constitutive appraisals of rationality are not *wholly* independent of evaluative appraisals. If some creature *never* acts as it has reason to, is *entirely* unmoved by reasons, is *completely* insensitive to relations of rational consequence and incompatibility among its attitudes, goals, and performances, there might simply be no point in holding it rationally responsible, in treating it as a rational agent and knower at all. Still, there is no definite threshold of heedlessness to reasons that in principle precludes assessment of reasons—of what someone is rationally committed or entitled to.

Taking something to be subject to appraisals of its reasons, holding it rationally responsible, is treating it as some*one:* as one of *us* (rational beings). This normative attitude toward others is *recognition,* in the sense of Hegel's central notion of Anerkennung (discussed in the second chapter of Part One). Adopting that attitude is acknowledging a certain kind of *community* with the one recognized. It is the fellowship of those we acknowledge not only as *sentient* (a factual matter of biology), but also as *sapient* (a normative matter of responsibility and authority). It is attributing a kind of rational personhood, treating others as *selves,* in the sense of knowers and agents, ones who are *responsible* for their doings and attitudes. What they are principally responsible for is having reasons for those doings and attitudes.

The core of the notion of <u>recognition</u> is the idea that normative statuses such as rational responsibility and authority (commitment and entitlement) are fundamentally *social* statuses. They are in principle unintelligible apart from consideration of the practical attitudes of those who *hold* each other responsible, *acknowledge* each other's authority, *attribute* commitments and entitlements to one another. Because the space of reasons is a *normative* space, it is a *social* space.

Not all norms are rational norms. What is it for it to be *reasons* that one is sometimes obliged or responsible for having, that some sort of authority is conditioned on? The answer developed here understands reasons in terms of *inferences*. Reasons are construed as *premises,* from which one can draw *conclusions.* Although this is, I think, a natural enough approach, it is worth noticing that it is not obligatory. Work is required to wrestle our talk of reasons around into inferential shape. If I am asked why I stacked the flowerpots next to the wall, I may reply "Because she asked me to." That is giving a reason. But it is not immediately clear what relation it bears to any inference. Indeed, when any *fact* is cited as a reason (whether as the justification of a cognitive or a practical commitment), a story would need to be told about how that fact is supposed to be understood to show up as a *premise* in some inference. Inferring is reasoning, but there may be other kinds of reasoning besides inferring. Activities such as making distinctions or comparisons, exploring analogies and disanalogies, conceptual construction and analysis also seem to be kinds of reasoning. It is at least not obvious that they should be either assimilated to or understood in terms of inference. Even in the light of these considerations, I am concerned to see what sort of story can be told, what sort of illumination one can get, by focusing to begin with on the central inferential kind of reasons and the dimension of reasoning they pick out.

One important issue in the vicinity concerns the *semantic* presuppositions of one's account of reasoning and rationality. A methodological fork in the road is marked out by whether one is prepared to take for granted the *meaning* or *content* of whatever serves as or stands in need of reasons. One program that is committed to this order of explanation is rational choice theory (for instance, in its paradigmatic decision-theoretic and game-theoretic forms). It assumes as inputs probabilities and utilities assigned to definite propositionally contentful possible states of affairs. These are part of the specification of the choice situation. It then yields as outputs verdicts about the comparative rationality of various choices and strategies. An explanatory strategy of this shape assumes that the semantic contents of states such as beliefs and desires, contents that can be expressed by declarative sentences, can be settled independently and in advance of thinking about their role in reasoning. It then addresses questions of the form: what conclusions (practical and theoretical) do commitments of this sort rationally entitle us to? How good are the reasons they give us to do or think one thing rather than another?

Rational choice theory has no indigenous semantics. It outsources that job. Such a division of theoretical labor makes sense, so long as the assumption of independence it presupposes is well-founded. But what if it is not? What if the questions of what a sentence means and what its role in reasoning is are two sides of one coin, needing to be addressed together? Then a different methodological strategy is called for.[1] The broadly Carnapian picture has two stages: semantic and epistemic. First, *meanings* must be fixed: a language. Then, and on that basis, *beliefs* are to be settled: a theory, what sentences with those meanings one has reason to endorse or commit oneself to. This procedure makes sense for artificial languages, but it is arguable that for natural languages there is no way to separate the semantic and the epistemic tasks—not just in practice, but in principle. An alternative Quinean approach does not attempt to address the question of what is a reason for what, independently of the question of what we have reason to believe. The semantic and epistemic dimensions of thought and language use are not only understood as inextricably intertwined, their common structure is the *inferential* articulation characteristic of the space of reasons. In this picture, <u>justification</u> (and so its cousins <u>reason</u> and <u>inference</u>) is not only a key concept in epistemological investigations of the nature of *knowledge,* but also and equally a key concept in semantic investigations of the nature of *meaning.*

Another potentially illuminating broad-brushstroke sketch of a historical path that led to the same constellation of ideas portrays it as the culmination of a three-phase process. The classical American pragmatists were properly impressed by the role beliefs play in the explanation of action. With admirable theoretical ambition, they accordingly tried out the idea that one could not only deduce what people *believe* from what they *do,* but also understand the *concept* of <u>belief</u> (including the *contents* of those

---

1. I have expressed similar concerns about the parallel semantic assumptions implicit in reliabilist epistemologies. See Chapter Three of *Articulating Reasons* (Cambridge, MA: Harvard University Press, 2000).

beliefs) wholly in terms of the concept of <u>agency</u>. The line of thought that issued in contemporary rational choice theory saw that this could not be right. What people do depends not only on what they *believe,* but also on what they *want.* Intentional actions (they were less concerned than the pragmatists with habitual ones) are to be explained by appeal to beliefs *and* desires, preferences, or some other sort of pro-attitude. (I would prefer to say: "by appeal to *practical* as well as *cognitive* commitments.") The pragmatists show up as having taken for granted a background of needs and wants that played no explicit role in their theorizing. But since beliefs can be held constant and actions varied by varying the accompanying goals,[2] it can be seen that a more articulated scheme is required. Manifesting the same admirable theoretical ambition as the pragmatists, some rational choice theorists likewise proposed turning this model of the explanation of action around and both inferring subjective probabilities and preferences from choice behavior and understanding the notions of <u>probability</u> and <u>preference</u> in terms of their role in explaining choice behavior. The third, Davidsonian phase of this development then consists in pointing out that unless one excludes *verbal* behavior from the scope of one's explanatory ambitions (a drastic, unmotivated, and unnecessary restriction—one that would be particularly bizarre for a theory aimed at *rational* agency), a *third* factor that is being taken for granted is the *meanings* expressed by the sentences the agent utters, including those by which he makes his beliefs and preferences explicit. For once again we could hold fixed an agent's subjective probabilities and preferences and change what she would say and do (for instance, in response to the utterances of others) by varying the meanings she associates with her sentences—most evidently, the sentences expressing the propositions to which she attaches probabilities and preferences. Davidson, too, shares the aspiration of exploiting this form of explanation of action (now tripartite: appealing to beliefs, desires, and meanings) in the service of an order of explanation that starts with specifications of what people *do* and on that basis not only

2. In some contexts, it makes a lot of difference whether one thinks of the practical component in terms of desires, preferences, values, practical commitments, or goals (to mention just a few of the prime contenders). I suppress such complications here in the interests of generality, and because they do not make a difference to the points I am making about various general structures of explanation.

imputes beliefs, desires, and meanings, but also explains theoretically what beliefs, desires, and (especially) meanings *are*.

One lesson we should draw both from Davidson's development of Quine's criticisms of Carnap and from his own criticisms of the theoretical shortcomings that remain, even after rational choice theory substantially improved on classical pragmatist ideas, is that the *inferential* relations sentences stand in to one another are an essential element of the *meanings* that they express. This is a point we can also come at from another direction. Wilfrid Sellars says:

> . . . although describing and explaining (predicting, retrodicting, understanding) are *distinguishable,* they are also, in an important sense, *inseparable.* It is only because the expressions in terms of which we describe objects, even such basic expressions as words for perceptible characteristics of molar objects, locate these objects in a space of implications, that they describe at all, rather than merely label. The descriptive and explanatory resources of language advance hand in hand.[3]

Labels distinguish things. If two objects have different labels, we may conclude that they are different in some respect. But a *mere* label tells us nothing about *which* respect. If two objects have different *descriptions,* however, we not only may conclude *that* they are different, but can consult the *content* of the description to learn something about *how* they are different. Sellars's claim is that we cannot understand that descriptive content apart from the "space of implications" in which the descriptive terminology is embedded. That is, in order to understand the content of the description, we must know something about what other descriptive contents its applicability gives us sufficient reason to apply, which other descriptions would give us reason to apply that one, and which further descriptions it rules out. 'Red' is a description, and not just a label, in part because **being red** follows from **being scarlet,** entails **being colored,** and

3. "Counterfactuals, Dispositions, and the Causal Modalities," in *Minnesota Studies in the Philosophy of Science,* vol. 2, ed. H. Feigl, M. Scriven, and G. Maxwell (Minneapolis: University of Minnesota Press, 1957), sec. 108.

rules out **being green.** Understanding a description, as opposed to being
able to apply a label, is a matter of practically mastering the *inferential*
relations it stands in to other descriptions: its place in the space of reasons or implications. The parrot we have trained reliably to respond to
the visible presence of red things by squawking "That's red" is applying a
label. A three-year-old child who knows that red lollipops have a cherry
taste and red traffic lights mean "Stop" is already applying a descriptive
*concept.*

So one of the things I take it we have learned is that *reasoning* and *concept use* are two sides of one coin. *Discursive* activity, applying concepts
paradigmatically in describing how things are, is inseparable from the *inferential* activity of giving and asking for *reasons.* Elsewhere[4] I have elaborated a view along these lines under the rubric "semantic inferentialism."
Three ever more committive versions of such a view can be distinguished.
*Weak* semantic inferentialism claims only that inferential articulation is a
*necessary* condition of conceptual contentfulness. *Strong* semantic inferentialism claims further that inferential articulation in a broad sense is a
*sufficient* condition. *Hyper*inferentialism claims that inferential articulation in a narrow sense is a sufficient condition. In *Making It Explicit* I
developed and defended a version of strong semantic inferentialism. In
this book, I explore some of the motivations and consequences of such a
view.

Understanding conceptual content in terms of role in reasoning, and
reasoning in terms of inference, entails giving pride of place to *propositional* content. For propositional contents, in the first instance expressed
by declarative sentences, can play the role both of premise and of conclusion in inferences—and so, on the inferential conception of reasoning,
both serve as and stand in need of reasons. When I was in elementary
school, I was solemnly taught that "a sentence is the grammatical expression of a whole thought." Even at the time, I found the confident endorsement of this order of explanation quaint and unmotivated. Surely the two
ideas *sentence* and *whole thought* come as a package. The issue being implicitly raised is the vexed philosophical topic of the "unity of the propo-

---

4. *Making It Explicit* (Cambridge, MA: Harvard University Press, 1994) and *Articulating
Reasons.*

sition." What is the unity characteristic of basic thinkables (namely judge-ables), as such? The suggestion is that this question, too, should be addressed in terms of role in *reasoning*—and hence, given the specifically inferentialist version of rationalism being pursued here, *inference*. What is propositionally contentful is what can stand in inferential relations. (In this sense, it is not only *declarative* sentences that exhibit propositional contentfulness. Expressions of intention or preference, requests, and commands can do so as well.)

What is the relation between reasoning (inferring) and inferential rela-tions (among propositionally contentful items)? A traditional strategy seeks to derive proprieties of inferential practice from inferential relations. But there are reasons to adopt a converse strategy. Gilbert Harman has famously and provocatively argued that there is no such thing as deduc-tive inference.[5] If there were, he suggests, then it would be conducted ac-cording to rules such as "If you believe that *p,* and you believe that *if p then q,* then you should believe that *q.*" But that would be a terrible rule. One might have much better evidence against *q* than one has in favor of either *p* or *if p then q.* Deductive implicational relations tell us that we ought not to believe all of *p, if p then q,* and ~*q.* But they don't tell us what to *do,* which of the many options for repairing the situation to pur-sue, if we are threatened by commitment to such an inconsistent triad. Inferential relations constrain, but do not determine, inferential pro-cesses.

A *pragmatist* strategy looks to impute inferential *relations* on the basis of inferential *processes* or *practices.* (Think here of the heroic functionalist inversion strategy mentioned earlier: the idea of turning on its head the form of an explanation of action in terms of reasons—whether in terms of beliefs, beliefs plus desires, or beliefs plus desires plus meanings—so as to explain the nature of the explainers, including their contents, in terms of their role in such explanations.) The fundamental termini of inferring moves—the acts or statuses that are givings of reasons and for which rea-sons are given—are judgings, claimings, assertings, or believings. They are the undertakings or acknowledgments of *commitments.* It is the prop-ositional contents of those commitments that stand in inferential relations

5. "Logic and Reasoning," *Synthese* 60 (1984): 107–128.

to one another. The indissoluble package that includes <u>sentence</u> on the syntactic side, and <u>propositional content</u> on the semantic side, also includes the activities of <u>inferring</u> and (therefore) <u>asserting</u> on the pragmatic side. This is the iron triangle of discursiveness.

On this conception of the <u>discursive</u>, then, to say that we are discursive creatures is to say both that we are *normative* creatures and that we are *rational* ones. We undertake discursive commitments and responsibilities, and what makes them *discursive* commitments and responsibilities is that they stand in *inferential* relations to one another: relations that codify what is a *reason* for what. Because our commitments are inferentially articulated, they are *conceptually* contentful. The space of reasons is the space of concepts. What discursive beings as such do is apply concepts, undertaking cognitive commitments as to how things are and practical commitments as to how things shall be. Such discursive activity is the exercise of a distinctive kind of *consciousness.* It is *sapient,* rather than merely *sentient,* consciousness or awareness. For it depends on the sort of conceptual *understanding* that consists in practically knowing one's way about in the inferentially articulated space of reasons and concepts, rather than the sort of organic *feeling* we share with animals that are not *rational* animals.

This rationalist understanding of our characteristic discursive kind of consciousness also makes sense of a corresponding sort of semantic *self-consciousness.* For we can take things to be thus-and-so, *describe* them (rather than merely discriminate or label them), become discursively aware of them, in virtue of the inferential relations our commitments (including those we come to acknowledge by non-inferential responsive perceptual mechanisms) stand in to one another. And those same inferential relations can themselves become the topics of our discursive awareness. All that is required for that is practical mastery of the use of vocabulary expressing the right kind of concepts. These are concepts that let us make explicit—put into judgeable, thinkable, assertable, *propositional* form— the inferential relations that articulate the "space of implications" that is the context and horizon within which alone what we do acquires the significance of rational, discursive consciousness of what we respond to. These are concepts that let us *say that* one claimable content follows from or is a reason for or against another. The paradigmatic locution expressing such a concept is the *conditional*. "If *p* then *q*," tells us that a certain inferential relation holds between *p* and *q*.

In the rationalist picture I have been sketching, inferential relations are the medium of discursive understanding and consciousness in the sense of sapience. The expressive role characteristic of *logical* vocabulary is to codify inferential relations in propositional form. That is to bring them into the practices of giving and asking for reasons as themselves items that can be given as reasons and for which reasons can be sought—that is, as things that can themselves be objects of discursive understanding and consciousness. Where before the advent of logical vocabulary and the concepts it expresses rational creatures had to be able in practice to discriminate (however fallibly and incompletely) materially good from materially bad inferences, the new expressive capacity provided by logical locutions lets them reason about what is a reason for what. Logic is the organ of semantic self-consciousness.[6]

So one consequence of this way of thinking about things (a potentially controversial one, to be sure) is that one need not be a *logical* being to be a *rational* one. The sort of semantic (because inferential) *self-consciousness* that is afforded by mastery of the use of specifically logical vocabulary is not, as far as I can see, a necessary condition of the sort of sapient consciousness afforded by mastery of the use of ordinary empirical descriptive vocabulary. One can be good enough at distinguishing what follows from what and what is a reason for or against what other claims to be held responsible for having reasons for one's cognitive and practical commitments even if that ability remains at the implicit level of knowing *how*, and is not something one could formulate explicitly in rules or principles at the level of knowing (and being able to say) *that* certain inferences are good and others not. The sort of self-consciousness that is exhibited in making *explicit* (in judgeable, sayable, thinkable, *propositional* form) what otherwise remains *implicit* in the inferentially articulated practical capacities in virtue of which one can be consciously aware of anything (make something explicit, by judging, saying, or thinking

6. This is the doctrine that I call "logical expressivism" in *Making It Explicit*, chap. 2, and *Articulating Reasons*, chap. 1, and have articulated in most detail in *Between Saying and Doing* (Oxford: Oxford University Press, 2008), chaps. 2 and 5.

something, applying concepts) is *sui generis,* and not to be understood on the traditional Tarski-Carnap model of metalanguages. Logical vocabulary and concepts make possible a distinctive kind of self-reflection about reasons and reasoning, and so about the semantogenic features characteristic of specifically discursive practice.

This is to say that philosophy begins in logic. For as I remarked in the opening sentence of this Introduction, in the broadly rationalist tradition to which this work belongs, philosophy is demarcated by its concern to understand, articulate, and explain the notion of *reason* that distinguishes us as *rational* animals, *discursive, concept-using, sapient* beings. Specifically *logical* self-consciousness is a matter of being able to make claims and reason about reasoning, about inference and the inferential relations that articulate the contents of *non*-logical concepts. So logic makes possible already a kind of distinctively *philosophical* reflection.

Of course there is more to philosophy than logic. Put slightly more carefully, not all the concepts whose use is the exercise of specifically philosophical self-consciousness (consciousness of ourselves as *rational* animals) are logical concepts. I have emphasized that on my way of understanding it, rationality is a normative concept. The space of reasons is a normative space. I have also registered a methodological commitment (though in these introductory remarks I have not tried to entitle myself to it by argument) to a pragmatist order of explanation—to accounting for *meaning* in terms of *use;* more specifically, to abstracting the inferential relations that articulate conceptual (paradigmatically propositional) content from the reasoning practices and inferential processes of discursive practitioners. This is a broadly functionalist explanatory strategy. It is a rationalist (more specifically, inferentialist) functionalism, because conceptual content is to be understood in terms of role in reasoning, in the form of inferential role. And it is a normative functionalism, rather than a causal-dispositional functionalism. That is, the roles in question are to be specified in a normative vocabulary of what would commit or entitle one to apply a concept and what else doing that would commit or entitle one to, rather than with what would dispose one to apply that concept and what else doing that would dispose one to do. (For reasons discussed in Chapter Two, my understanding of normativity then requires a social functionalism, in which the functional system in question is a linguistic community and its practices, rather than confining the functional system to what is inside the skin of some individual organism. But that further commitment can be ignored here.)

So according to an account that founds an inferentialist semantics on a normative pragmatics, philosophical reflection on us as rational creatures must deploy not only *logical,* but also *normative* concepts. The latter have the expressive job of making explicit what it is we are *doing* in engaging in discursive practices, applying concepts, and exercising our sapient consciousness. For what we are doing is claiming authority and undertaking responsibility, altering our commitments and entitlements in ways that depend on what is a reason for what. Besides developing and deploying logical concepts and vocabulary to express inferences in explicit, propositional, conceptual form, philosophers must develop and deploy normative concepts and vocabulary to express the acknowledgment and attribution of discursive deontic statuses such as responsibility and authority, commitment and entitlement. Philosophy is concerned not only with the semantics, but with the pragmatics of discursivity. That much follows already from the most basic characterization of its task as understanding us as rational creatures, once the normativity of that characterization is appreciated.

This constellation of ideas provides the framework within which the more specific investigations reported in the body of this work are conducted. The book has two parts. The first finds in normative rationalism an organizing principle that guides us to a new way of understanding both Kant's most basic ideas and what Hegel made of those ideas. These three chapters are tightly integrated with one another, presenting a single, cumulative story culminating in a unified, articulated picture of the rational activity that makes us what we are: knowers and agents, creatures able to undertake and attribute determinate, conceptually contentful commitments and responsibilities. The second part of the book comprises five chapters that discuss various topics in contemporary philosophy, viewed from the perspective of what it has to tell us about ourselves as rational creatures.

Part One of the book consists of my three Woodbridge lectures.[7] The first of these, "Norms, Selves, and Concepts," begins with what I take to be Kant's principal innovation: his normative characterization of the mental. This is the idea that what distinguishes judging and intentional doing from the activities of non-sapient creatures is not that they involve some special sort of mental processes, but that they are things knowers and agents are in a distinctive way *responsible* for. Judgments and actions make knowers and agents liable to characteristic kinds of *normative* assessment. What one must *do* in order to be taking responsibility for or committing oneself to a judgeable content (or practical maxim) in the sense that matters for apperceptive (sapient) awareness is *synthesize* an original unity of apperception, by *integrating* the content in question into the whole that comprises all of one's commitments, in the light of the relations of material inferential consequence and incompatibility they stand in to one another. This is the synthesis of a rational self or subject: what is responsible *for* the commitments. It has a *rational* unity in that the commitments it comprises are treated as *reasons* for and against other commitments, as normatively *obliging* one to acknowledge some further commitments and *prohibiting* acknowledgment of others. This is Kant's normative inferential conception of awareness or experience. Further, he pursues a pragmatist order of explanation, in that concepts and their contents are understood in terms of the role they play in this synthetic process of taking rational responsibility (judging). As predicates of judgment, concepts are rules determining what is a reason for what. The final move in this first chapter is to explain in these terms the notion of <u>representation</u>. Kant understands this, too, in normative terms. What is represented is what representings (judgments) are responsible *to,* what exercises a distinctive kind of *authority* over assessments of their correctness. I offer an account of this sort of normativity in terms of the more basic inferential sort that governs the rational synthetic process, and so provide a reading

7. Originally presented at Columbia University in November of 2007. I delivered them again at the University of Pittsburgh, in January of 2008, and once more at the Humboldt University in Berlin, in July of 2008. I have profited greatly from the comments of all those audiences.

of Kant's dark but central claim that "it is the unity of consciousness that alone constitutes the relation of representations to an object."[8]

The first chapter, then, presents Kant's pragmatist version of a normative rationalist account of intentionality, along both its expressive dimension and its representational dimension. For both propositional (and, more generally, conceptual) contentfulness and what it is for our judgments to purport to be about objects (which play the normative role of what those judgments answer or are responsible to for their correctness) are explained in terms of the activity of judging, understood as a process of synthesizing a unity of apperception by rational integration of commitments. The second chapter, "Autonomy, Community, and Freedom," explores Kant's theory of *normativity*. (The shift in topic corresponds to that from concern with *rational* normativity to concern with rational *normativity*.) Earlier Enlightenment thinkers (for instance, in the social contract tradition of political thought, culminating in Rousseau) had already had the idea that normative *statuses* such as responsibility and authority (commitment and entitlement) are not independent of the normative *attitudes* of those who acknowledge such responsibility or authority. Kant radicalizes that idea into a criterion of demarcation of the normative—a way of distinguishing normative constraint from various sorts of non-normative compulsion—in terms of *autonomy*. One is genuinely *normatively* bound only by rules one has bound *oneself* by, concepts one has oneself applied in judging or acting. The central role accorded to normativity in understanding concept use generally (in Chapter One) turns out here to have as a consequence that the significance of the concept of *autonomy* for Kant's thought extends far beyond the practical use of reason, penetrating deeply into his account of rationality and discursivity in general—in their theoretical no less than their practical forms of expression.

At this point Hegel's reciprocal recognition model of normativity is introduced. It takes its place as a way of developing Kant's autonomy model, so as to make sufficient room for the relative *independence* of conceptual contents from the attitudes of those who endorse them. That independence is in turn required to make intelligible the notion that in applying concepts one is undertaking a determinately contentful rational responsi-

8. *Critique of Pure Reason* B137.

bility. Hegel's social model manages to satisfy that criterion of adequacy while still respecting the original Enlightenment insight. It does so by acknowledging the crucial role played by the attitudes of *others*—those I recognize (as authoritative) and am in turn recognized by—in constituting the authority I have to make myself responsible to conceptual norms.

Kant introduced a new normative conception of positive freedom. Freedom in his sense consists in the capacity to bind oneself by norms. It is the authority to make oneself responsible. The chapter closes with a discussion of how this looks when it is transposed into Hegel's new social key, and given, as it is by Hegel, a further, specifically *linguistic* twist. The positive expressive power achievable only by constraining oneself by the norms constitutive of the use of a public natural language provides a paradigm of the Hegelian version of Kant's normative conception of positive freedom.

The third chapter, "History, Reason, and Reality," describes how Hegel fits together the model of the synthesis of an original unity of apperception by rational integration (discussed in the first chapter) and the model of the synthesis of normative-status-bearing apperceiving selves and their communities by reciprocal recognition (discussed in the second chapter) by placing both within a larger *historical* developmental structure. Further, he does so in such a way as to make intelligible the sense in which the discursive commitments that arise in that process should be understood as having determinate conceptual contents. Conceptual contents are determined by rational integration that includes historical reflection. The Kantian account of rational integration of new commitments into a synthetic unity with prior commitments is recontextualized as merely one aspect of a more general rational integrative-synthetic activity. What Hegel adds is a *retrospective* notion of *rationally reconstructing* the process that led to the commitments currently being integrated (not just the new one, but all the prior ones that are taken as precedential for it, too). This is a kind of *genealogical* justification or vindication of those commitments, showing why previous judgments were correct in the light of still earlier ones—and in a different sense, also in the light of subsequent ones. Hegel calls this process "Erinnerung," or *recollection*. A successful recollective reconstruction of the tradition shows how previously endorsed constellations of commitments were unmasked, by internal instabilities, *as appearances,* representing how things *really* are only incompletely and partially incorrectly—but also how each such discovery contributed to filling in or correcting the picture they present of how it really is with what they were all along representing, by more closely approximating the actual consequential and incompatibility relations of the concepts and making more correct applications of them. So they were not *mere* appearances, in that they did genuinely reveal something of how things really are. Exhibiting a sequence of precedential concept applications-by-integration as *expressively progressive*—as the gradual, cumulative making explicit of reality as revealed by one's current commitments, recollectively made visible as having all along been implicit— shows the prior, defective commitments endorsed, and conceptual contents deployed, as nonetheless genuinely appearances representing, however inadequately, how things really are.

The new notion of *reason,* expanded to include both *integration* and *recollection,* is the centerpiece of an account of what discursive practitioners must *do* in order to be intelligible as granting *authority* over the correctness of what they say and think (in a sense of 'correct' corresponding to a distinctive normative dimension of assessment they institute by those very practical attitudes) to an objective reality they count, by making themselves *responsible* to it, thereby in this normative sense as talking and thinking *about.* In fact the systematic account of reason and concepts, normativity and freedom, of the social and historical dimensions of self-consciousness, and of intentionality and objectivity that is recounted in these three chapters itself exhibits this same structure. These chapters recollectively reconstruct an expressively progressive rational path leading from Kant's central ideas to Hegel's. They exhibit Kant and Hegel as developing a sophisticated account of the unity of the various central features that distinguish discursive beings from merely natural ones. We are social, normative, rational, free, self-consciously historical animals. This powerful and finely conceptually articulated vision of ourselves is the crowning philosophical achievement of German Idealism.

The material in Part Two of the book is less intricate and more accessible. These chapters should be intelligible not only to philosophers, but also to more general audiences. They try to extract lessons that might matter in other corners of the culture from the particular way of working out the rationalist tradition of thinking about us that I have been waving my hands at. They take this same constellation of considerations developed in Part One and apply them to more specific issues of contemporary philosophical significance.

Chapter Four, "Reason, Expression, and the Philosophic Enterprise," begins where Chapter Three left off: considering us as creatures with histories rather than natures. It then takes a metaphilosophical turn, addressing the question of what philosophy is. The overall view is that it is the discipline that thinks about what *we* are, first as beings who live and move and have our being in a *normative* space, and second as *rational, discursive* creatures. Its conclusion is that the topic of philosophy is normativity in all its guises, and inference in all its forms. And its task is an *expressive, explicative* one. Philosophy is a discipline whose distinctive concern is with a certain kind of *self-consciousness:* awareness of ourselves as specifically *discursive* (that is, concept-mongering) creatures. Its task is understanding the conditions, nature, and consequences of conceptual norms and the activities—starting with the social practices of giving and asking for reasons—that they make possible and that make them possible. As concept users, we are beings who can make explicit how things are and what we are doing—even if always only in relief against a background of implicit circumstances, conditions, skills, and practices. Among the things on which we can bring our explicitating capacities to bear are those very concept-using capacities that make it possible to make anything at all explicit. Doing that is philosophizing.

Chapter Five, "Philosophy and the Expressive Freedom of Thought," takes a different path through what should now be familiar material. It, too, is metaphilosophical in intent.[9] The argument proceeds by way of a consideration of the relative roles of our sentience and sapience in thinking about who *we* are—in our ownmost being, as Heidegger liked to say. Three models of the sapience of rational animals are considered: an instrumental one, which considers rationality as a matter of being good at

9. It was originally written as a contribution to a popular lecture series at Yale in which different advocates spoke in favor, respectively, of a life of pleasure, of philosophical activity, and of philosophical reflection. Their original agreed-upon avatar for the life of pleasure was Mick Jagger—but at the last minute he begged off. Something about a banquet, I understand.

getting what we want, a Kantian normative one, and a Hegelian social-historical one. The conclusion, for what it is worth, is the Hegelian one: that what we are *in* ourselves depends on what we are *for* ourselves. We are the kind of being whose self-conception is essential to our selves. These different self-conceptions correspond to different aims for political activity. And they correspond to different conceptions of philosophy. The piece ends with an encomium to the philosophical life. It is not meant, *pace* Rousseau, to claim that one must first be a philosopher in order truly to be one of us,[10] only to recommend the special virtues of the special form of self-consciousness that philosophers (those who just can't help doing it) aim to practice and promote.

Chapter Six, "Why Truth Is Not Important in Philosophy," addresses a question that might well have occurred to the reader very early on in the exposition of this Introduction: why <u>reason</u> and not <u>truth</u> as the master idea in terms of which to approach both the question of who we are and the question of what philosophy is and by rights ought to be? After all, the two concepts have equally august pedigrees in the philosophical tradition. As the point is put at the end of this chapter, we are not only "makers and takers of reasons," but "seekers and speakers of truth." The methodological route I took here looks first to our sapience, and then to a specifically *semantic* account of the conceptual contents it is our fate, mission, and glory as sapients to shape and be shaped by. But that very sort of semantic story is, in the recent tradition, typically told in terms of truth and truth conditions, rather than reason and inference (which come into the story only later). I am concerned here (as in *Tales of the Mighty Dead*) retrospectively to discern and provide a provenance for a contrary explanatory strategy. But surely its competitor should at least be addressed.

My general view is that once the *expressive* role distinctive of the vocabulary of 'truth' and 'reference' is properly appreciated, it will be seen that the concepts expressed by these locutions are not suitable to be recruited for semantic *explanatory* purposes. This is a conclusion that my allies in the semantic deflationist camp have not always sufficiently emphasized. (In the context of the general direction of explanation I have been recommending, such a view will have substantial consequences for

10. I have in mind his remark in the preface to the *Discourse on the Origin of Inequality*.

how one thinks about us as rational animals, sapients, and discursive practitioners—and hence how one thinks about philosophy as the study of us as such.) More deeply, from my pragmatist perspective, I am impressed that inferring and asserting are things that one *does*. (*Representing,* for instance, is only something one does in a seriously derivative, parasitic sense—something one does *by* doing something more fundamental.) Of course, speaking *truly* is also something one does. But 'truly' is an adverb, not a verb. And saying something *true* is also something one does. Yet 'true' is an adjective, not a verb. Obviously, grammar is not destiny. But pragmatists (or just functionalists) want to know how these assessments are related to what people *do* in engaging in discursive practices: in thinking and saying things.

This chapter is divided into two parts. The critical bit describes the expressive role characteristic of semantic vocabulary. Truth-talk generally ought to be understood anaphorically, as a way of forming prosentences, which relate to their antecedents in ways analogous to the ways pronouns relate to theirs. If that is right, then there are various explanatory roles that philosophers have hoped to recruit the concept of *truth* to pursue that it turns out not to be suitable for. The constructive bit of the chapter explores how the notion of *inference* can be used to pursue many of those same philosophical projects for which *truth* traditionally seemed to be essential, or at least helpful.

One cause for complaint about this chapter is that in taking success semantics as a target along the way, I have chosen a minority view that is well out of the mainstream of truth-conditional semantics. That is true. I have seized on it because it seems to me to be one of the most sophisticated truth-conditional approaches that takes broadly pragmatist considerations seriously in its larger philosophical motivations. Overall, my aim is to show how things look from a point of view that emphasizes reason. And I have nothing against working out a different approach. But it is also important to register some of the drawbacks of a popular competing approach.

Chapter Seven, "Three Problems with the Empiricist Conception of Concepts," begins by distinguishing four ways in which a broadly functionalist approach to the conferral of conceptual content might be pursued: the empiricist strategy, which looks exclusively to the causal antecedents that reliably elicit a (therefore) contentful state; the pragmatist strategy, which looks exclusively to the causal consequences reliably elicited by a (therefore) contentful state; the rationalist strategy, which looks to the role in reasoning of a (therefore) contentful state; and the combined strategy, which appeals to all these sorts of functional involvements, both causal and inferential. The aim is to show some of the ways in which the rationalist criterion of demarcation of the *conceptual* in terms of specifically inferential articulation remedies specific shortcomings of empiricist and pragmatist accounts of conceptual content that appeal only to causal inputs (in perception) and outputs (in action). To that end, the chapter considers three difficulties that confront such non-inferential conceptions of conceptual content: inability to distinguish the sort of complexity distinctive of the *conceptual* as such, failure to make sense of the crucial notion of responsive *reliability,* and liability to *proximal* interpretations of what empirical concepts are applied to. In each case, it is claimed, the rationalist insight supplies what is missing from the empiricist approach.

The final chapter, "How Analytic Philosophy Has Failed Cognitive Science," argues that concept use is intrinsically stratified. It exhibits at least four basic layers, with each capacity to deploy concepts in a more sophisticated sense of 'concept' presupposing the capacities to use concepts in all of the more primitive senses. The three lessons that generate the structural hierarchy oblige us to distinguish between

- concepts that only *label* and concepts that *describe,*
- the *content* of concepts and the *force* of applying them, and
- concepts expressible already by *simple* predicates and concepts expressible only by *complex* predicates.

Artificial intelligence (AI) researchers and cognitive, developmental, and animal psychologists need to take account of the different grades of conceptual content made visible by these distinctions.

Considerations that have been in play since the dawn of analytic philosophy, well over a century ago, yield a four-stage hierarchy of ever more demanding senses of "concept" and "concept use." At the bottom are concepts as reliably differentially applied, possibly learned, *labels* or classifications. This is the empiricist construal of concepts which I argued in the previous chapter needs to be supplemented in order to be adequate. At the next level, concepts as *descriptions* emerge when merely classifying concepts come to stand in *inferential, evidential, justificatory* relations to one another—when the propriety of one sort of classification has the practical significance of making others appropriate or inappropriate, in the sense of serving as *reasons* for them. This is the rationalist construal of concepts.

Building on the capacity to use inferentially articulated descriptive concepts to make propositionally contentful judgments or claims, the capacity to form sentential *compounds*—paradigmatically *conditionals,* which make endorsements of material inferences relating descriptive concept applications propositionally explicit, and *negations,* which make endorsements of material incompatibilities relating descriptive concept applications propositionally explicit—brings with it the capacity to deploy a further, more sophisticated kind of conceptual content: *ingredient* (as opposed to freestanding) content. Conceptual content of this sort is to be understood in terms of the contribution it makes to the content of compound judgments in which it occurs, and only thereby, indirectly, to the force or pragmatic significance of endorsing that content. Ingredient conceptual content is what can be *negated,* or *conditionalized.*

The first step was from merely *discriminating* classification to *rational* classification ('rational' because inferentially articulated, according to which classifications provide reasons for others). The second step is to *synthetic logical* concept formation, in which concepts are formed by logical compounding operators, paradigmatically conditionals and negation. The final step is to *analytical* concept formation, in which the sentential compounds formed at the third stage are *decomposed* by noting invariants under substitution. Systematically assimilating sentences into various equivalence classes accordingly as they can be regarded as substitutional variants of one another is a distinctive kind of *analysis* of those compound sentences, as involving the application of concepts that were not *components* out of which they were originally constructed. Concepts formed by this sort of analysis are substantially and in principle more expressively powerful than those available at earlier stages in the hierarchy of conceptual complexity.

This hierarchy is not a *psychological* one, but a *logical* and *semantic* one. Concepts at the higher levels of complexity presuppose those at lower levels not because creatures of a certain kind cannot in practice, as a matter of fact, deploy the more complex kinds unless they can deploy the simpler ones, but because in principle it is impossible to do so. Nothing could count as grasping or deploying the kinds of concepts that populate the upper reaches of the hierarchy without also grasping or deploying those drawn from its lower levels. The dependencies involved are not empirical, but (meta)conceptual.

The five chapters that make up the second part of this book thus represent a number of different paths that can be taken through what are essentially the same rationalist woods explored in the first three. The desire to make it possible to read them also as self-contained essays means that some prominent features of that landscape show up many times, from somewhat different perspectives. Those landmarks provide orientation, and a potentially calming reminder on unfamiliar ground that at least one already knows what is to be found in a neighboring region. The hope is that by the end of these journeys, the reader will feel thoroughly at home in this terrain.

The book as a whole describes a narrative arc that takes us from Kant to the frontiers of contemporary analytic philosophy. It presents a rationally reconstructed tradition that ties these endpoints together in an expressive progression, in which a promising constellation of ideas gradually becomes more explicit. One of Hegel's big ideas is that this recollective form of rationality is the way one moves forward, by looking backward. (Traditions are lived forward and understood backward.) An understanding of how we got to where we are is a distinctive form of an idea about where we can go. It is of the essence of this form of understanding that it is not unique. There are many different diagnoses possible, leading to different proposed therapies. There are eight million stories out there, and this is one of them.

# PART ONE

# Animating Ideas of Idealism: A Semantic Sonata in Kant and Hegel

# CHAPTER ONE

# Norms, Selves, and Concepts

**1.** In the first three chapters I consider some of the ideas that animated the philosophical tradition, anchored and epitomized by Kant and Hegel, which they called 'idealism'. My aim is to reanimate some of those ideas, breathing life into them by exhibiting a new perspective from which they show up as worthy of our interest and attention today. I do that by retrospectively rationally reconstructing a coherent, cumulative trajectory of thought, carving it out of the context in which it is embedded, ruthlessly ignoring elements near and dear to Kant and Hegel that are not essential to the line of thought on which I am focusing. This will seem to some a perverse sort of enterprise. At the end of Chapter Three I assemble conceptual raw materials drawn from all three chapters, in order to address the methodological issue of how to think about the nature, justification, and possible value of this sort of undertaking.

**2.** At the heart of Descartes' innovations in epistemology and the philosophy of mind lies a revolutionary semantic idea. He saw that the rising new science required giving up the old ways of thinking about the relations between appearance and reality. Since the Greeks, the idea had been that, at least when things go well, the way things appear to us *resembles* the way they really are. Resemblance in this sense is a matter of sharing properties (or some more general sort of form), as a realistic picture shares some elements of shape and perhaps color with what it pictures. But on Copernicus's account, the reality behind the appearance of a stationary Earth and a revolving Sun is a rotating Earth and a stationary Sun. No resemblance there. And Galileo's reading of what he calls the "book of nature, written in the language of mathematics" finds the best way of getting a grip on the reality of motion to be by manipulating geometrical appearances, in which a period of time shows up as the length of a line, and acceleration as the area of triangle. The category of <u>resemblance</u> is of little help in understanding the connections that are being exploited. And in Descartes' own algebraized geometry, the equations of lines and circles do not at all resemble the geometrical figures about which they let us reason so effectively. Descartes sees that a more abstract notion of *representation* is needed. We've been worrying about it ever since.[1]

For Descartes, the way discursive algebraic equations represent geometrical figures serves as a paradigm of representational relations generally, and in particular of the relation between appearance and reality—between the concept-manipulating mind and the geometrical Galilean world of extended things in motion that mind thinks about by representing it. What makes it possible to use algebraic formulae to reason about geometrical objects—the phenomenon I am claiming provided Descartes with his semantic paradigm—is the *global isomorphism* between the two systems. One can, if one likes, still think of a formula and the figure it represents as sharing something or being alike in some way. But what they share must be thought about in terms of the role each plays in the *system* of which it is a part: the structure-preserving way in which a formula's relations to other formulae can be mapped onto a figure's relations to other figures. Apart from those horizontal relations between representings and other representings, the vertical semantic relations between representings and representeds are invisible and unintelligible. This holistic character of the new notion of representation was not lost on Spinoza, for whom thought of the world is possible only because "the order and con-

---

1. John Haugeland tells this story well, in the opening chapter of his *Artificial Intelligence: The Very Idea* (Cambridge, MA: MIT Press, 1989). On Kant's early rejection of resemblance in favor of representation, see his *Dissertation*, sec. 4, Ak. 2:383–393.

nection of things is the same as the order and connection of ideas," nor on Leibniz, who required each monad to represent its whole universe in order to represent any of it.[2]

**3.** Where Descartes' semantic concerns center on the nature of representational *success,* Kant addresses more fundamental questions about the nature of representational *purport.* What is it, he wants to know, for our ideas so much as to *seem* to be about something? What is it for us to take or treat them as, for them to show up to us as, representings, in the sense of something that answers for its correctness to what thereby counts as being represented?[3] This issue is the core around which cluster the other elements of Kant's concern with what he calls "objectivity." The line of thought he develops to answer these questions begins with the identification of a critical shortcoming of the account of judgment he inherited. That account finds its place as part of the traditional *classificatory theory of consciousness.* This is the idea that to be aware of something is to take it *as* something: paradigmatically, to classify something particular as being of some general kind. In its form as a theory of judgment, it becomes the view that judging is *predicating* one concept of another: putting two concepts into a relation, marked by a copula, whose paradigm once again is bringing a particular concept under a general one, or subordinating a less general to a more general one.

In a radical break with the whole of the logical tradition he inherited, Kant rejects this way of thinking about judgment. The reason he gives is that it does not apply to logically compound judgments:

> I have never been able to accept the interpretation which logicians
> give of judgment in general. It is, they declare, the representation of a

---

2. I discuss some of the details of their holistic accounts of representation in chaps. 4 and 5 of *Tales of the Mighty Dead: Historical Essays in the Metaphysics of Intentionality* (Cambridge, MA: Harvard University Press, 2002).

3. Already in the letter to Herz of 1772, Kant says: "I noticed that I still lacked something essential, something that in my long metaphysical studies I, as well as others, had failed to pay attention to and that, in fact, constitutes the key to the whole secret of hitherto still obscure metaphysics. I asked myself: What is the ground of the relation of that in us which we call 'representation' to the object?" *Philosophical Correspondence 1759–99,* ed. Arnulf Zweig (Chicago: University of Chicago Press, 1967), 71.

relation between two concepts . . . [W]hat is defective in this interpretation . . . [is] that it applies only to categorical, not to hypothetical and disjunctive judgments (the two latter containing a relation not of concepts but of judgments), an oversight from which many troublesome consequences have followed.[4]

It will be instructive to fill in some of those "troublesome consequences." The same logical tradition distinguishes between mental *acts* and their *contents*—that is, between the two sides of what Sellars calls the "notorious 'ing'/'ed' ambiguity," which affects concepts such as <u>judgment</u>, <u>representation</u>, <u>experience,</u> and <u>perception</u>—between what one is *doing* in judging, representing, experiencing, or perceiving, on the one hand, and what is judged, represented, experienced, or perceived, on the other. Sensitivity to that distinction should prompt the question whether understanding judgment as consisting in predication or the relation of two concepts is intended to address the activity of judging or the propositional contents of such acts. It is in the context of that question that the invocation of the sorts of compound judgment that populate Kant's Table of Judgments—negative, hypothetical, disjunctive, and modal judgments—makes most visible the inadequacy of the traditional way of thinking about judgment.

For it then becomes clear that in the traditional theory, the notion of *predication* is being asked to do two incompatible jobs. On the one hand, it serves as a structural way of building up new judgeable contents. On the other hand, it is thought of as a kind of doing that has the significance of endorsing such contents. The collision between these two senses in which predication is an 'operation' is clearest when one thinks about judgeable contents appearing as unasserted (unendorsed) components of more complex sentences (judgments). The conditional is a paradigm. When I assert "If $Pa$ then $Pb$," I have *not* asserted $Pa$. Have I predicated $P$ of $a$? If so, then predication does not amount to endorsement: predicating is not judging. If not, then it looks as though there is an equivocation when I detach from the conditional, reasoning:

4. *Critique of Pure Reason* B140–141.

If *Pa* then *Pb*

*Pa*

So: *Pb*

For the second premise *is* a predication, and the antecedent of the first premise is *not* a predication.

Geach picks up this Kant-Frege point, using it in his masterful, gem-like essay "Ascriptivism" to argue against emotivist semantic analyses of terms of moral evaluation.[5] His target is theories that understand the normative significance of terms such as 'good' not as part of the *content* of what is said about an act, not as specifying a characteristic that is being attributed, but rather as marking the *force* of the speech act. Calling something good is thought of as *doing* something distinctive: commending. Geach first asks what the limits of this ploy are. He points to the lovely archaic English verb 'to macarize', which means to characterize someone as happy. Does the possibility of understanding calling someone happy as macarizing her mean that happiness is not a property being invoked in specifying the content of the claim that someone is happy, because in saying that we are really *doing* something else, namely performing the special speech act of macarizing? If we can do that with 'happy', why not with 'mass' or 'red'? What are the rules of this game? He then suggests the embedding test: look to see if an expression can be used to construct a judgeable content that is *not* directly used to perform a speech act, paradigmatically in the antecedent of a conditional. Because imperatival force *is* grammatically marked, we cannot say:

*"If shut the door, then. . . ."

But we *can* say things like "If he is happy, then I am glad," and "If that is a good thing to do, then you have reason to do it." In the first of these, I have *not* macarized anyone, and in the second, I have not commended any action. So the terms 'good' and 'happy' contribute to the specification of content, and are not to be understood as mere force indicators. (I called

5. *Philosophical Review* 69, no. 2 (1960): 221–225.

this essay "masterful" and "gemlike." Geach exhibits a deep fault line in an entire philosophical approach, nails down his point, and leaves it at that. The essay is five pages long.)[6]

Worrying about compound forms of judgment containing unendorsed judgeable contents as components required Kant to distinguish the operations by which such contents are constructed from the activity of endorsing the results of those operations. Further, once we see that the doctrine of judgment as predication is trying to have things both ways, and that no single 'operation' can be taken both to form contents and to be the adoption of an attitude toward those contents, the need to deal with compound judgments shows that predication is inadequate for *both* purposes. Endorsing hypothetical (conditional) judgeable contents is not happily thought of as predicating, and those contents are not happily thought of as formed by predication.[7]

**4.**    For this reason, Kant could not take over the traditional classificatory theory of consciousness, which depends on understanding judging as predicating. But what can go in its place? Here is perhaps Kant's deepest and most original idea, the axis around which I see all of his thought revolving. What distinguishes judging and intentional doing from the activities of non-sapient creatures is not that they involve some special sort of mental processes, but that they are things knowers and agents are in a distinctive way *responsible* for. Judging and acting involve *commitments.* They are *endorsements,* exercises of *authority.* Responsibility, commitment, endorsement, authority—these are all *normative* notions. Judgments and actions make knowers and agents liable to characteristic kinds of *normative* assessment. Kant's most basic idea is that minded creatures

6. Of course this argument does not make it forever impossible to pursue emotivist-expressivist theories. It just obliges those who do to have something to say about embedded uses as well as freestanding ones. Addressing just this issue is what marks the divide between classical expressivists such as C. L. Stevenson and the more sophisticated generation of neo-expressivists epitomized by Allan Gibbard and Simon Blackburn.

7. At this point some (even Frege himself, briefly) have been tempted to think of judging as predicating *truth* of a sentence—at the cost of seeing the *same* predicate as involved in all judgings. But sentences formed by applying ". . . is true" to a sentence can also appear as the antecedents of conditionals, and the same question arises: in asserting such a conditional, has one "predicated" truth of the sentence that appears in the antecedent?

are to be distinguished from unminded ones not by a matter-of-fact onto-logical distinction (the presence of mind-stuff), but by a normative *deon*-tological one. This is his *normative characterization* of the mental.

Drawing on a jurisprudential tradition that includes Grotius, Pufen-dorf, and Crusius, Kant talks about norms in the form of *rules.* Judging and acting—endorsing claims and maxims, committing ourselves as to what is or shall be true—is binding ourselves by norms. It is making our-selves subject to assessment according to rules that articulate the *contents* of those commitments. Those norms, those rules, he calls 'concepts'. In a strict sense, all a Kantian subject can do *is* apply concepts, either theo-retically, in judging, or practically, in acting. Discursive, that is to say, concept-mongering, creatures are normative creatures—creatures who live and move and have their being in a normative space.

It follows that the most urgent philosophical task is to understand the nature of this normativity, the bindingness or validity (Verbindlichkeit, Gültigkeit) of conceptual norms. For Descartes, the question was how to think about our grip on our concepts, thoughts, or ideas (Is it clear? Is it distinct?). For Kant the question is rather how to understand their grip on us: the conditions of the intelligibility of our being bound by concep-tual norms.

**5.**   This master idea has some of Kant's most characteristic innovations as relatively immediate consequences. The logical tradition that under-stood judging as predicating did so as part of an order of semantic expla-nation that starts with concepts or terms, particular and general, advances on that basis to an understanding of judgments (judgeables) as applica-tions of general to particular terms, and builds on that basis an account of inferences or consequences, construed syllogistically in terms of the sort of predication or classification exhibited by the judgments that appear as premises and conclusions. In a radical break with this tradition, Kant takes the whole judgment to be the conceptually and explanatorily basic unit at once of meaning, cognition, awareness, and experience.[8] Concepts and their contents are to be understood only in terms of the contribu-tion they make to judgments: concepts are predicates of judgment. Why?

---

8. As we might say, judgment is for Kant the Ur-teil of discourse.

Kant adopts this order of semantic explanation because judgments are the minimal units of *responsibility*—the smallest semantic items that can express *commitments*. The semantic primacy of the propositional is a consequence of the central role he accords to the *normative* significance of our conceptually articulated doings. In Frege this thought shows up as the claim that judgeable contents are the smallest units to which pragmatic force can attach: paradigmatically, assertional force. In the later Wittgenstein, it shows up as the claim that sentences are the smallest linguistic units with which one can make a move in the language game.

Understanding judging in normative terms, as undertaking a distinctive kind of responsibility, is also responsible for the most general features of Kant's account of the *form* of judgment. The subjective form of judgment is the "I think," which, we are told, can accompany all our judgings, and so, in its pure formality, is the emptiest of all representations. Thought of in terms of the normative pragmatics of judgment, it is the mark of *who* is responsible for the judgment. (A corresponding point applies to the endorsement of practical maxims.) It indicates the relation of a judging to the "original synthetic unity of apperception" to which it belongs. I will say something more soon about the use Kant makes of this central concept. But the idea behind it is that the sorting of endorsements into co-responsibility classes is a basic condition of the normative significance of commitments. Committing myself to the animal's being a fox, or to driving you to the airport tomorrow morning, normatively precludes *me* from committing myself to its being a rabbit, or to my sleeping in tomorrow (in the sense that I cannot be entitled to such commitments), but it does not in the same way constrain the commitments *others* might undertake.

The objective form of judgment, Kant says, is "the object=X," to which judgments always, by their very form as judgments, make implicit reference. Thought of in terms of the normative pragmatics of judgment, it is the mark of what one has made oneself responsible *to* by making a judgment. It expresses the objectivity of judgments, in the sense of their having intentional objects: what they purport to represent. The understanding of the intentional directedness of judgments—the fact that they *represent* or are *about* something—is through-and-through a *normative* one. What the judgment is about is the object that determines the *correct-*

*ness* of the commitment one has undertaken by endorsing it. (On the practical side, it is normative assessments of the *success* of an action for which the object to which one has made oneself responsible by endorsing a maxim must be addressed.) In endorsing a judgment one has made oneself liable to distinctive kinds of normative assessment. What one is thinking and talking *about* is what plays a special role, exercises a special sort of *authority* in such assessments. Representing something, talking *about* or thinking *of* it, is acknowledging its semantic *authority* over the correctness of the commitments one is making in judging. Representational *purport* is a normative phenomenon. As we shall see, representational *content* is to be understood in terms of it.

**6.**  Besides *who* is responsible for a judging, and what that judging is responsible *to,* there are two other elements a normative pragmatics of judgment should address:

- What is it that one makes oneself responsible *for* by judging?

and

- What is it that one is *doing* in making oneself responsible, committing oneself, endorsing?

The first is a question of how to understand judgeable *contents.* The second is the challenge to fill in the bare-bones picture of judging as a normative doing, the alteration of one's normative status, the undertaking of some sort of responsibility. This is the key issue, for it is in terms of the answer to this question that we will have to understand both dimensions of content—what one makes oneself responsible *for* in judging, and what one makes oneself responsible *to*—as well as the nature of the subject of those responsibilities. Here, I think, we get Kant's next big idea.

That is that the responsibility one undertakes in judging (and there is a parallel story about endorsing a practical maxim) is generically a kind of *task* responsibility: the responsibility to *do* something. Specifically, it is the responsibility to *integrate* the judgment into a *unity of apperception.* Synthesizing a unity of apperception is the activity that provides

the background and the context in which episodes can have the significance of judgings. Engaging in that activity produces, sustains, and develops a synthetic unity of apperception: a *self* or *subject*. What must one do
to be doing that? One must *integrate* new endorsements into the whole
that comprises one's previous endorsements. Synthesis by successive integration can be thought of as involving three sorts of activity: critical,
ampliative, and justificatory. One's *critical* responsibility is to weed out
materially incompatible commitments.[9] This means rejecting candidate
judgments that are incompatible with what one is already committed to
and responsible for, or relinquishing the offending prior commitments.
Judgers as such are obliged to renounce commitment to contents that are
*incompatible* with their other commitments, or which have such commitments as their consequences. For if two commitments are incompatible,
each serves as a reason to give up the other.

One's *ampliative* responsibility is to extract the material inferential
consequences of each commitment, including new ones, in the context
of the auxiliary hypotheses and collateral premises provided by the rest
of one's commitments. Each commitment gives one reason to accept others, which one ought to accept in the sense that one has already implicitly
committed oneself to them by acknowledging the commitment from
which they follow. One's *justificatory* responsibility is to be prepared to
offer reasons for the commitments (both theoretical and practical) that
one acknowledges, by citing prior commitments (or undertaking further
commitments) that inferentially entitle one to those new commitments.
Seeking to fulfill the first sort of responsibility is aiming at a whole constellation of commitments that is *consistent*. Seeking to fulfill the second
is aiming at one that is *complete*. And seeking to fulfill the third is aiming
at a constellation of commitments that is *warranted*. (Perhaps it will be
clear at this point how it is that Kant can take it that the systematic obliga-

---

9. My use (here and in what follows) of the terminology of "material" relations of incompatibility and inferential consequence is adapted from Sellars's usage. It refers to incompatibility and inferential relations that hold in virtue of what is expressed by *non-logical* vocabulary. Thus claiming that Pittsburgh is west of New York City has as a material inferential
consequence that New York City is east of Pittsburgh, and is materially incompatible with the
claim that Pittsburgh is a prime number. I discuss this idea further in chap. 1 of *Articulating
Reasons* (Cambridge, MA: Harvard University Press, 2000).

tions of philosophers are merely the explicit form of the very same obligations that are implicitly incumbent on rational knowers and agents as
such.)

What is produced, sustained, and developed by practically acknowledging these critical, ampliative, and justificatory integrative task responsibilities is a *unity* precisely in the sense of being governed by, subject to
assessment according to, those norms of integration. It is a *synthetic* unity
in that it is produced by the activity of synthesis that is integrating dispa-
rate commitments into such a unity.[10] It is an *original* synthetic unity of
*apperception* because what makes an act or episode a *judging* in the first
place is just its being subject to the normative demand that it be integrated
into such a systematically unified whole,[11] and awareness in the sense of
apperception (a matter of sapience, rather than mere sentience) is judgment (apperceiving is judging).[12] Kant also, tellingly, calls the product of
this synthetic activity a *transcendental* unity of apperception. It is transcendental in that it is that in terms of which we must understand the relation to objects—representation—which is an essential dimension of the
*content* of judgments. The key to Kant's account of representation is to be
found in the story about how representational purport is to be under-

10. This is not the only sort of "combination" that Kant calls "synthesis" (cf. *CPR*
B130–131). But the claim that this is the basic species is an important element of the reading I
am offering. Cf. the claim at A79/B104: "The same function which gives unity to the various
representations in a judgment also gives unity to the mere synthesis of various representations
in an intuition; and this unity, in its most general expression, we entitle the pure concept of the
understanding. The same understanding, through the same operations by which in concepts,
by means of analytical unity, it produced the logical form of a judgment, also introduces a
transcendental content into its representations, by means of the synthetic unity of the manifold in intuition in general." (I have said—and will here say—nothing about the move from
unifying judgments into an original synthetic unity of apperception to the unification of concepts and intuitions in judgments.)

11. This is what I take to be the idea behind Kant's apparently awkward claim that representations must both already "stand under" a synthetic unity and "be brought under" it by the
activity of synthesis: "I am conscious to myself *a priori* of a necessary synthesis of representations—to be entitled the original synthetic unity of apperception—under which all representations that are given to me must stand, but under which they have also first to be brought by
means of a synthesis" (*CPR* B135).

12. "[T]hat act of understanding by which the manifold of given representations . . . is
brought under one apperception, is the logical function of judgment" (*CPR* B143).

stood in terms of the activity of synthesizing an original unity of apperception, as I have described it so far. It will help to approach that story in stages.

**7.** So far I have attributed to Kant two positive moves in response to his principled rejection of traditional accounts of judgment as predication:

- understanding the activity of judging in *normative* terms, as the undertaking of a kind of responsibility or commitment;

and

- understanding that kind of responsibility as a *task*-responsibility, a commitment to *do* something, namely to integrate the judgeable content one endorses into a synthetic unity of apperception.

In light of the justificatory, ampliative, and critical dimensions of that practical synthetic-integrative responsibility, another way of putting this last point is that what one is responsible for is having *reasons* for one's endorsements, using the contents one endorses *as* reasons for and against the endorsement of other contents, and taking into account possible *countervailing* reasons. And that is to say that as *normative* creatures, we are *rational* creatures—not in the sense that we always or even generally think or act as we have reason to, or that we usually have good reasons for thinking and doing what we do, but in the sense that whether we do or not, we are always liable to normative *assessment* concerning our reasons for thinking as we do or doing what we do. However *sensitive* we are in fact on any particular occasion to the normative force of reasons (that peculiar force, at once compulsory and yet not always compelling, that so fascinated and puzzled the ancient Greek philosophers), we are the kind of creatures we are—knowers and agents, creatures whose world is structured by the *commitments* and *responsibilities* we undertake—only because we are always liable to normative assessments of our *reasons*.

The norms that articulate the contents of judgments are *concepts*. The conceptual faculty, the understanding, is the faculty of judgment. Concepts articulate the contents of judgments by determining what one would make oneself responsible for, what one would be committing oneself to, were one to endorse those contents. Kant thinks of concepts as a kind of *rule*. What are they rules for doing? They are rules for synthesizing a unity of apperception. And that is to say that they are rules articulating what is a *reason* for what. The concepts being applied determine what *follows* from a given claim(able), hence what (else) one would have committed oneself to or made oneself responsible for by endorsing it. They determine what counts as rational *evidence for* or against, or *justification of* a judgeable content, hence would count as a *reason for* or against endorsing it.

The task of integrating a judgment (or practical maxim) into a synthetic unity of apperception has determinate conditions of success and failure only insofar as the judgments have contents that stand in relations of material inferential consequence and incompatibility to one another. A knower can have a determinate *critical* integrative task-responsibility only if it is settled which judgeable contents are materially incompatible with which others, so that endorsing some provides good reasons to reject others. And a knower can have a determinate *ampliative* or *justificatory* integrative task-responsibility only if it is settled which judgments inferentially commit or entitle one to which others, and so provide good reasons for accepting those further judgments. The concepts applied in judging articulate the content of the judgment (the judgeable *content* one becomes responsible *for*) by specifying the material inferential and incompatibility relations that content stands in to other such contents. For that is what settles what one is responsible for *doing* in making the judgment. Conceptual content in that sense provides the details of the synthetic-integrative responsibility one is undertaking thereby. Here the paired notions of a judgeable content and of being responsible for such a content in the sense of endorsing or committing oneself to it are being made sense of in terms of a basic kind of task-responsibility: being responsible for *doing* something (namely integrating the judgment into a normative unity of apperception).

Kant's ideas about the act or activity of judg*ing* settle how he must understand the content judg*ed*. In conditioning the semantic account of *content* on the pragmatic account of *force* (in Frege's sense)—the way the story about what is endors*ed* is shaped by the story about what endors*ing* is—Kant exhibits a kind of methodological *pragmatism.* In this sense, that pragmatism consists not in the explanatory privileging of *practical* discursive activity over *theoretical* discursive activity, but in the explanatory privileging of *act* over *content,* within *both* the theoretical and the practical domain. Kant's explanatory privileging of the *activity* of synthesizing a unity of apperception would reverberate through subsequent German Idealism, and be embraced and exploited in particular by Fichte and Hegel.

**8.**　The argumentative and explanatory structure I have been indicating as guiding and working out (in a pragmatist spirit) Kant's master idea of the fundamentally *normative* character of judging is a way of thinking about the relations between four things:

(1) What one must *do* in order in the relevant sense to be taking responsibility for or committing oneself to a judgeable content (or practical maxim). This is engaging in the activity of *synthesizing* an original unity of apperception, by *integrating* the content in question into the whole that comprises all of one's commitments in the light of the relations of material inferential consequence and incompatibility they stand in to one another.

(2) What one creates, sustains, and develops by doing that: the constellation of commitments that is an original synthetic unity of apperception (OSUA).

(3) The elements of that synthetic unity, what one takes responsibility *for* or commits oneself to. These are the judgeable contents that are integrated into the OSUA.

(4) What one thereby makes oneself responsible *to.* These are the *objects* that one comes to *represent,* in the sense of making oneself answerable (*for* the correctness of the endorsed judgeable contents that make up the OSUA) *to* objects, which one in that normative sense thereby counts as thinking (talking, judging) *about.* It is because of this dimension of conceptual contentfulness that the

synthetic unity of apperception deserves to count as a *transcendental* unity of apperception. For in Kant's usage, *transcendental* logic differs from *general* logic in addressing the *content,* and not just the *form,* of judgments, in the sense of their representation of, or reference (in the sense of normative answerability) to, *objects.*

This list amounts to an order of explanation. The strategy is to make sense of each of these elements in terms of those that precede it. Because the kind of normative *unity* distinctive of the synthetic unity of apperception must be understood in terms of the synthetic-integrative *activity* that produces it, the cognitive-practical subject or self that is identified with a synthetic unity of apperception is not happily thought of using the traditional category of <u>substance</u>. It is the moving, living constellation of its "affections," that is, of the concomitant commitments that compose and articulate it. The significance of each of the component commitments that contingently and temporarily are included in a particular synthetic unity of apperception depends holistically on its rational consequential and incompatibility relations to its fellows. This reciprocal dependence of the whole and its parts, together with the dynamic character of such relational structures as sustained by rational synthetic-integrative activity, made it irresistible for subsequent idealists (following Kant himself, in his *Critique of Judgment*) to appeal to and apply *organic* metaphors.

The two-sided notion of <u>conceptual content</u> adverted to in the last two items on the list—what one makes oneself responsible *for* and what one makes oneself responsible *to,* by judging—is also to be explained in terms of the original synthetic activity of integrating one's commitments according to their rational relations to one another. I have claimed that we can think of this as a *pragmatist* explanatory strategy, in the sense that we find in contemporary philosophers of language who want to understand the *meanings* expressed by various locutions in terms of the *use* of those expressions—that is, in suitably broad senses of the terms, to give explanatory priority to *pragmatics* over *semantics.* But I have so far said nothing about the relations between the two dimensions of conceptual content that show up as the third and fourth items on the list. I have suggested that the target notion of <u>representational purport</u> should itself be understood as a normative (meta)concept: as a matter of taking or treating one's commitments as subject to a distinctive kind of *authority,* as being *responsible* (for its correctness, in a characteristic sense) *to* things that in that normative sense count as represent*ed* by those represent*ing* states, which are what must be integrated into an original synthetic unity. What remains to be seen is how that rational synthetic integrative activity can be understood as instituting a specifically *representational* normative dimension of authority and responsibility. That is what is required to justify the claim that the original rational synthetic unity of apperception as so far described also deserves to be thought of as a *transcendental* unity of apperception, the subject studied by *transcendental* logic, which goes beyond *general* logic precisely in its concern not with the *form* of judgments, but of their *content,* in particular their *representational* content.

Intentionality—semantic contentfulness—comes in two flavors: 'of'-intentionality and 'that'-intentionality. The first, or *representational,* dimension is semantic directedness at objects: what one is thinking *of* or talking *about.* The second, or *expressive,* dimension concerns the *content* of our thought and talk: *what* one is thinking or saying (*about* what one is thinking or talking *about*). So one can think *of* or *about* foxes, *that* they are nocturnal omnivores. What falls within the scope of the 'of' in such a specification is a term, while what follows the 'that' in such phrases as "I think (or John thinks) *that* foxes are nocturnal omnivores" is a declarative sentence. The pre-Kantian early modern philosophical tradition took it for granted that one ought first to offer an independent account of representational 'of'-intentionality, of what it is to represent something, and only then, on that basis, to explain expressive 'that'-intentionality, what it is to judge or claim *that* things are thus-and-so.

That commitment is not strictly entailed by the traditional bottom-up order of logical-semantic explanation that begins with an account of concepts, builds on that an account of judgments, and on that in turn an account of inferences. For one might pursue such a three-stage account first for what expressions of the various orders of complexity *express,* and only then turn to consideration of what they *represent* (for instance: objects-and-properties, facts, and laws). So Kant's rejection of the traditional logic, in light of the normative-pragmatic priority of judgment (which we have seen in his hands already has a substantial inferential component)— his treating concepts as "functions of judgment"—is not tantamount to a prioritizing of the expressive over the representational dimensions of semantic content.[13] But in fact, once again Kant turns the traditional order of explanation on its head. The fact that Kant's approach to judging appeals to integration of judgments by synthesizing them into a whole according to their *rational* relations to one another brings into view in the first instance a notion of the <u>content</u> a declarative sentence expresses, what one has become responsible *for*, that is understood in terms of the broadly inferential relations of *in*clusion and *ex*clusion it stands in to other contents (both those included in the current synthetic unity of apperception and candidates not currently endorsed). But for what thereby becomes visible to be intelligible as a notion of <u>conceptual content</u>, it must exhibit also a representational dimension. Thinking *about* something is not a special kind of thinking. It is an aspect of *all* thinking.

So the question is how reference to or representation of objects (representational 'of'-intentionality) can be made intelligible or shown to be a necessary sub-structure of inferential 'that'-intentionality, when the latter is understood in terms of the rational synthetic integrative activity that is judging. Here is how I think that story goes (and this is really the punch line of my story in this chapter, the "one far-off, divine event" toward which this whole creation has been moving): the relations of material incompatibility and inferential consequence among judgeable contents that we have seen are a necessary condition of synthesizing a rational unity of apperception (which is to say judging) already implicitly involve commitments concerning the identity and individuation of *objects* they can accordingly be understood as representing or being *about*. Why? The judgment that *A* is a dog is *not* incompatible with the judgment that *B* is a fox. The judgment that *A* is a dog *is* incompatible with the judgment that *A* is a fox. That means that taking a dog-judgment to be materially incompatible with a fox-judgment *is* taking them to refer to or represent an object: the *same* object. And the same thing holds for relations of material infer-

---

13. In terms of later developments, we can see it as a question of the relative explanatory priority of the notions of the *sense expressed* by a sentence and the *object represented* by a singular term. With the wisdom of hindsight vouchsafed us by Frege's analysis (still opaque to Russell), we can see that the two issues that need to be disentangled are the distinction between the content associated with declarative sentences and that associated with singular terms, and the distinction between sense and reference.

ential consequence. Taking it that $A$ is a dog does *not* entail that $B$ is a mammal. But taking it that $A$ is a dog *does* entail that $A$ is a mammal. So drawing the inference is taking it that the two judgments refer to one and the same object.[14]

This *triangulation* by acknowledging material incompatibilities and inferences is, in a nutshell, how the *normative* demand for a *rational* unity of apperception (judgments) makes intelligible *representational* purport: what it is to take or treat judgments as *representing* or being *about objects*. It shows how the *representational* dimension of conceptual content can be understood as already implicit in its articulation by relations of inference and incompatibility, which is how we understood the *expressive* dimension. It provides a sense in which making oneself rationally responsible *for* an inferentially articulated judgeable content, in the sense of being committed to integrating it into a rational unity of apperception, involves

14. It doesn't matter that these examples appeal only to sentences formed by applying monadic predicates. Inferential and incompatibility relations among sentences formed using relational predicates exhibit corresponding phenomena. For instance, the identities of the terms are essential to the goodness of the inference from "Kant admired Hamann" and "Hamann was a teacher of Herder" to "Kant admired a teacher of Herder." One might also worry about logically compound premises and conclusions (especially in light of the emphasis placed on these in motivating the whole line of thought being considered). I'll say more about those in the next section, in the context of the categories. But once again, the goodness of *material* inferences involving the paradigmatic negative, hypothetical, and disjunctive judgments, for instance, depends on the identity of the objects addressed by the premises and conclusions. "If my dog Coda broke any home furnishings, I will be angry with Coda" entails "If my dog Coda broke my favorite lamp, I will be angry with Coda," but not "If my dog Coda broke my favorite lamp, I will be angry with John," or even "If John broke my favorite lamp, I will be angry with John."

One might think that if I believe that $A$ is the mother of $B$, then "$A$ is a dog" *is* incompatible with "$B$ is a fox." But we should rather say that "$A$ is the mother of $B$," "$A$ is a dog," and "$B$ is a fox" form an incompatible triad. Here there is still triangulation, pointing to *common* objects: "$A$ is the mother of $B$" invokes objects common to each of the other two elements.

If there are not "enough" other claims in play, we may not be able to tell whether an incompatible triad has the structure of this example, involving a relational predicate, rather than that exhibited by "$A$ is a blackberry," "$A$ is red," and "$A$ is ripe," which also are irreducibly triadically incompatible. This sort of possible under-determination would be a problem if the aim were to produce a theory of reference that would say what objects any given claim referred to, given only the rational relations it stands in to other claims. But the aim is only something much weaker: to say what it is to take or treat a claim as so much as purporting to refer to some object or other. For that purpose, it is enough that all the patterns of multiadic incompatibility involve some sort of triangulation-by-coreference.

taking or treating those judgments as *about* objects, and so as making oneself responsible *to* them. It puts us in a position to understand Kant's otherwise dark claim that "it is the unity of consciousness that alone constitutes the relation of representations to an object, and therefore their objective validity."[15] Represented objects show up as something like *units of account* for the inferential and incompatibility relations judgeable contents stand in to one another. If two properties are incompatible, then it is impossible for *one and the same* object to exhibit both, but not impossible for *two different* objects to do so. And if possession of one property entails possession of another, then any object that exhibits the first will necessarily exhibit the second. But it is not necessary that some other object do so.

Here, then, is an answer to the question with which we began: what is it for something so much as to *seem* to be a representation (a representing of something represented)? What does one have to *do* to count as taking or treating it *as* a representing *of* something? The answer is that treating it as standing in relations of material incompatibility and inferential consequence to other such things *is* taking or treating it as a representation, as being *about* something. This decidedly non-atomistic way of thinking about representational purport is recognizably a way of picking up Descartes' idea (endorsed and developed by Spinoza and Leibniz) that horizontal relations among representings are what is needed to make intelligible the vertical relations between them and representeds. The account of what one must *do* in order to synthesize a unity of apperception provides the context in which it is possible to understand *both* dimensions of conceptual content: the inferential-expressive and the referential-representational.

**9.**  In order to be able to integrate a judgeable content into a unity of apperception, we have seen, one must be able to distinguish in practice what follows from it and would be evidence for it, and what is incompatible with it.[16] But that means that those abilities can be recruited to introduce

15. *CPR* B137.

16. That is, one must make such distinctions. It is not to say that for any judgeable whatsoever one must be disposed to put it into one of these classes. And it is not to say that one must always get it *right*—though if one gets *enough* of it wrong, one will throw into doubt the attribution of commitment to *that* content—in extreme cases, perhaps to *any* content.

a new kind of claim, the conditional *if p then q,* for instance, according to the rules:

- One is committed to the conditional *if p then q* if and only if one takes it that the material inference from $p$ to $q$ is a good one.
- The inference from the conditional *if p then q* and $r$ to $q$ is good just in case the material inference from $r$ to $p$ is good.
- The conditional *if p then q* is incompatible with $r$ just in case the material inference from $r$ to $p$ is good, and there is some $s$ incompatible with $q$ such that the material inference from $r$ to $s$ is good.

(Many different ways of introducing conditionals present themselves at this point. I offer these rules just for definiteness.)[17] These amount to rules for forming *conditional* (Kant's "hypothetical") judgments. They specify the *conceptual content* of such judgments, for they associate a definite set of material inferential and incompatibility relations with each such judgment. And those relations are what settle what counts as successfully integrating such hypothetical judgments into a synthetic unity of apperception. But that means that anyone who can integrate *any non-*hypothetical judgments into a synthetic unity of apperception already knows how to do everything in principle needed to integrate hypothetical judgments involving those same judgeable contents into such a synthetic unity. In a similar way, it is possible to use the practical mastery of the notion of material incompatibility exhibited by anyone capable of engaging in basic synthetic-integrative activity to introduce explicit notions of *negation* and *necessity*—the idea being that one counts as committed to $\sim(p\&q)$ whenever one treats $p$ and $q$ as materially incompatible.[18]

17. Another way to go starts with material incompatibilities. Say that $p$ entails $q$ ($p \vDash q$) iff everything incompatible with $q$ is incompatible with $p$. (So Coda's being a dog entails Coda's being a mammal, in the sense that everything incompatible with his being a mammal is incompatible with his being a dog.) Then what is incompatible with $p \rightarrow q$ is just whatever is incompatible with $q$ and *not* incompatible with $p$. Those incompatibilities will in turn settle the entailments of $p \rightarrow q$. The possibility of doing everything with material incompatibilities is significant in understanding the metaphysical and logical primacy Hegel assigns to *determinate negation,* which is just his version of that concept.

18. I show in detail how one might do something like this in the appendices to the fifth of my 2006 John Locke lectures, *Between Saying and Doing: Toward an Analytic Pragmatism* (Oxford: Oxford University Press, 2008).

Now a concept, on Kant's usage, is a rule for forming a judgment. In this sense, "forming" a judgment (that is, a judgeable) is settling what counts as successfully integrating it into a synthetic unity of apperception. The concepts according to which hypothetical, modal, and negative judgments are formed, then, are *a priori,* not in the first instance in an *epistemological* sense, but in the *semantic* sense that any subject of apperception, which is to say any subject that can engage in judging (and hence be aware of anything in the sense of sapient or apperceptive awareness), at least implicitly always already possesses (can deploy) those concepts. They are in this sense "pure" concepts: what Kant calls "categories." And each is associated with a form of judgment. In these cases, they are associated with forms of *compound* judgment: the very kind of judgment consideration of which turned out to require a new theory both of the activity of judging and of the contents judged. In this case of the hypothetical, Kant thinks the category is that of *causation* in the sense of one thing *necessitating* another. Thereon hangs a tale. The only conclusion I want to draw from this line of thought at this point is that here we have an example of at least some of Kant's central categories that we can understand entirely in terms of the process of synthesizing a rational unity of apperception. And notice that in this way of telling the story, we did *not* have to *presuppose* the possibility of something called "synthetic knowledge *a priori,*" and then search for the conditions of its possibility.

What we *have* had to presuppose, in telling this story about the activity of synthesizing a transcendental unity of apperception, is the availability, as raw materials, of judgeable (or practically endorsable) items possessing *determinate conceptual contents.* That is, it must already be settled, at each stage of the process of rational critical and ampliative integration, what relations of material incompatibility and inferential consequence the conceptual contents that are to be integrated stand in to one another. In order to assess the status of that presupposition concerning conceptual *contents,* we need to look more closely at the kind of normative *force* that is involved in taking responsibility for the *use* of concepts in judgment and intentional action. That is the topic of the next chapter.

**10.**　I pointed out above that when we understand *represented objects*—what one makes oneself responsible *to* in becoming responsible *for* a judgeable content by judging (integrating it into a synthetic unity of apperception)—in terms of triangulation of the material incompatibility and inferential consequence relations that articulate the contents of those judgeable contents, those objects show up as something like units of account for properties, which stand in those relations of exclusion and inclusion (or consequence) (Hegel's 'ausschliessen' and 'schliessen') to one another. *Representing subjects,* understood as original synthetic unities of apperception, can also be understood as something like units of account, for commitments (judgings, and, in the extended system, also endorsements of practical maxims), which stand in relations of exclusion and consequence to one another. Subjects and objects are alike in "repelling" material incompatibilities and encompassing material consequences. They are different in that while it is *impossible* for one and the same object at the same time to exhibit two incompatible properties (or stand in incompatible relations) and *necessary* that it have all the properties entailed by any properties it does have, it is merely *inappropriate* for one and the same subject at the same time to undertake incompatible commitments, and *obligatory* that it acknowledge all the commitments entailed by any commitments it does acknowledge. In the case of *objects,* the relations of exclusion and inclusion are *alethic modal* ones: a matter of what is and is not possible and what is and is not necessary. In the case of *subjects,* the relations of exclusion and inclusion are *deontic* or *normative* ones: a matter of what one is and is not entitled and committed to or responsible for, hence of liability to normative assessment and criticism.

Objects play the conceptual functional role of *units of account for alethic modal incompatibilities.* A single object just is what cannot have incompatible properties (at the same time). That is, it is an essential individuating feature of the metaphysical categorical sortal metaconcept <u>object</u> that objects have the metaproperty of *modally* repelling incompatibilities. And in a parallel fashion, subjects too are individuated by the way they normatively "repel" incompatible commitments. It is *not* impermissible for two *different* subjects to have incompatible commitments—say, for me to take the coin to be copper and you to take it to be an electrical insulator. What *is* impermissible is for one and the *same* subject to do so. Subjects play the conceptual functional role of *units of account for deontic normative incompatibilities.* That is, it is an essential individuating feature of the metaphysical categorical sortal metaconcept <u>subject</u> that subjects have the metaproperty of *normatively* repelling incompatibilities. A single subject just is what *ought* not to have incompatible commitments (at the same time).[19]

When Hegel looks back at Kant's account of the nature of the subject, construed as an original unity of apperception and marked by the subjective form of all judgments, the "I think," and of the objects to which subjects make themselves responsible in judging, marked by the objective form of all judgments, the "object=X," it strikes him that both are to be understood in terms of the synthetic *activity* of integrating judgments with one another, by critical exclusion and ampliative inclusion or extension. That sort of *doing* is what makes the concepts both of <u>subject</u> and of <u>object</u> intelligible: as what is responsible *for* judgments and what judgments are responsible *to*, respectively. This is one of the core ideas around which Hegel elaborates his *idealism*. Consciousness, in the sense of apperception, a relation between subjects and objects, presupposes and is to be explained in terms of the *process* of synthesizing a self—the process that is *self*-consciousness. What now show up as symmetric subjective and objective poles of consciousness (the intentional nexus) are to be understood as corresponding to two aspects of the activity of synthesizing a unity of apperception that can, in the way we have rehearsed, be seen to be necessarily a *transcendental*, that is, object-representing, unity. Alethic and deontic modalities, what is expressed by modal and normative vocabulary, show up as two sides of one coin, intimately bound together by the synthetic-integrative systematizing activity that is the ultimate source of the *senses* of both kinds of locution. I'll have more to say about this idea, and the demarcation of the normative, in Chapter Two, "Autonomy, Community, and Freedom."

**11.** I have now finished telling the substantive part of the story to which this chapter is dedicated. I want to close by briefly addressing a methodological question that will have occurred to just about everyone who has

---

19. I am suppressing many complications in these formulations. In one sense, it is the whole objective world that "repels" incompatible *facts*, and so is analogous to *each* subject. Thought of this way, it is clusters of intersubstitutable singular terms that are analogous to objects. The general point I am after does not require considering this level of fine structure.

come this far with me: "What in the world do you think you are doing?"
How could I think that I have been talking about anything that *Kant*
thought, given all the concepts absolutely central to his project that do
*not* appear at all in my tale? Among the topics I did not find it necessary
so much as to mention are intuition, sensibility, receptivity, the fact that
concepts without intuitions are empty, space and time, conditions of the
possibility of experience, synthetic truths known *a priori,* the distinction
between phenomena and noumena, transcendental idealism, the Coper-
nican revolution . . . and a lot more. One might well think that these topics
are somewhat important to Kant; certainly they loom large in his own telling of his story.

Of course they are important. There is a lot more going on, even just in
his theoretical philosophy, than I have adverted to. For instance, Kant is
the first philosopher to try to think through the consequences of moving
from Aristotelian principles of identity and individuation of empirical objects, in terms of substance and accident, to Newtonian ones, which appeal instead to spatiotemporal location. (This is a naturalist idea, but not
one the British empiricists—even the "celebrated Mr. Locke"—had con-
templated, never mind endorsed.) He thinks that this metaconceptual
transformation has profound consequences for what it is to be semantically in touch with—to be able to represent—objects so conceived. Those
considerations are interwoven with a line of thought about sensibility and
receptivity and neither are in any obvious way necessarily connected to
the story about representational purport that I have told here. That there
is nonetheless a deep connection, indeed a necessary harmony, between
them is what the Transcendental Deduction aims to explain.

But the fact that one of Kant's central preoccupations is synthesizing
these two thoughts about content—one, as Kant seems to have thought of
it, having to do with the *form* of the metaconcept <u>conceptual content</u>, and
the other having to do with its *content*—does not at all mean that it is not
possible to dissect from the results of his synthesis one of the constellations of commitments he is concerned to integrate into a larger whole.
There is an internal coherence to the line of thought about concepts,
judging, hence apperception and understanding, that I have been laying
out. And we can consider it in abstraction from the other elements with
which Kant combines it. Indeed, we *must* distinguish it if we are to ask

the potentially interesting philosophical question of whether you get a better story about intentionality, semantics, and representation with or without the considerations concerning sensibility that he is concerned to integrate with those I have indicated. And I think we must discern the train of thought I have picked out here in order to address the historically interesting question of how to understand the paths that lead from Kant's to Hegel's most interesting ideas.

Of course, there are many such paths. In Chapter Two, I will lay out another one, centering on practical rather than theoretical philosophy.

# Autonomy, Community, and Freedom

**1.** My theme in Chapter One was the innovative *normative* conception of intentionality that lies at the heart of Kant's thought about the mind. He understands judging and willing as taking on distinctive kinds of *responsibility*. And he understands *what* one endorses by doing that—judgeable contents and practical maxims—in terms of what one is thereby committing oneself to *do*, the kind of *task*-responsibility one is taking on. The practical activity one is obliging oneself to engage in by judging and acting is *integrating* those new commitments into a unified whole comprising all the other commitments one acknowledges. What makes it a *unified* whole is the *rational* relations among its parts. One is obliged to resolve material incompatibilities one finds among one's commitments, by rejecting or modifying some of the offending elements. This is one's *critical* obligation. And one is obliged to acknowledge commitment to the material inferential consequences of one's commitments. This is one's *ampliative* obligation.

Engaging in those integrative activities is synthesizing a *self* or *subject*, which shows up as what is responsible *for* the component commitments into which it is articulated. Kant's core *pragmatist* commitment consists in his methodological strategy of understanding *what* one is in this sense responsible for or committed to, the *contents* of one's judgings and will-ings, in terms of the role they play in what acts with those contents to make one responsible for *doing:* criticizing and amplifying the commitments one thereby undertakes. Such a strategy accordingly demands that those contents determine the relations of material incompatibility and inferential consequence in which they stand to each other (since that is what is needed to make possible resolution of conflicts and extraction of consequences). The rules that settle those rational relations are the *concepts* one counts as applying in judging or willing, which activities then become visible as endorsings of specifically *discursive* (that is, *conceptual*) contents.

We saw that in taking two commitments to be materially incompatible, or to stand in material inferential-consequential relations, one is in effect taking them to *refer to* or *represent* a single *object:* to attribute to that object properties that exclude or include one another, that is, that are themselves incompatible or stand in a consequential relation. As a result, the synthetic-integrative process, with its aspects of critical and ampliative activity (what Hegel with characteristic imagery talks about as the "exhaling and inhaling" that maintain the rational organic integrity of the discursive subject), provides the basis for understanding both the subjective and the objective poles of the intentional nexus. Subjects are what repel incompatible commitments in that they *ought* not endorse them, and objects are what repel incompatible properties in that they *can*not exhibit them. (Subjects are *obliged* to endorse the consequences of their commitments, and objects *necessarily* exhibit the properties that are consequences of their properties.)

On this account, there is an intimate connection—grounded in the fundamental process or activity of rational synthesis or integration—between the (vertical) *semantic-intentional* relations between representing subjects and represented objects, on the one hand, and the (horizontal) *deontic normative* relations among subjective commitments and *alethic modal* relations among objective properties, on the other. The way I have told this bit of the story perhaps owes more to what Hegel makes of Kant's thought than to Kant's own understanding of it. But Kant himself did, as no one had done before, connect deontic and alethic modalities as pure concepts expressing related species of *necessity:* practical and natural necessity, respectively.

**2.** For Kant read Hume's practical and theoretical philosophies as raising variants of a single question. On the side of *practical* reasoning, Hume asks what our warrant is for moving from descriptions of how things *are* to prescriptions of how they *ought* to be. How can we rationally justify the move from 'is' to 'ought'? On the side of *theoretical* reasoning, Hume asks what our warrant is for moving from descriptions of what *in fact* happens to characterizations of what *must* happen and what *could not* happen. How can we rationally justify the move from descriptions of matter-of-factual regularities to formulations of necessary laws? In Kant's terminology, these are both kinds of 'necessity', practical and natural necessity, because for him, 'necessary' (notwendig) just means "according to a *rule.*" Hume's predicament is that he finds that even his best understanding of *facts* doesn't yield an understanding of either of the two sorts of *rules* governing and relating those facts, underwriting assessments of which of the things that actually happen (all he thought we can directly experience) *ought* to happen (are *normatively* necessary) or *must* happen (are *naturally* necessary). (I have been expounding the fundamental *idealist* idea that to understand, in terms of our normative, rational, synthetic activity, why there must be these two flavors of rules, deontic and alethic, and how they are related to one another as they are, is to understand the basic nature and structure of *intentionality,* in the sense of the expressive and representational relations between subjects and objects.)

Kant's response to the proposed predicament is that we cannot be in the position Hume envisages: understanding matter-of-factual empirical claims and judgments perfectly well, but having no idea what is meant by modal or normative ones. To judge, claim, or believe that the cat is on the mat, one must have at least a minimal practical ability to sort material inferences in which that content is involved (as premise or conclusion) into good ones and bad ones, and to discriminate what is from what is not materially incompatible with it. Part of doing that is associating with those inferences ranges of counterfactual robustness: distinguishing collateral beliefs functioning as auxiliary hypotheses that would, from those that would not, infirm the inference. So, for example, one must have such dispositions as to treat the cat's being on the mat as compatible with a nearby tree being somewhat nearer, or the temperature a few degrees higher, but not with the sun being as close as the tree or the temperature being thousands of degrees higher. One must know such things as that the cat might chase a mouse or flee from a dog, but that the mat can do neither, and that the mat would remain essentially as it is if one jumped up and down on it or beat it with a stick, while the cat would not. It is not that there is any one of the counterfactual inferences I have mentioned that is necessary for understanding what it is for the cat to be on the mat. But if one makes *no* distinctions of this sort—treats the possibility of the cat's jumping off the mat or yawning as on a par with its sprouting wings and starting to fly, or suddenly becoming microscopically small; does not at all distinguish between what can and cannot happen to the cat and what can and cannot happen to the mat—then one does not count as understanding the claim well enough to endorse it, in any sense save the derivative, parasitic one in which one can believe of a sentence in Turkish, which one does not at all understand, that it is true. Sellars puts this Kantian point well in the title of one of his essays: "Concepts as Involving Laws, and Inconceivable without Them."

If that is right, then in being able to employ concepts such as <u>cat</u> and <u>mat</u> in ordinary empirical descriptive claims one already knows how to do everything one needs to know how to do in order to deploy concepts such as <u>possible</u> and <u>necessary</u>—albeit fallibly and imperfectly. Grasp of what is made explicit by judgments formed using those alethic modal concepts is *implicit* in and *presupposed* by grasp of *any* empirical descriptive concepts. This is part of what Kant means by calling them "pure" concepts, that is "categories," and saying that our access to them is *"a priori"*—in the sense that the ability to deploy them is presupposed by the ability to deploy *any* concepts, including especially ordinary empirical descriptive concepts. This latter claim is not at base *epistemological*, but *semantic*.

What about the concern, on the side of practical philosophy, with the question of how grasp of *normative* vocabulary is related to grasp of empirical descriptive vocabulary? A closely analogous argument applies. Any rational agent, anyone who can act intentionally, must practically understand the possibility of acting for *reasons*. That means making some distinction in practice between sample bits of practical reasoning that do and those that do not entitle or commit those who endorse their premises to their conclusions. For being an intentional agent means being intelligible as responding differentially to the goodness of practical reasons for action provided by one's discursive attitudes. The sort of force such reasoning gives to its conclusion is *normative* force. Good bits of practical reasoning give the agent *reason* to act in one way rather than another, in the sense of showing that it is rationally *permissible* or *obligatory* to do so. If that is right, then being able to engage in practical reasoning at all, being able to act for practical reasons, which is to say to be an intentional agent, already involves exercising all of the abilities needed to deploy normative concepts. For concepts such as <u>commitment</u> or <u>obligation</u>, <u>entitlement</u> or <u>permission</u>, expressing various kinds of oughts, just make it possible to express *explicitly* (which is to say, in judgeable form) distinctions and attitudes that one *implicitly* acknowledges and adopts already in sorting practical inferences into materially good and bad ones (however fallibly).

In fact (though this is a fact Hegel makes more of than Kant does), Kant's normative account of theoretical judgments means that we do not even have to look to the practical sphere to mount an argument along these lines. Taking responsibility for or committing oneself to any judgeable content is integrating it into a synthetic unity of apperception. Doing that is practically acknowledging both critical and ampliative *obligations,* treating the embrace of incompatible contents and the failure to acknowledge consequential ones as not *permissible.* So in being apperceptively aware of anything at all one is already exercising all the abilities needed to master the use of at least some basic normative concepts. These, too, are "pure" concepts, which make explicit something implicit in the use of *any* concepts. Indeed, we saw last time that in Kant's picture, alethic modal and deontic normative concepts show up as intimately related. For they make explicit different but complementary aspects of the process of apperceptive synthesis, corresponding respectively to the subjective form of judgment, which gives us our grip on the concept of <u>represent*ing* subjects</u>, and the objective form of judgment, which gives us our grip on the concept of <u>represent*ed* objects</u>.

A central observation of Kant's is that what we might call the framework of empirical description—the commitments, practices, abilities, and procedures that form the necessary practical background within the horizon of which alone it is possible to engage in the cognitive theoretical activity of describing how things empirically are—essentially involves elements expressible in words that are *not* descriptions, that do *not* perform the function of describing (in the *narrow* sense) how things are. These include, on the objective side, what is made explicit as statements of *laws,* using alethic modal concepts to relate the concepts applied in descriptions. Kant addresses the question of how we should understand the semantic and cognitive status of those framework commitments: are they the sort of thing that can be assessed as *true* or *false?* If true, do they express *knowledge?* If they are knowledge, how do we come to know and justify the claims expressing these commitments? Are they a kind of *empirical* knowledge? I think that the task of crafting a satisfactory idiom for discussing these issues and addressing these questions is still largely with us, well into the third century after Kant first posed them.

Now Kant already realized that the situation is much more complicated and difficult than is suggested by this way of putting the issue: as though all that were needed were to distinguish framework-constitutive commitments from commitments that become possible only within the framework (what becomes the dichotomy between language and theory, meaning and belief, that Carnap endorses and Quine rejects). For it is one thing to acknowledge that the existence of "lawlike" relations among concepts or properties (that is, ones that support counterfactually robust inference) that are expressed explicitly by the use of alethic modal vocabulary is a necessary part of the framework of empirical description, that (as Sellars puts the point) no *description* is possible except in a context in which *explanation* is also possible, and that the function of the modal vocabulary that expresses those explanatory relations is not descriptive in the narrow sense whose paradigm is the statement of particular empirical facts. That is, *that* there must be laws (reflected in rules of inference) governing the properties (reflected in concepts) appealed to in empirical descriptions is a necessary part of the framework of description(-and-explanation). *That* claim will not itself be an *empirical* claim, in the sense of one that can only be established by investigating what descriptions actually apply to things. If it is true and knowable, it is so, we could say, *a priori.* It is, we would be tempted to say in Kant's hylomorphic terms, a matter of the *form,* rather than the *content,* of empirical knowledge. But the further point must then be granted that *which* lawlike statements express *genuine* laws (are "objectively valid") and which do not *is* an *empirical* question. So we need a way of talking about broadly *empirical* claims that are not in the narrow sense *descriptive* ones, codifying as they do *explanatory* relations among ground-level particular descriptive applications of determinate empirical concepts. Responding to this challenge (and to its analog on the side of practical activity) is one of the central animating and orienting themes of Kant's and Hegel's work (as it would be later for Peirce's and Sellars's).

**3.** Upstream from all these considerations, in the order of explanation I am pursuing, is Kant's *normative* understanding of mental activity, on both the theoretical and the practical side: his taking judging and endorsing practical maxims both to consist in *committing* oneself, taking on distinctively discursive sorts of *responsibility*. This is what corresponds on the subjective side to the framework elements made explicit on the objective side in terms of alethic modal vocabulary. In Chapter One, I suggested that this idea about the centrality of normativity is the axis around which all of his thought should be understood to turn, and that in light of that, understanding the nature of the *bindingness* of conceptual norms becomes a central philosophical task. That is the topic of this chapter.

An integral element of Kant's normative turn is his radically original conception of *freedom*. His theory is unusual (though not wholly without precedent) in putting forward a conception of *positive* rather than negative freedom. That is, it is a conception of freedom *to* do something, rather than freedom *from* some sort of constraint. Freedom for Kant is a distinctive kind of practical ability. What *is* unprecedented, I think, is the way he thinks about that ability. The philosophical tradition, especially its empiricist limb, had understood the issues clustering around the notion of <u>human freedom</u> in alethic modal terms. Determinism asserted the *necessity* of intentional performances, given non-intentionally specified antecedent conditions. The freedom of an intentional action was thought of in terms of the *possibility* of the agent's having done otherwise. The question was how to construe the subjection of human conduct to *laws* of the sort that govern the natural world. For Kant, though, these categories apply to the *objective* side of the intentional nexus: the domain of represented objects. Practical freedom is an aspect of the spontaneity of discursive activity on the *subjective* side: the domain of representing subjects. The modality that characterizes and articulates this dimension is not alethic but deontic. What is distinctive of it is being governed not by laws but by *conceptions* of laws, that is, normative attitudes. Kant's conception of freedom, too, is a *normative* one.

*Spontaneity,* in Kant's usage, is the capacity to deploy concepts. Deploying concepts is making judgments and endorsing practical maxims. Doing that, we have seen, is *committing* oneself, undertaking a distinctive sort of discursive *responsibility.* The positive freedom exhibited by exercises of our spontaneity is just this normative ability: the ability to commit ourselves, to become responsible. It can be thought of as a kind of *authority:* the authority to bind oneself by conceptual norms. That it is the authority to *bind* oneself means that it involves a correlative kind of *responsibility.* That the norms in question are *conceptual* norms means that the responsibility involved in exercising that sort of authority is a *rational* responsibility. We have seen that it is a kind of *practical* responsibility, the responsibility to *do* something. It is the responsibility to integrate the commitment one has undertaken with others that serve as *reasons* for or against it. Kantian positive freedom is the *rational* capacity to adopt *normative statuses:* the ability to *commit* oneself, the *authority* to make oneself *responsible.*

To get an intuitive sense of how such a capacity can sensibly be thought of as a kind of positive *freedom,* it is helpful to think of an example suggested by the guiding metaphor of Kant's popular essay "Was ist Aufklärung?" Consider what happens when a young person achieves her legal majority. Suddenly she has the authority to bind herself legally, for instance by entering into contracts. That gives her a host of new abilities: to borrow money, take out a mortgage, start a business. The new authority to bind oneself normatively, to take on these new normative statuses, involves a huge increase in positive freedom. The difference between discursive creatures and non-discursive ones is likewise to be understood in terms of the sort of *normative positive freedom* exhibited by the concept users.

Further, for Kant this sort of normative positive freedom is a kind of *rational* freedom. For the exercise of that spontaneity is *rational* activity. Rationality in this sense does not consist in knowers and agents generally, or even often, having good reasons for what they believe and do. It consists rather just in being in the space of reasons, in the sense that knowers and agents count as such insofar as they exercise their normative authority to bind themselves by conceptual norms, undertake discursive commitments and responsibilities, and so make themselves liable to distinctive kinds of normative *assessment*. For they are liable to assessment as to the goodness of their *reasons* for exercising their authority as they do, for taking on *those* specific commitments and responsibilities. Assessment of those reasons is assessment of their success at integrating the new commitments with others they have similarly adopted and acknowledged. Whatever the actual causal antecedents of their judgings and intentional doings, Kantian knowers and agents are *obliged* (committed) to have *reasons* for their judgments and actions. (This rational justificatory obligation is a kind of resultant of the critical and ampliative obligations we have already registered.)

On this account, far from being incompatible with constraint, freedom *consists* in a distinctive kind of constraint: constraint by norms. This sounds paradoxical, but it is not. The positive freedom Kant is describing is the practical capacity to be bound by discursive norms. This is a capacity that is compatible with but extends beyond being bound by the laws that govern natural beings. It is by exercising this capacity that we raise ourselves above the merely natural, and become beings who live and move and have our being in the normative space of commitments and responsibilities, and so (because it is the rational relations they stand in that articulate the contents of those normative statuses) *reasons*.

4.   The aspiration to be entitled to a conception of *normative positive freedom* along these lines makes all the more urgent the philosophical project of understanding normative statuses such as commitment, responsibility, and authority. One of the permanent intellectual achievements and great philosophical legacies of the Enlightenment—and perhaps the greatest contribution modern philosophers have ever made to the wider culture—is the development of secular conceptions of legal, political, and moral normativity. In the place of traditional appeals to authority derived ultimately from divine commands (thought of as ontologically based upon the status of the heavenly lord as creator of those he

commands), Enlightenment philosophers conceived of kinds of responsibility and authority (commitment and entitlement) that derive from the practical attitudes of human beings. So for instance in social contract theories of political obligation, normative statuses are thought of as instituted by the intent of individuals to bind themselves, on the model of promising or entering into a contract. Political authority is understood as ultimately derived from its (perhaps only implicit) *acknowledgment* by those over whom it is exercised.

This movement of thought is animated by a revolutionary new conception of the relations between normative *statuses* and the *attitudes* of the human beings who are the subjects of such statuses, the ones who commit themselves, undertake responsibilities, and exercise authority, and who acknowledge and attribute (practically take themselves and others to exhibit) those statuses. This is the idea that normative statuses are *attitude-dependent.* It is the idea that authority, responsibility, and commitment were not features of the non- or pre-human world. They did not exist until human beings started taking or treating each other *as* authoritative, responsible, committed, and so on—that is, until they started adopting normative *attitudes* toward one another. Those attitudes, and the social practices that make adopting them possible, *institute* the normative statuses—in a distinctive sense that it is a principal task of philosophy to investigate and elucidate. This view of the global attitude-dependence of norms contrasts with the traditional objectivist one, according to which the norms that determine what is "fitting" in the way of human conduct are to be read off of features of the non-human world that are independent of the attitudes of those subject to the norms. The job of human normative subjects on this traditional picture is to conform their attitudes (what they *take* to be correct or appropriate conduct) to those attitude-independent norms—to discover and acknowledge the objective normative facts, on the practical side, just as they are obliged to discover and acknowledge objective non-normative facts on the theoretical side.

Kant identifies himself with this modern tradition in that he embraces the Enlightenment commitment to the attitude-dependence of basic normative statuses (a commitment that, in the context of a normative approach to cognitive-practical activity, and a pragmatist approach to understanding conceptual contents in terms of what one is *doing* in endorsing them, has considerable significance for subsequent idealism). This is a thought that can be developed in a number of ways. (Further along, I'll consider some paths opened up by beginning to disambiguate it along two crucial dimensions.) One of Kant's big ideas is that it can be exploited to provide a criterion of demarcation for the normative. To be entitled to a normative conception of positive human freedom as discursive spontaneity, Kant must be able to distinguish the *normative* constraint characteristic of knowing and acting *subjects* from the necessitating *causal* constraint characteristic of the *objects* they know about and act on. In his terms, he must be able to distinguish constraint by *conceptions*[1] of laws from constraint by laws. What is the difference between adopting a *normative status* and coming to be in a *natural state?* What is the difference between how norms and causes "bind" those subject to them?

Following his hero Rousseau, Kant radicalizes (what he and his followers thought of as) the Enlightenment discovery of the attitude-dependence of normative statuses into an account of what is distinctive of normative bindingness, according to a model of *autonomy*. This model, and the criterion for demarcating normative statuses from natural properties that it embodies, is intended as a successor-conception to the traditional model of *obedience* of a subordinate to the commands of a superior. On that traditional conception, one's normative statuses are determined by one's place in the great feudal chain of normative subordination—which may itself be thought of either as an objective feature of the natural (and supernatural) world, or as determined normatively by some notion of the deserts of those ranked according to their asymmetric authority over and responsibility to one another. The contrasting autonomy idea is that we, as subjects, are genuinely *normatively* constrained only by rules we constrain *ourselves* by, those that we adopt and acknowledge *as* binding on us. Merely natural creatures, as objects, are bound only by rules in the form of laws whose bindingness is not at all conditioned by their attitudes of acknowledging those rules *as* binding on them. The difference between non-normative *compulsion* and normative *authority* is that we are genuinely *normatively* responsible only to what we *acknowledge as* authoritative. In this sense, only we can bind ourselves, in the sense that we

1. Or representations: "Vorstellungen."

are only *normatively* bound by the results of exercises of our freedom: (self-constitutive) *self*-bindings, commitments we have undertaken by acknowledging them.[2] This is to say that the positive freedom to adopt normative statuses, to *be* responsible or committed, is the same as the positive freedom to *make* ourselves responsible, by our attitudes. So Kant's normative conception of positive freedom is of *freedom* as a kind of *authority*. Specifically, it consists in our *authority* to *make* ourselves *rationally responsible* by *taking* ourselves to be responsible. The capacity to *be* bound by norms and the capacity to *bind ourselves* by norms are one and the same. That they are one and the same is what it is for it to be *norms* that we are bound by—in virtue of binding ourselves by them. Here authority and responsibility are symmetric and reciprocal, constitutive features of the normative subject who is at once authoritative and responsible.

This whole constellation of ideas about normativity, reason, and freedom, initiated by Kant and developed by his successors, is, I think, what Heidegger means when he talks about "the dignity and spiritual greatness of German Idealism."

**5.** In Chapter One, I claimed that Kant's rejection of the traditional classificatory theory of consciousness and the need for a new theory both of judging and of what is judged result from considering the distinction between pragmatic force and semantic content, the act of judging and judgeable content, as it shows up in the context of *compound* forms of judgment. That same distinction now combines with the autonomy thesis (which is a thesis about pragmatic *force,* or what one is *doing* in judging) to yield a demand for the relative *independence* of force and content: attitude-*dependence* of normative force turns out to require attitude-*independence* of content. The Kant-Rousseau autonomy criterion of demarcation of the normative tells us something about normative *force*—about the nature of the bindingness or validity of the discursive commitments

2. The acknowledgment of authority may be merely implicit, as when Kant argues that in acknowledging others as concept users we are implicitly also acknowledging a commitment not to treat their concept-using activities as mere means to our own ends. That is, there can be background commitments that are part of the implicit structure of rationality and normativity as such. But even in these cases, the source of our normative *statuses* is understood to lie in our normative *attitudes*.

undertaken in judging or acting intentionally. That force, it tells us, is *attitude-dependent*. It is important to realize that such an approach can only work if it is paired with an account of the *contents* that normative force is invested in that construes those contents (and in that regard, the normative statuses whose contents they are) as attitude-*independent*.

The autonomy criterion says that it is in a certain sense up to us (it depends on our activities and attitudes) *whether* we are bound by (responsible to) a particular conceptual norm (though acknowledging *any* conceptual commitments may involve further implicit rationality- and intentionality-structural commitments). However, if not only the normative *force*, but also the *contents* of those commitments—*what* we are responsible for—were *also* up to us, then, to paraphrase Wittgenstein, "whatever seems right to us would be right." In that case, talk of what is right or wrong could get no intelligible grip: no norm would have been brought to bear, no genuine commitment undertaken, no normative status instituted. Put another way, autonomy, binding oneself by a norm, rule, or law, has two components, corresponding to 'autos' and 'nomos'. One must bind *oneself*, but one must also *bind* oneself. If not only *that* one is bound by a certain norm, but also *what* that norm involves—what is correct or incorrect according to it—is up to the one endorsing it, the notion that one is *bound,* that a distinction has been put in place between what is correct and incorrect according to that norm, goes missing. The attitude-dependence of normative *force,* which is what the autonomy thesis asserts, is intelligible in principle *only* in a context in which the boundaries of the *content*—what I acknowledge as constraining me and by that acknowledgment *make* into a normative *constraint* on me in the sense of opening myself up to normative *assessments* according to it—are *not* in the same way attitude-dependent. That is a condition of making the notion of <u>normative constraint</u> intelligible. We may call it the requirement of the relative *independence* of normative *force* and *content*.

Kant secures this necessary division of labor by appeal to *concepts,* as rules that determine what is a reason for what, and *so* what falls under the concepts so articulated. (If being malleable is a conclusive consequence of being gold, then only malleable particulars can fall under the concept <u>gold</u>. His picture of empirical activity as consisting in the application of concepts—of judging and acting as consisting in the endorsement of propositions and maxims—strictly separates the *contents* endorsed from the *acts* of endorsing them. The latter is our responsibility, the former is not.[3] In Kant's picture, the judging or acting empirical consciousness always already has available a stable of completely determinate concepts. Its function is to choose among them, picking which ones to invest its authority in by applying to objects, hence which conceptually articulated responsibility to assume, which discursive commitments to undertake. Judging that what I see ahead is a <u>dog</u>—applying that concept in perceptual judgment—may initially be successfully integratable into my transcendental unity of apperception, in that it is not incompatible with any of my other commitments. Subsequent empirical experience may normatively require me to withdraw that characterization, and lead me to apply instead, say, the concept <u>fox</u>. That is my activity and my responsibility. But what other judgments are compatible with something being a dog or a fox (so what would oblige me to withdraw the application of those concepts) is *not* at that point up to me. It is settled by the contents of those concepts, by the particular rules I can choose to apply and so to bind myself by.

In taking this line, Kant is adopting a characteristic rationalist order of explanation. It starts with the idea that empirical experience presupposes the availability of determinate concepts. For apperception—awareness in the sense required for sapience, awareness that can have *cognitive* significance—is judgment: the application of concepts. Even classification of something particular as of some general kind counts as *awareness* only if the general kind one applies is a *concept:* something whose application can both serve as and stand in need of *reasons* constituted by the application of *other* concepts. When an iron pipe rusts in the rain, it is in some sense classifying its environment as being of a certain general kind, but is in no interesting sense *aware* of it. So one must already have concepts in order to be aware of anything at all.

Of course, this is just the point at which the pre-Kantian rationalists notoriously faced the problem of where determinate concepts come from. If they are presupposed by experiential awareness, then it seems that they

---

3. This does not require that the constitution of conceptual contents be wholly independent of our activity. Kant in fact sees "judgments of reflection" as playing a crucial role in it. It requires only that each empirical ("determinate") judgment be made in a context in which already determinately contentful concepts are available as candidates for application.

cannot be thought of as derived from it, for instance by abstraction. Once the normative apperceptive enterprise is up and running, further concepts may be produced or refined by various kinds of judgments (for instance, reflective ones), but concepts must always already be available for judgment, and hence apperception, to take place at all. Empirical activity, paradigmatically apperception in the form of judgment, presupposes transcendental activity, which is the rational criticism and rectification of one's commitments, making them into a normatively coherent, unified system. Defining that normative unity requires the availability of concepts with already determinate contents (roles in reasoning). Leibniz's appeal to innateness is not an attractive response to the resulting explanatory demand. And it would not be much improvement to punt the central issue of the institution of conceptual norms from the realm of empirical into the realm of noumenal activity. I think it is a nice question just how Kant's account deals with this issue.

**6.** As I read him, Hegel criticizes Kant on just this point. He sees Kant as having been uncharacteristically and culpably uncritical about the origin and nature of the *determinateness* of the contents of empirical concepts. Hegel's principal innovation is his idea that in order to follow through on Kant's fundamental insight into the essentially *normative* character of mind, meaning, and rationality, we need to recognize that normative statuses such as authority and responsibility are at base *social* statuses. He broadens Kant's account of synthesizing normative individual selves or subjects (unities of apperception) by the activity of *rational integration,* into an account of the simultaneous synthesizing of apperceiving individual selves (subjects of normative statuses) and their communities, by practices of *reciprocal recognition.* How does this response fit into the space of possibilities defined by the considerations I have been putting forward as motivating Kant?

The problem is set by a tension between the autonomy model of normative bindingness, which is a way of working out and filling in the Enlightenment commitment to the attitude-dependence of normative statuses, on the one hand, and the requirement that the contents by which autonomous subjects bind themselves be at least relatively attitude-*independent*, in the sense that while according to the autonomy thesis the subject has the authority over the judg*ing,* in the sense of *which* concepts are applied, which judgeable content is endorsed (responsibility is taken for), *what* one then becomes responsible for must be independent of one's taking responsibility for it, on the other. This is to say that the content itself must have an *authority* that is independent of the *responsibility* that the judger takes for it. And the problem is to reconcile that requirement with the autonomy model of the bindingness of normative statuses such as authority. Whose attitudes is the authority of conceptual contents dependent on? The autonomy model says it must be dependent on the attitudes of those responsible to that authority, namely the subjects who are judging and acting, so undertaking commitments with those contents and thereby subjecting themselves to that authority. But the requirement of relative independence of normative force and content forbids exactly that sort of attitude-dependence.

To resolve this tension, we must disambiguate the basic idea of the <u>attitude-dependence of normative statuses</u> along two axes. First, we can ask: *whose* attitudes? The autonomy model takes a clear stand here: it is the attitudes of those who are responsible, that is, those over whom authority is exercised. This is not the only possible answer. For instance, the traditional subordination model of normative bindingness as *obedience,* by contrast to which the autonomy view defines itself, can be understood not only in objectivist terms, as rejecting the attitude-dependence of normative statuses, but also in terms compatible with that insight. So understood, it acknowledges the attitude-dependence of normative statuses but insists that it is the attitudes of those *exercising* authority, the superiors, rather than the attitudes of those *over whom* it is exercised, the subordinates, that are the source of its bindingness. (It is in this form that Enlightenment thinkers fully committed to attitude-dependence, such as Pufendorf, could continue to subscribe to the obedience model.)

Hegel wants to respect both these thoughts. The trouble with them, he thinks, is that each of them construes the reciprocal notions of <u>authority</u> and <u>responsibility</u> in a one-sided (einseitig) way: as having an *asymmetric* structure that is unmotivated and ultimately unsustainable. If $X$ has authority over $Y$, then $Y$ is responsible to $X$. The obedience view sees only the attitudes of $X$ as relevant to the bindingness of the normative relation between them, while the autonomy view sees only the attitudes of $Y$ as mattering. Hegel's claim is that they *both* do. The problem is to understand how the *authority* to undertake a determinate responsibility that for Kant is required for an exercise of freedom is actually supplied with a correlative determinate *responsibility*, so that one is intelligible as genuinely *committing* oneself to something, constraining oneself. This coordinate structure of authority and responsibility ('independence' and 'dependence' in the normative sense Hegel gives to these terms) is what Hegel's *social* model of *reciprocal recognition* is supposed to make sense of. He thinks (and this is an Enlightenment thought, of a piece with that which motivates the autonomy criterion of demarcation of the normative) that all authority and responsibility are ultimately *social* phenomena. They are the products of the *attitudes,* on the one hand, of those who *undertake* responsibility and *exercise* authority, and on the other, of those who *hold* others responsible and *acknowledge* their authority. In spite of the formal parity of both models as asymmetric, the modern autonomy model represents for Hegel a clear advance on the traditional obedience model in that it *does* aspire to endorse symmetry of authority and responsibility. But it does so by insisting that these relations of authority and responsibility obtain only when $X$ and $Y$ are *identical:* when the authoritative one and the responsible one coincide. That immediate collapse of roles achieves symmetry, but only at the cost of making it impossible to satisfy the demand of relative independence of normative force and content.[4]

4. I think that the reason why the structural deficiency in the Kantian notion of autonomy that I take Hegel to be responding to has not been much discussed in contemporary treatments of that concept (which are extensive and sophisticated) is that those discussions typically take place within a substantially more limited horizon of concerns than that in which the issue is being situated here. If one thinks of autonomy exclusively as a principle in *practical* philosophy, one will be liable, and may be entitled, to take for granted the conceptual contents deployed in autonomously endorsed reasons for action (as opposed to heteronomous inclinations to act). If instead one sees it playing the pivotal role of providing a criterion of demarcation for normativity in the context of Kant's normative conception of apperception, subjectivity, and intentionality in *both* the theoretical and practical spheres and of the pragmatist order of semantic explanation that seeks to understand conceptual *content* in terms of normative *force* (in terms of what one is *doing,* the responsibilities one is undertaking, the authority one is exercising, in judging or endorsing a practical maxim), one does not have that luxury. For it is in that wider context that the requirement of relative independence of force and content arises, and needs to be reconciled (rationally integrated) with both the attitude-dependence of normative statuses at the core of autonomy and the pragmatist commitment to understanding content in terms of force. Cf. Kant's remark: "In respect of the faculties of the soul generally, regarded as higher faculties, i.e., as faculties containing an autonomy, understanding is the one that contains the constitutive *a priori* principles for the faculty of cognition (the theoretical knowledge of nature)" (*Critique of Judgment,* introduction, sec. 9).

The next clarificatory question that must be asked about the basic idea of the attitude-dependence of normative statuses is: what *sort* of dependence? In particular, are the attitudes in question *sufficient* to institute the normative statuses? Or are they merely *necessary?* The stronger, sufficiency claim seems to be required to sustain the tension between the autonomy model and the requirement of relative independence of force from content. When I introduced the attitude-dependence idea, I characterized it in two different ways. On the one hand, I said it was the idea that

> [a]uthority, responsibility, and commitment were not features of the non- or pre-human world. They did not exist until human beings started taking or treating each other *as* authoritative, responsible, committed, and so on—that is, until they started adopting normative *attitudes* towards one another.

This asserts only the *necessity* of normative attitudes for normative statuses. But I also put it as the idea that

> [t]hose attitudes, and the social practices that made adopting them possible, *institute* the normative statuses.

Here the suggestion is of the *sufficiency* of attitudes to bring normative statuses—genuine obligations and rights—into existence. A moderate version of the normative attitude-dependence thesis rejects objectivism by insisting that the notions of responsibility and authority essentially involve (in the sense of being unintelligible apart from) the notion of *acknowledging* responsibility and authority. One can say that political legitimacy is not possible without the consent of the governed without thereby being committed to the possibility of reducing legitimacy without remainder to such consent. And a moderate autonomy thesis might treat subjects as responsible only to what they acknowledge as authoritative without dissolving the authority wholly into that acknowledgment. The one-sided obedience view took the attitudes of the superior to be sufficient all by themselves to institute a normative status of authority and corresponding responsibility on the part of the subordinate. And the one-sided autonomy view took the acknowledgment of responsibility by the one bound to be sufficient all by itself to institute the authority by which he is bound. What Hegel sees as wrong about the obedience view is accordingly not that it makes each subject's normative statuses dependent on the attitudes of others, but that its asymmetric treatment of those attitudes is sufficient to institute those statuses all by themselves, independently of the attitudes of the one whose statuses they are.

Taking someone to be responsible or authoritative, attributing a normative deontic status to someone, is the attitude-kind that Hegel (picking up a term of Fichte's) calls 'recognition'.(Anerkennung). Hegel's view is what you get if you take the attitudes of *both* recognizer and recognized, both those who are authoritative and those who are responsible, to be essential *necessary* conditions of the institution of genuine normative statuses, and require in addition that those attitudes be symmetric or reciprocal (gegenseitig). In a certain sense (which it will be our business to investigate more closely in the next chapter), Hegel also takes it that those *individually necessary* normative attitudes are *jointly sufficient* to institute normative statuses. What institutes normative statuses is *reciprocal* recognition. Someone becomes responsible only when others *hold* him responsible, and exercises authority only when others *acknowledge* that authority. One has the authority to *petition* others for recognition, in an attempt to become responsible or authoritative. To do that, one must recognize others as able to *hold* one responsible or *acknowledge* one's authority. This is according those others a certain kind of authority. To achieve such statuses, one must be recognized by them in turn. That is to make oneself in a certain sense responsible to them. But they have that authority only insofar as one grants it to them by recognizing them as authoritative. So the process that synthesizes an apperceiving normative subject, one who can *commit* himself in judgment and action, become responsible cognitively and practically, is a *social* process of reciprocal recognition that at the same time synthesizes a normative recognitive community of those recognized by and who recognize that normative subject: a community bound together by reciprocal relations of authority over and responsibility to each other.

Here is a mundane example. Achieving the status of being a good chess player is not something I can do simply by coming subjectively to adopt a certain attitude toward myself. It is, in a certain sense, up to me whom I regard as good chess players: whether I count any wood pusher who can play a legal game, only formidable club players, masters, or grand masters. That is, it is up to me whom I recognize as good chess players, in the sense in which I aspire to be one. But it is not then in the same sense up to me whether I qualify as one of them. To earn their recognition in turn, I must be able to play up to their standards. To *be,* say, a formidable club player, I must be recognized as such by those I recognize as such. (The same is true of being a good philosopher.) My recognitive attitudes can define a virtual community, but only the reciprocal recognition by those I recognize can make me actually a member of it, accord me the status for which I have implicitly petitioned by recognizing them. My attitudes exercise recognitive authority in determining whose recognitive attitudes I am responsible to for my actual normative status.

As in the Kantian autonomy model of normative bindingness, according to the recognitive model we bind ourselves, collectively and individually. No one has authority over me except that which I grant by my recognitive attitudes. Those attitudes of mine are accordingly a necessary condition of my having the status I do. But as on the traditional obedience model, others do exercise genuine authority over my normative statuses: what I am committed to, responsible for, and authoritative about. Their attitudes are also a necessary condition of my actually having the status I do. The two aspects of normative dependence, authority and responsibility, are entirely mutual, reciprocal, and symmetrical. And together, the attitudes of myself and my fellows in the recognitive community, of those I recognize and who recognize me, are sufficient to institute normative statuses that are *not* subjective in the same way in which the normative attitudes that institute them are.

Hegel diagnoses the incompatibility of commitment to the attitude-dependence of normative statuses according to the Kantian autonomy model and the relative independence of normative content from normative force as resulting from the autonomy model's asymmetric insistence on the *sufficiency* of the attitudes of the committed one to institute the normative status in question, without acknowledging also any normative dependence, in the sense of a *necessary* condition, on the attitudes of others (due to an insufficiently nuanced appreciation of the dimensions along which the autonomy model of normative force or bindingness represents an advance over the obedience model). The reciprocal recognition model he recommends to resolve this incompatibility balances moments of normative *independence* or authority of attitudes over statuses, on the part of both recognizer and recognized, with corresponding moments of normative *dependence* or responsibility to the attitudes of others, by reading both of these aspects as individually only necessary, and only jointly sufficient to institute normative statuses in the sense of giving them binding force.

**7.** For Hegel, social substance (a community) is synthesized by reciprocal recognition. It is articulated into individual recognizing and recognized *selves,* which are the *subjects* of normative statuses of commitment, authority, and responsibility—statuses instituted collectively by those recognitive attitudes. He sees these social recognitive practices as providing the context and background required to make sense of the Kantian process of integrating conceptual commitments so as to synthesize a rational unity of apperception. Hegel's term for the whole normatively articulated realm of discursive activity (Kant's "realm of freedom") is 'Geist': spirit. At its core is *language:* "Language is the Dasein of Geist," Hegel says.[5] That is where concepts (which for Hegel, as for Kant, is to say norms) have their actual, public existence. (To look ahead: we might here think of Sellars's principle that "[g]rasp of a concept is mastery of the use of a word.")

Here is how I think the social division of conceptual labor understood according to the recognitive model of reciprocal authority and responsibility works in the paradigmatic linguistic case, so as to resolve the tension with which we have been concerned. It *is* up to me which counter in the game I play, which move I make, which word I use. But it is *not* then in the same sense up to me what the *significance* of that counter is—what other moves playing it precludes or makes necessary, what I have said or claimed by using that word, what the constraints are on successful rational integration of the commitment I have thereby undertaken with the rest of those I acknowledge. It *is* up to me what concept I apply in a particular

5. *Phenomenology of Spirit,* trans. A. W. Miller (Oxford: Oxford University Press, 1979), sec. 652.

judgment—whether I claim that the coin is made of copper or silver, for instance. But if I claim that it is copper, it is *not* then up to me what *move* I have made, what *else* I have committed myself to by using that term. So, for instance, I have thereby committed myself to the coin melting at 1084°C, but not at 1083°C—in the sense that if those claims are not true, then neither is the one I made. And I have made a claim that is incompatible with saying that the coin is an electrical insulator. I can bind myself by these determinate conceptual norms because they are always already there in the always already-up-and-running communal linguistic practices into which I enter as a young one. An essential part of what maintains them is the attitudes of *others*—in this case, of the metallurgical experts who would hold me responsible for those commitments on the basis of my performance, if the issue arose. My authority to commit myself using public words is the authority at once to make myself responsible for and authorize others to hold me responsible for determinate conceptual contents, about which I am *not* authoritative. It is a petition for determinate recognition (attribution of specific commitments) by those I implicitly recognize as having authority, and thereby grant the authority so to recognize me. That is granting them the authority to assess the correctness or success of my rational integrative performances.

The point with which I want to close is that Hegel's social, linguistic development of Kant's fundamental insight into the essentially normative character of our mindedness provides a model of positive *freedom* that, while building on his notion of *autonomy,* develops it substantially. One of the central issues of classical political philosophy was always how to reconcile individual freedom with constraint by social, communal, or political norms. Kant's vision of us as rational creatures opens up space for an understanding of a kind of freedom that consists in being able to constrain ourselves by norms—indeed, by norms that are rational, in the sense that they are conceptual norms: norms articulating what is a reason for what. The normative conception of positive freedom then makes possible a distinctive kind of answer to the question of how the loss of individual negative freedom—freedom from constraint—inevitably involved in being subject to institutional norms could be *rationally justified* to the individual. (Even if it could be justified from the point of view of the collective—which cannot exist without such constraints on individual behavior—it is important that it can also be understood as rationally justifiable from the point of view of the individual herself.) In the Kantian context, such a justification could in principle consist in the corresponding increase in positive freedom.

The positive expressive freedom, the freedom *to* do something, that is obtainable only by constraining oneself by the conceptual norms implicit in *discursive* social practices, speaking a public language, is a central case where such a justification evidently is available. Speaking a particular language requires complying with a daunting variety of norms, rules, and standards. The result of failure to comply with enough of them is unintelligibility. This fact can fade so far into the background as to be well-nigh invisible for our home languages, but it is an obtrusive, unpleasant, and unavoidable feature of working in a language in which one is *not* at home. The same phenomenon is manifest in texts that intentionally violate even a relatively small number of central grammatical and semantic norms, such as Gertrude Stein's prose. But the kind of positive freedom one gets in return for constraining oneself in these multifarious ways is distinctive and remarkable.

The astonishing empirical observation with which Chomsky inaugurated contemporary linguistic theory is that almost every sentence uttered by an adult native speaker is radically *novel*. That is, not only has that speaker never heard or uttered just that sequence of words before, but neither has anyone else—ever. "Have a nice day" may get a lot of play in the States, and "Noch eins" in Germany, but any tolerably complex sentence is almost bound to be new.

Quotation aside, it is for instance exceptionally unlikely that anyone else has ever used a sentence chosen at random from the story I have been telling. And this is not a special property of professor-speak. Surveys of large corpora of actual utterances (collected and collated by indefatigable graduate students) have repeatedly confirmed this empirically. And it can be demonstrated on more fundamental grounds by looking at the number of sentences of, say, thirty words or less that a relatively simple grammar can construct using the extremely minimal 5,000-word vocabulary of Basic English. There hasn't been time in human history for us to have used a substantial proportion of those sentences (even the true ones), even if every human there had ever been always spoke English and did nothing but chatter incessantly. Yet I have no trouble producing, and you have no trouble understanding, a sentence that (in spite of its ordinariness) it is quite unlikely anyone has happened to use before, such as

> We shouldn't leave for the picnic until we're sure that we've packed my old wool blanket, the thermos, and all the sandwiches we made this morning.

This capacity for *radical semantic novelty* fundamentally distinguishes sapient creatures from those who do not engage in linguistic practices. Because of it we can (and do, all the time) make claims, formulate desires, and entertain goals that no one in the history of the world has ever before so much as considered. This massive positive expressive freedom transforms the lives of sentient creatures who become sapient by constraining themselves by linguistic—which is at base to say conceptual—norms.

So in the conceptual normativity implicit in linguistic practice we have a model of a kind of constraint—loss of negative freedom—that is repaid many times over in a bonanza of positive freedom. Anyone who was in a position to consider the tradeoff rationally would consider it a once-in-a-lifetime bargain. Of course, one need not be a creature like us. As Sellars says, one always could simply *not speak*—but only at the price of having nothing to say. And non-sapient sentients are hardly in a position to weigh the pros and cons involved. But the fact remains that there *is* an argument that shows that at least *this* sort of normative constraint is rational from the point of view of the individual—that it pays off by opening up a dimension of positive expressive freedom that is a pearl without price, available in no other way. Hegel's idea is that this case provides the model that every other social or political institution that proposes to constrain our negative freedom should be compared to and measured against. The question always is: what new kind of positive expressive freedom, what new kinds of life-possibilities, what new kinds of commitment, responsibility, and authority are made possible by the institution?

**8.** Kant's normative conception of intentionality moves to the center of the philosophical stage the question of how we should think about the force or bindingness ('Gültigkeit', 'Verbindlichkeit') of normative statuses such as commitment, authority, and responsibility. Kant's response is to develop and extend the Enlightenment commitment to the attitude-dependence of normative statuses in the form of his *autonomy* model, which serves also as a criterion demarcating the realm of the normative from that of the natural.[6] Hegel sees that the very distinction of force and content that called forth Kant's new normative conception of judging and intending demands a relative independence of those two aspects that cannot be accommodated on the autonomy model, so long as that model is construed as applying to individual normative subjects conceived in isolation from one another—that is, apart from their normative attitudes toward one another. He notices to begin with that the requisite dependence and independence claims can be reconciled if they are construed in terms of individually necessary conditions, rather than individually sufficient ones. And understanding the sort of *normative* dependence and independence in question as ways of talking about relations of *responsibility* and *authority,* he offers a *social* model of normative statuses as instituted by reciprocal recognition, according to which each recognitive relation (recognizing and being recognized) combines aspects of authority over and responsibility to those who are recognized or who recognize.

We have seen how the reciprocal recognition model (and criterion of demarcation) for normative bindingness underwrites all of the following:

- A strong version of the Enlightenment idea of the *attitude-dependence* of normative statuses, since the recognitive attitudes of individual members of a recognitive community, while individually only necessary, are understood as jointly sufficient for the institution of determinately contentful normative statuses of commitment, responsibility, and authority;

- A *social* version of the structure of *autonomy*—one that incorporates the dependence on or responsibility to the attitudes of others characteristic of the obedience model in the weaker form of merely nec-

---

6. Notice that on the reading I am presenting here, the significance of autonomy for Kant extends far beyond the realm of the moral, or even the practical. It encompasses the whole realm of the conceptual: the theoretical and cognitive applications of concepts just as much as practical.

essary conditions—since each individual is responsible only for what she has authorized others to hold her responsible for; and

- Provision for the relative independence of the content of each commitment from the authority of the one who undertakes that commitment—a way normative statuses outrun normative attitudes.

Finally, we saw how Hegel's distinctively *linguistic* version of the social recognitive model of normativity opens up a powerful and original notion of positive *expressive* freedom and normative selfhood, as the product of the rationality-instituting capacity to constrain oneself by specifically *discursive* norms.

# CHAPTER THREE

# History, Reason, and Reality

**1.** In Chapter Two I discussed Hegel's account of what we need to *do* in order thereby to count as adopting normative statuses: committing ourselves, taking responsibility, exercising authority. To be a self in this normative sense, one must authorize others to *hold* one responsible, must petition them to *acknowledge* one's authority to commit oneself to specific claims and actions, and they must respond by actually doing so. The subjects of normative statuses, those statuses, and their communities are understood as all simultaneously synthesized by such a process of mutual recognition—the taking up of reciprocal practical normative attitudes. I motivated this social model of the nature and origin of normative force or bindingness as a response to the requirement of relative independence of the *content* of conceptual norms from their normative *force* that shows up as a criterion of adequacy for Kant's way of working out the Enlightenment idea of the attitude-dependence of normative statuses in the form of his autonomy model.

According to that model, I have a certain sort of authority over what I am genuinely responsible for or committed to. In the most basic case, it is at least a necessary condition of my *being* responsible or committed, of something *having* normatively binding authority over me, that I *acknowledge* that responsibility, commitment, or authority. Because my normative statuses are in this way conditioned on my normative attitudes, I have a certain kind of (meta-)authority concerning them; they are in this sense up to me. That is my autonomy. I am only *normatively* bound when I have bound *myself*. But for this to be intelligible as a model of normative force or bindingness, we must be able to understand what I have done as *binding* myself by undertaking a responsibility or commitment, a normative status, whose content is not simply determined by my attitudes. For if the content were so determined—if whatever *seems* right to me *is* right— then the notion that I am genuinely *bound* (that I have *bound* myself) has no application. That is to say that in order to be intelligible as determinately contentful, my autonomous (meta-)authority to bind or commit myself, to make myself responsible (a matter of the normative force of my attitudes to institute statuses), must be balanced by some authority associated with the content, with what I have become responsible *for*.

Hegel's reciprocal recognition model stems from the idea that, accepting the overarching Enlightenment commitment to the attitude-dependence of normative statuses, the way to make sense of the independent, counterbalancing (meta-)authority associated with the content to which I commit myself or for which I make myself responsible is to have that authority administered by others, *to* whom I make myself responsible, *by* authorizing them to *hold* me responsible for the content I have exercised my authority to make myself responsible for. I suggested that this idea makes sense if we think about the paradigm of discursive (conceptually contentful) norms as *linguistic* norms. What I do is intelligible as binding myself by the norms associated with the concept <u>copper</u> when I use the word 'copper', because in doing so I subject myself to normative assessment as to the correctness of my commitment (for instance, about the temperature at which a particular coin would melt) according to standards of correctness that are administered by metallurgical experts.

The reciprocal recognition model of normative bindingness preserves cardinal features of the autonomy model it seeks to develop and succeed. What any subject is actually responsible for depends essentially on that subject's own attitudes—though the attitudes of others now play an equally essential role. Authority and responsibility are fully coordinate, and the attitudes of all the recognized recognizers are jointly sufficient to institute normative statuses. And from an engineering point of view,

the social account provides a good solution to the demand for relative independence of what one is responsible for from the attitudes that make
one responsible for it. Nonetheless, there are a number of important questions concerning the nature of conceptual contents that are left open by
this social model of normativity as instituted by practical attitudes of reciprocal recognition. In the context of the story as I have been telling it
here, the most general question is: how is the Hegelian social-recognitive
form of the autonomy model of what one must do in order to count as
thereby binding oneself normatively (adopting a normative status) related
to the prior Kantian story about synthesizing an original unity of apperception (a normative self or subject of normative statuses) by rational integration?[1]

That Kantian story, which I told in Chapter One, pursues a distinctive
pragmatist order of explanation. It starts with an account of what one
must *do* in order to take responsibility for a claim or a plan—to make it
one's own—that understands it as rationally integrating such a commitment with one's other theoretical and practical commitments. It then
elaborates an account of the nature of the conceptual contents one becomes responsible for on the basis of that notion of what it is to invest
them with normative force so understood. For the ampliative and critical
dimensions of the activity of rational integration by which apperceiving
normative subjects are synthesized require that the conceptual contents
that are integrated stand to one another in relations of material inferential
consequence and incompatibility. This overarching pragmatist explanatory strategy in turn imposes constraints on the way different dimensions
of conceptual or intentional content are thought of as related to one
another. We saw how (at least the form of) the vertical, representational
dimension of content could be made intelligible in terms of the horizontal, expressive dimension—that is, how the notion that one is talking or
thinking *of* or *about* objects could be made sense of in terms of the relations of material inferential inclusion and material incompatibility ex-

---

1. One way of thinking about the relations between synthesis-as-rational-integration and
synthesis-as-reciprocal-recognition is to ask how we understand the significance of the expository transition from *Force and Understanding* to *Self-Consciousness* in the *Phenomenology*.

clusion among claimable contents of the form *that*-p. Couched in the vocabulary Frege will later introduce, this is a semantic strategy of explaining <u>reference</u> in terms of an antecedent notion of <u>sense</u>, which itself is derived from a particular way of understanding normative <u>force</u>.

What becomes of all this when the autonomy model of normative bindingness is elaborated into the reciprocal recognition model, as I suggested in Chapter Two? At this point we have visible *two* pragmatist stories about how to get from force to content. For both the Kantian rational integrative and the Hegelian social recognitive models specify what sort of thing one must *do* in order thereby to count as binding oneself by conceptual norms. But how should they be understood as related to one another? And what sort of understanding do they make possible of the determinate contentfulness of the conceptual norms which the pragmatist order of explanation wants us to understand in terms of those practices, processes, or activities?

**2.  It is by placing both within a larger *historical* developmental structure that Hegel fits the model of the synthesis of an original unity of apperception by rational integration together with the model of the synthesis of normative-status-bearing apperceiving selves and their communities by reciprocal recognition so as to make the discursive commitments instituted thereby intelligible as determinately contentful.** The process by which the commitments undertaken by members of a discursive recognitive community—and with them the concepts that articulate and constrain what counts as successfully integrating them— change and develop over time Hegel calls "experience" (Erfahrung). In that process the various deliverances of sensuous immediacy—commitments practitioners acquire non-inferentially, by observation[2]—are rationally integrated into a continually evolving whole unified by the exclusion of materially incompatible contents and the inclusion of material inferential consequences. Understanding the sense in which such development can be *expressively progressive,* in the sense of putting into claimable, thinkable form more and more of how things really are, then underwrites a distinctive and original account of aspects of semantic content that have

2. And on the practical side, inclinations they immediately find themselves with.

not been addressed in my discussion of the previous models. It is that story that I want to tell in this chapter.

In Chapter One, I pointed to some features of conceptual contents—their standing to one another in relations of inclusion and exclusion, that is, material inferential consequence and incompatibility—that are presupposed by the process of synthesis as rational integration. For the contents of the concepts one applies in judging and intending must be understood as exercising a kind of *authority* over that process, which is accordingly responsible to them in the sense that those relations among contents determine standards of correctness according to which the integration of commitments is assessed as more or less correct or successful. In Chapter Two, I claimed that the social model of normative bindingness (the force of normative statuses) as instituted by attitudes of reciprocal recognition makes room in principle for an account of the authority exercised by conceptual contents to constrain the process/practice of rational integration that respects both the *attitude-dependence* of normative statuses and the requirement that the authority of conceptual contents to which a knower and agent makes himself responsible by applying concepts in judging and intending be sufficiently *independent* of the attitudes of that very knower-agent to make sense of the notion that in applying those concepts he has *bound* himself, made himself *responsible* to them, adopted a normative status. But we have *not* seen how the reciprocal recognition model makes intelligible the availability of determinate conceptual contents to the normative subjects who are rationally integrating their commitments. A striking constitutive feature of that model is the thoroughgoing *symmetry* of authority and responsibility that it sees as integral to the institution of those normative statuses. Applied to the case at hand, this means that the reciprocal recognition model requires that the authority of conceptual contents over the activities of practitioners (their responsibility to those contents) be balanced by a reciprocal authority of practitioners over those contents, a responsibility of those contents to the activities of the subjects of judgment and action who apply them. And that is to say that Hegel is committed to understanding the practice of acknowledging commitments by rational integration as a process not only of *applying* conceptual contents, but also as the process by which they are *determined*.

I think it useful to think about this move in connection with a later one in the philosophy of language that (not at all coincidentally) has the same structure. Carnap told a two-phase story about meaning and belief, language and theory. He thought of the activity of fixing meanings as in principle prior to the subsequent activity of endorsing claims or forming beliefs that could be expressed in terms of those meanings. First one settles the language, determines the meanings or conceptual contents associated with various expressions, and so how the world would have to be for claims formulated using those expressions to be true. In this phase, the language user has complete authority. Then one looks at the world to see which applications of those concepts, which of the claims that can be expressed in the vocabulary one has introduced, are true. Here the whole authority lies with the world, which determines what theory couched in those terms is true. Quine objects that while this two-stage procedure might make perfect sense for introducing *artificial* languages, it is completely unrealistic when applied to *natural* languages. In that case, we cannot neatly separate the two aspects of language use that correspond to Carnap's two-phase picture. For here we cannot appeal to some expressively stronger metalanguage in which to stipulate or otherwise fix the meanings of our expressions in advance of using them. All there is to fix those meanings *is* our *use* of them. And what we use them to do, the kind of doing that is their use, is making claims and inferences[3]—in effect, making discursive commitments and rationally integrating them. For natural languages, and the thought conducted in them, that activity of rational integration must accordingly be able to be understood not only as consisting in the process of *applying* concepts by using expressions to make judgments, but also as the process that *determines* what concepts are expressed by those locutions: what fixes the determinate content and boundaries of those concepts.

Carnap had followed Kant in seeing the prior determination of conceptual contents as a condition of the possibility of applying those concepts in judging—which, we have seen, is intelligible only as part of the activity of synthesizing a unity of apperception integrating such commitments into a rational whole. Hegel proposes a transformation of Kant's

---

3. And undertaking practical commitments, but for simplicity, I'll focus on the theoretical side here.

picture that corresponds structurally to Quine's replacement of Carnap's two-phase picture with one that sees only two functions of or perspectives on a unified, ongoing discursive practice. In this respect, Hegel stands to Kant as Quine stands to Carnap. (Those who do not understand history are destined to repeat it.)

**3.** How could one understand the process of *applying* concepts in judgment, and their rational integration with one another by extracting consequences and extruding incompatibilities, as also being the process of *determining* the contents of those concepts, including their relations of material inferential consequence and incompatibility? Here again I think it is useful to think of an analogy that is not one that Hegel himself appeals to. Consider the development of concepts of English and American common law. Unlike the creatures of statutory law, there are no explicit original definitions or initial principles laying down circumstances and consequences of application for these concepts. All there is to give them content is the actual applications that have been made of them over the years. They are case law all the way down.

The judge must decide, for each new case, *both* what to endorse—that is, whether or not to take the concept in question to apply to the situation as described—*and* what the material incompatibility exclusions and consequential inclusions articulating the content of the concept are. And for *both* these tasks the only raw materials available are provided by how previous cases have been decided. It will help to think of a simplified, stylized version of this process. Cases consist of a set of facts specified in an antecedent, non-legal vocabulary. The task in each case is to decide the applicability of some distinguished legal vocabulary (such as "strictly liable" or "contractually obliged"). The judge in each new case makes a decision, to apply or not to apply the legal concept in question, given the facts of the case. For each such decision, the judge may be conceived of as supplying also a justifying rationale. That rationale can be thought of as having two parts. First, it points to and privileges some respects of similarity and dissimilarity between the case at issue and the facts of other, previously decided cases involving the application of the same legal concept. It might rationalize applying the concept in the present case by pointing to other cases that shared some descriptions of the facts with this one, in which the concept was applied, and pointing to differences from some prior cases in which application of the concept was rejected. The cases selected are normatively privileged by the current judge as *precedential* with respect to the present case, and the respects of similarity and dissimilarity to them that are cited delineate implicit rules of inference from the applicability of non-legal concepts in specifying the facts of the case to the applicability of the legal concepts. Second, the rationale can appeal to the explicit rationales associated with these precedential decisions. In this process, each new decision, with its accompanying rationale, including a selection of precedents, relevant considerations, and rules of inference and incompatibility, helps to determine further the conceptual content of the legal term whose application is up for adjudication.

In engaging in this kind of practice, participating in this kind of process, the judge is performing what is recognizably a kind of synthesis by rational integration. For his selection of precedents, privileging of respects of similarity and difference, and construction of an explicit rationale for a commitment *is* the integration of that commitment with the commitments undertaken by the adjudicators of previous cases. On the ampliative side, the judge is extracting material inferential consequences from their commitments—at least according to the accompanying rationale. And on the critical side, the judge is rejecting prior commitments that would be materially incompatible with the current decision—by *not* treating those decisions, or the considerations they turn on, as valid or binding precedents. But it is clear how what the judge is doing is *also* intelligible as *developing* and *determining* the conceptual contents (thought of now in terms of relations of material consequence and incompatibility) that in turn constrain the process going forward.

What kind of structure of authority and responsibility is exhibited by a process like this? One might first be struck by the fact that the legal concepts that develop in this way are, as the point is often put, "judge-made law." There is nothing to them that is not the cumulative result of judicial decisions to apply or not to apply the concepts in particular cases. The deciding judge exercises authority both over the content of the legal concepts being applied and thereby over future judges. For in selecting the prior cases he treats as precedential and the features of the facts he takes as salient in making the decision and providing a rationale for it, the judge both further determines the content of the concept and provides potential precedents and rationales to which future judges are responsible.

But that description shows that there is also a sense in which any deciding judge is *responsible to* the content of the concept whose applicability is being assessed, by being responsible to the authority exercised by the commitments of the prior judges whose decisions are available to provide precedents and rationales. For the justification of a judge's decision can appeal only to the authority of prior decisions, and to the conceptual content those decisions have conferred on or discovered in the legal term in question. Here the current judge is responsible to the *conceptual content* (semantic responsibility) expressed by the legal term, *by* being responsible to the *commitments* of previous judges (responsibility to, acknowledgment of the authority of the *attitudes* of *others*), in accepting the *task*-responsibility (the responsibility to *do* something) to synthesize a rational (including consequences and excluding incompatibles) *contemporary* unity *by* integrating the commitments of *past* judges. *Stare decisis,* the authority of precedent, is a matter of how the relations of material consequence and incompatibility that have actually been endorsed (normative attitudes) determine what one is actually responsible for (normative statuses).

In offering a rationale, a justification for a decision, the judge presents what is in effect a rational reconstruction of the tradition that makes it visible as authoritative insofar as, so presented, the tradition at once *determines* the conceptual content one is adjudicating the application of and *reveals* what that content is, and so how the current question of applicability ought to be decided. It is a *reconstruction* because some prior decisions are treated practically as irrelevant, non-precedential, or incorrect. It is a *rational* reconstruction insofar as there is a standing obligation that the commitments, considerations, and implicit relations of material inclusion and exclusion that are embraced by a rationale as precedential, salient, and implicit must fit together with the new commitment that is the decision being made, so as to constitute the very sort of rational unity Kant saw as the ideal or standard normatively governing the synthesis of an original unity of apperception. The rationale is an account delineating the boundaries of the authority of the conceptual content associated with a legal term, determined by the attitudes of the prior judges' precedential decisions and rationales, to which the current judge is responsible, in the sense that that content sets the standards for normative assessments of the correctness of that judge's decision.

Here is my first major claim: this sort of practice or process of sequential rational integration of new commitments into a constellation of prior commitments institutes normative statuses of authority and responsibility according to the model of reciprocal recognition. This is how the model of synthesis of a unity of apperception by rational integration, which I discussed in Chapter One, is combined with the model of the synthesis of normative subjects or selves and their communities by mutual recognition, which I discussed in Chapter Two. In our example, each deciding judge recognizes the authority of past decisions, and the contents they institute and acknowledge, over the assessment of the correctness of the decision being made. That judge also exercises authority over future judges, who are constrained by that judge's decisions, insofar as they are precedential. But the currently deciding judge is also responsible to (and held responsible by) future judges, who can (by their practical attitudes) either take the current decision (and rationale) to be correct and precedential or not. For the current judge actually to exercise the authority the decision implicitly petitions for recognition of, it must be recognized by future judges. And if that precedential authority *is* recognized by the later judges, then it is real (a normative status has been instituted by those attitudes), according to the model of reciprocal recognition. Both in acknowledging and in claiming the authority of precedent, the judge is implicitly acknowledging the authority also of future judges, who administer that authority. For they assess whether the new commitment has been appropriately integrated with prior commitments, and decide on that basis whether to acknowledge it as authoritative, as normatively constraining future commitments in that they must be integrated with it. So each judge is recognized (implicitly) as authoritative by prior judges (the ones whose decisions are being assessed as precedential or not) and (explicitly) by future judges (the ones who assess the current decision as authoritative, that is precedential, or not). And each judge recognizes the authority both of prior judges (to whose precedential decisions the judge is responsible) and of future judges (on whose assessments of the extent to which the present judge has fulfilled his responsibility to the decisions of prior judges the present judge's authority wholly depends). Because the future stands to the present as the present does to the past, and there is no final future, hence no final authority, every judge is symmetrically recognized and recognizing.

**4.** In making a decision, a judge undertakes a commitment. The model of reciprocal recognition explains how that attitude, together with the attitudes of others, institutes normative statuses of authority and responsibility intelligible as commitment. The sequences of successive rational integration of new commitments with previous ones exhibit this historical structure of reciprocal recognition. What we now need to see is how that fact makes sense *also* of a dimension of symmetric authority over and responsibility to *determinate conceptual contents* for *both* specific recognitive attitudes of attributing and acknowledging commitments *and* the normative statuses those attitudes institute. One of Hegel's key ideas, as I read him, is that in order to understand how the historical process of *applying* determinately contentful concepts to undertake discursive commitments (taking responsibility for those commitments by rationally integrating them with others one has already undertaken) can also be the process of *determining* the contents of those concepts, we need a new notion of determinateness.

What we might call "*Fregean* determinateness" is a matter of sharp, complete boundaries. For Frege, each concept must be determinate in the sense that it must be semantically settled for every object, definitively and in advance of applying the concept epistemically, whether the object does or does not fall under the concept. No objects either both do and do not, or neither do nor do not, fall under it. I'll discuss this representational dimension of conceptual content in the next section. The dimension of conceptual content that is made intelligible in the first instance by the synthetic activity of rational integration, we have seen, is articulated by relations of material inferential consequence and incompatibility. What corresponds to Fregean determinateness for conceptual contents specified in terms of these relations is that for every potential material inference in which any judgment that results from applying the concept figures as a premise or conclusion, it is definitively settled semantically, in advance of any actual applications, whether it is a good inference, and similarly for the relations of material incompatibility that hold between those judgments and any others. Here the sharp, complete boundaries that must be semantically settled definitively are those around the sets of materially good inferences and materially incompatible sets of sentences.

Hegel associates the demand for conceptual contents that are definite in this sense with the early modern tradition that culminates in Kant. It is the central element in the metaconceptual framework Hegel calls 'Verstand'. He proposes to replace this static way of thinking about the determinateness of the *relations* that articulate conceptual contents with a dynamic account of the *process* of determin*ing* those contents, which he calls 'Vernunft'. Roughly, he thinks that Verstand is what you get if you assume that those applying concepts always already have available the contents that would result from *completing* the process of determining those contents by sequential rational integration exhibiting the historical structure of reciprocal recognitive authority and responsibility. He is very much aware of the *openness* of the use of expressions that is the practice at once of applying concepts in judgment and determining the content of the concepts those locutions express. This is the sense in which prior use does *not* close off future possibilities of development by settling in advance a unique correct answer to the question of whether a particular concept applies in a new set of circumstances. The new circumstances will always resemble any prior, settled case in an infinite number of respects, and differ from it in an infinite number of respects. There is genuine room for choice on the part of the current judge or judger, depending on which prior commitments are taken as precedential and which respects of similarity and difference are emphasized.[4] After all, in the absence of any prior governing statute or definition, all there is to the content of the concept in question is what has been put into it by the applica-

---

4. This way of putting things highlights the features of the situation that encourage the temptation to think that the judge is totally unconstrained by the tradition. But to emphasize the fact that the judge is obliged to *privilege* some respects of similarity and dissimilarity out of this wide-open field is not yet to say that every way of doing so is as good as every other, given the tradition of prior authoritative privilegings constituted by previous judgments. Of course, judgments of better and worse in this regard, as in any other, are a matter of the attitudes of some actual participants in the practice—in this case, later judges.

tions of it that have actually been endorsed or rejected. Prior uses do not determine the correctness of all possible future applications of a concept "like rails laid out to infinity," as Wittgenstein would later put the point.

**5.**    So is Hegel's idea that we can take conceptual contents that turn out to be *in*determinate in the Kant-Frege sense—because no amount of prior use settles once and for all and in principle which of all possible future uses are correct—and just *call* them 'determinate', in his new sense? He does in the end want to do that, but not in the immediate, stipulative, ultimately irresponsible way that would have, as Russell says, "all the advantages of theft over honest toil." Instead, he takes on the hard work needed to entitle himself to a move of this shape. For, first, he wants us to step back and ask a more basic question: what *kind of fact* is it that prior uses constrain, but do not settle, in the Kant-Frege sense, how it would be correct to go on? His answer is that what is correct is a matter of a normative status, of what one is and isn't committed or entitled to, responsible for, and what would authorize such commitments. On his account, that kind of fact is a social recognitive fact—one, further, that is instituted by a process with the distinctive *historical* version of the structure of reciprocal recognition. Second, he uses that structure to fill in the details of a structurally new notion of determinateness, in which the Kantian Verstand conception takes its place as merely one recognitive moment in a larger whole.

For that to happen, the Kantian account of rational integration of new commitments into a synthetic unity with prior commitments must also be recontextualized as merely one aspect of a more general rational integrative-synthetic activity. For the original account appeals to fixed, definite relations of material inferential consequence and incompatibility, construed as given, settled in advance, and determinate according to the Verstand framework. What Hegel adds is a *retrospective* notion of *rationally reconstructing* the process that led to the commitments currently being integrated (not just the new one, but all the prior ones that are taken as precedential for it, too). This is a kind of genealogical justification or vindication of those commitments, showing why previous judgments were correct in the light of still earlier ones—and in a different sense, also in the light of subsequent ones. Hegel calls this process "Erinnerung," or *recollection.*

A good example of it is the sort of Whiggish, triumphalist, rationally reconstructed history of their disciplines to be found in old-fashioned science and mathematics textbooks. Such a story supplements an account of what we now know with an account of how we found it out. What from the point of view of our current commitments appear retrospectively to have been wrong turns, dead ends, superseded theories, and degenerating research programs are ignored—however promising they seemed at the time, however good the reasons for that were, and however much effort was devoted to them. What is picked out and presented instead is a trajectory of cumulative, unbroken progress—of discoveries that have stood the test of time. It is a story about how we found out what the real boundaries of our current concepts are, hence how they ought properly to be applied, by finding out what really follows from what and what is really incompatible with what. Hegel thinks that our activity of telling stories like this is reason's march through history. It is the way we retrospectively *make* our applications of concepts (have been) *rational,* in the sense of responsive to discursive norms, by finding a way concretely to *take* them to be rational, in that sense. For in rationally reconstructing the tradition concept users retrospectively discern conceptual norms that are determinately contentful in the Kantian Verstand sense, as having been in play all along, with different aspects of their boundaries (relations of material consequence and incompatibility) discovered by correct (precedential) applications at various critical junctures in the development of the tradition.

We can think of the way the theoretical metaconceptual role played by the Hegelian notion of <u>recollection</u> is related to the Kantian idea of <u>rational integration</u> in either of two ways. We can think of Hegel as adding a complementary, recognitively dual notion alongside rational integration. *Integrating* is taking *responsibility,* making a commitment, by petitioning future concept users to be recognized; *recollecting* is asserting *authority,* vindicating an entitlement, by recognizing past concept users. Together the two make up a recognitive whole. But we can also think of the basic Kantian idea that what one needs to *do* to count thereby as having undertaken a discursive commitment, taken responsibility for a claim or judgment, is rationally to integrate it with other commitments as being broadened and extended by the Hegelian move, so that the rational unity that must be synthesized (the "original synthetic unity of apperception") comprises the whole developmental process by which one arrived at one's current commitments, and not just the current time-slice of that ongoing enterprise. The new kind of rational unity requires not just that one have extracted the inferential consequences of one's commitments and excised the incompatibilities from among them, but also that one have shown how the process by which those commitments arose out of their predecessors was a rational one. The retrospective justificatory responsibility is not only to exhibit the doxastic commitments one now acknowledges as fitting together rationally, but also to exhibit the concepts applied in those judgments—the material inferential and incompatibility commitments that articulate their conceptual contents—as the products of a rational process.

**6.**　　The new Vernunft conception of <u>determinateness</u> that Hegel proposes is an essentially *temporally perspectival* one. Looked at *retro*spectively, the process of *determining* conceptual contents (and of course at the same time the correct applications of them) by applying them appears as a theoretical, epistemic task. One is "determining" the conceptual contents in the sense of *finding out* which are the right ones, what norms really govern the process (and so should be used to assess the correctness of applications of the concepts in question), that is, finding out what really follows from what and what is really incompatible with what. A *recollective reconstruction* of the tradition culminating in the current set of conceptual commitments-and-contents shows, from the point of view of that set of commitments-and-concepts, taken as correct, how we gradually, step by step, came to acknowledge (in our attitudes) the norms (normative statuses such as commitments) that all along implicitly governed our practices—for instance, what we were really, whether we knew it or not, committed to about the melting point of a piece of metal when we applied the concept <u>copper</u> to it. From this point of view, the contents of our concepts have always been perfectly determinate in the Kant-Frege Verstand sense, though we didn't always know what they were.

Looked at *pro*spectively, the process of *determining* conceptual concepts by applying them appears as a practical, constructive semantic task. By applying concepts to novel particulars one is "determining" the conceptual contents in the sense of *making it* the case that some applications are correct, by *taking it* to be the case that they are. One is drawing new, more definite boundaries, where many possibilities existed before. By investing one's authority in an application as being correct, one authorizes those who apply the concept to future cases to do so also. If they in turn recognize one in this specific respect, by acknowledging that authority, then a more determinate norm has been socially instituted. From this point of view, conceptual norms are never fully determinate in the Kant-Frege Verstand sense, since there is always room for further determination. The conceptual norms are not completely indeterminate either, since a lot of actual applications have been endorsed as correct by potentially precedent-setting judgments. All the determinateness the content has is the product of that activity.

So are the contents of empirical concepts *determinate,* in the Kant-Frege Verstand sense, as the retrospective epistemic perspective has it, or *in*determinate in that sense, as the prospective semantic perspective has it? Hegel thinks that if the only metaconceptual expressive tool one has available to describe the situation is that static, non-perspectival Verstand conception of determinateness, the answer would have to be "Both"—or, just as correctly, "Neither." That those two answers do not make any sense within the metaconceptual framework of Verstand just shows the expressive impoverishment and inadequacy of that framework. What we should say is that concepts have contents that are both determinate and further determinable, in the sense provided by the dynamic, temporally perspectival framework of Vernunft. Do we *make* our concepts, or do we *find* them? Are we authoritative over them, or responsible to them? Hegel's model entitles him to answer "Both." For both aspects are equally essential to the functioning of concepts in the ever-evolving constellation of concepts-and-commitments he calls "the Concept." Authority and responsibility are coordinate and reciprocal, according to the mutual recognition model of normativity that is Hegel's successor to Kant's autonomy model. And when such a structure of reciprocal recognitive attitudes takes the special form of a historical-developmental process, the contents of those attitudes and the statuses they institute can be considered from both prospective and retrospective temporal recognitive perspectives. Those perspectives are two sides of one coin. Hegel's Vernunft metaconception of <u>determinateness</u> is articulated by the complementary contributions of these two different aspects of one unitary process. That it is a *rational* unity, at each stage and across stages, is secured by the fact that new commitments are undertaken by a process of rational integration in the new, broader sense that includes justifying those commitments by recollective rational reconstruction of the tradition that produced them (in addition to the critical resolution of incompatibilities and ampliative extraction of inferential consequences, which Kant had already acknowledged).

If we revert for a moment to the jurisprudential example of judges at common law, with which I introduced the historical form of reciprocal recognition, we find a striking expression of the unhelpfulness of thinking about conceptual contents according to the Verstand model. A classic debate in jurisprudential theory pits two views against one another. According to one, the law is what some judge takes it to be. A statement of what is legal (a normative status) is a matter-of-factual *prediction* about what a judge would decide (the judge's normative attitude). Extreme forms of legal realism, within the scope of this legal positivism, in addition insist that what the judge says is typically determined by non-legal reasons or causes. Legal decisions are brought about causally by such factors as "what the judge had for breakfast," as the slogan has it (and, more realistically, by his training, cultural circle, and reading). On the other side is a view according to which the judge's job is not to *make* the law, but to *find out* what it already is (whether that is understood to be a matter of what norm the statutes or the precedents really institute, or of what natural law dictates, or any other conception). On the Hegelian view, both of these are literally "one-sided" (mis)conceptions. The former sees only the judge's authority, but not his responsibility, and the latter sees only his responsibility, but not his authority. What is needed is an account that does justice to both, to their essential interrelations with each other, and to the way the process of which both are aspects determines conceptual contents. Hegel's new notion of <u>determinateness</u> is constructed as a response to just these criteria of adequacy.

7. The pragmatist order of explanation, which we have seen in play throughout, seeks to understand discursive *content* in terms of the rational *activity* of normative subjects—to explain the *contents* of their commitments, what they in that special and derivative sense make themselves

responsible for, in terms of a more basic notion of what they are responsible for *doing*. By this point in the story, that activity is being considered in the broader sense that includes both the rational *integration* of *new* commitments and the rational *recollection* of *old* ones. The aim is to understand the relations that articulate conceptual content in terms of that kind of multifaceted process. I have said something about the Janus-faced, historically perspectival Hegelian Vernunft conception of <u>determinateness</u> of conceptual content, as regards the relations of material inferential consequence and incompatibility. But these remarks address only one dimension of conceptual content: the one that in Chapter One I called the "expressive" dimension, 'that'-intentionality. Another methodological aspiration that Hegel shares with Kant, as I read them, is to use the understanding of claimable contents in this sense (which, according to the pragmatist methodological commitment, is to be derived from thinking about what normative subjects *do* to take responsibility for such contents) in turn to explain the *representational* dimension of conceptual content: 'of'-intentionality. We saw how this worked for Kant: how at least a formal concept of representational purport, of treating one's claims as *about* objects, could be made intelligible in terms of the activity of rational integration constrained by relations of material inference and incompatibility. I want to close by saying how I think the corresponding Hegelian story about reference and representation goes.

In keeping with what I have presented as Kant's axial insight, representation, too, is understood in ultimately *normative* terms. What is represent*ed* is what exercises a distinctive kind of *authority* over represent*ings* of it. Representings as such must be understood to be *responsible* to what they represent; what is represented must provide a standard for normative assessment of their *correctness*, as representings. The explanatory task is to understand this special kind of representational normativity: the way what is said or thought is responsible for its correctness to what the subject thereby counts as talking or thinking *about*, in the normative sense of its being semantically or intentionally authoritative, its providing the standard for a distinctive kind of assessment of correctness.

In keeping with the overarching Enlightenment commitment to the *attitude-dependence* of normative statuses such as authority and responsibility, we need to understand what constellation of normative attitudes can *institute* the distinctively representational kind of authority and responsibility. What do knowing and acting subjects have to *do* in order thereby to count as having *deferred* or *accorded* authority over the correctness of their commitments to what they then in this distinctive normative sense count as making commitments *about?* More particularly, we want now to see how Hegel's *social* rendering of the attitude-dependence of the normative, in terms of the model of reciprocal recognition, and his account of how *historical* processes that exhibit that recognitive structure in virtue of incorporating the dual perspectival structure of prospective rational integration and retrospective rational recollection, can be understood as instituting a distinctively *representational* kind of normativity—as providing the standard for the assessment of a distinctive kind of correctness.

We do *not* need to move to this dimension of conceptual content in order to understand the idea that our judgments are *constrained,* that their evolution is subject to *friction.* For in the empirical, as opposed to the juridical, case, practitioners are trained to acquire some normative attitudes *immediately,* that is, *non*-inferentially. Under the right circumstances, properly trained observers are reliably disposed to respond to perceptible states of affairs by acknowledging commitments to corresponding perceptual judgments. The Verstand framework is not in a position to understand how there can be genuine *constraint* by norms (hence *friction* that constrains rational integration, going forward) unless the norms already instituted are *determinate* in the sense that they *necessitate* (*one* sense of 'determine') one rational unity rather than another. (Compare the jurisprudential theorists who think that if the law as previously instituted-determined does not *dictate* one unique result, then the only alternative is to understand judges as just making it up, unconstrained.) But this is a mistake. Like any other judgments, immediate perceptual judgments amount to petitions for recognition. The authority they claim may or may not be recognized by being incorporated in later rational integrations. But they exert constraint or friction just by making that petition for recognition. They help determine what one ought to be committed to, and in that sense increase empirical determinateness.

We have already in play a conception of the <u>sense</u> *expressed* by declarative sentences: what one thinks or says in endorsing such a sentence. That conception understands conceptual contents as articulated by relations of material inferential consequence and incompatibility among those contents. Besides that as it were *horizontal* dimension of conceptual contents, we are now seeking to underwrite the *vertical* dimension that depends on relations between those contents or senses and their referents in the world: what one is talking or thinking *about* in virtue of endorsing those claimable senses or contents. Hegel thinks that the representational relation between senses and the referents they normatively answer to for their correctness can be understood in terms of the prior notion of the sort of content judgments must possess in order to be eligible for integration into a rational unity of apperception, when we think about how those contents are shaped by an integrative process that includes symmetric, ultimately *recognitive* relations, both of *pro*spective rational synthesis and of *retro*spective rational recollection and reconstruction of the tradition that determines them. To do that, one must make a further move.

Frege thinks of the senses we grasp in thought and their referents in reality as two different *kinds* of things—as denizens of different ontological realms. It is a central part of Hegel's idealist strategy to take them to be things of the *same* generic kind. The conceptual contents of our thoughts are articulated by material consequential and incompatibility relations they stand in to one another. (Hegel calls these relations of "mediation" and "determinate negation.") But facts and objective states of affairs, too, stand in consequential and incompatibility relations to one another (and objects, we have seen, are to be understood in terms of the roles they play in those relations).[5] The fact that the coin is metal is a consequence of the fact that it is copper. And that same fact objectively rules out the possibility that it is an electrical insulator. The principled parallel between the *deontic* modal relations of inclusion and exclusion that articulate our thought on the subjective side and the *alethic* modal relations of inclusion and exclusion that articulate the world on the objective side, which I discussed at the end of Chapter One, define a structural conception of the <u>conceptual</u> according to which thought and the world thought about can

---

5. In fact, for reasons he discusses in the *Force and Understanding* chapter of the *Phenomenology*, Hegel is more holistic than this. In his preferred idiom, he does not talk about facts or states of affairs on the objective side, or about the determinate thoughts expressed by individual judgments on the subjective side, but only about the conceptually articulated wholes of which they are features. This holism is an important part of Hegel's picture, but I have chosen to suppress it in the interests of expository simplicity in focusing on other aspects of his views.

both be seen to be *conceptually* structured. This *conceptual realism* about objective reality is, in the context of the other metatheoretic commitments we have been considering, just a consequence of *modal realism:* taking it that objective states of affairs really do necessitate and rule out one another. I hope it is clear at this point that, given the conception of the conceptual in play, seeing the objective as well as the subjective realms as alike conceptually structured does not entail any claims about the causal "mind-dependence" of objective reality: of represented things on the activity of representing them. I have discussed elsewhere the crucial difference between seeing the *concept* of objective reality depending for its *sense* on our understanding of the rational activities of knowing subjects, on the one hand, and seeing the *referents* of that concept as depending on such activities, on the other. The idealism in play here is decisively of the former sort.[6]

Hegel's single-sort ontology of semantics takes both what things are *for* consciousness and what they are *in* themselves to be conceptually articulated. He thinks that any two-sort ontology that does not acknowledge this crucial generic similarity will be dualistic. (Slogan: "A dualism is a distinction drawn in such a way as to render unintelligible crucial relations between the distinguished items.") For it will underwrite a kind of semantic skepticism, according to which it is unintelligible that we should know how things actually are. On the single-sort approach, the content of my thought that these are my hands can be the fact itself—the two differing only in that the one has, as it were, deontic force, while the other has alethic force. ("A fact is a thought that is true.")[7] On the other hand, Hegel

---

6. "Holism and Idealism in Hegel's Phenomenology," chap. 6 of *Tales of the Mighty Dead* (Cambridge, MA: Harvard University Press, 2002).

7. This is, of course, Frege's slogan, in "The Thought." It depends on using 'thought' to mean *thinkable,* not *thinking.* In a way it is misleading for me to use Frege as the two-sorted foil for Hegel here. For Frege, what contrasts with thoughts (which are in the realm of sense) is objects-and-concepts (which are in the realm of reference, and are more like Tractarian facts). For Frege it is *not* the case that the world we are talking and thinking about consists of *facts.* For it does not, as it does for Hegel, consist of thinkables (not even true ones). For Frege, facts are facts *about* objects in the very same sense in which thoughts are about objects. The view I am associating with Hegel would take the sense in which facts are about objects to be secondary, derivative from and parasitic on the sense in which thoughts are. A more contemporary formulation would be that facts are about objects *only* in the sense that the sentences that express them contain singular terms that refer to objects.

also thinks that to assume that we know in advance of applying concepts epistemically in experience which relations of consequential inclusion and incompatibility exclusion articulate the contents of our concepts is to fall into a kind of semantic dogmatism. The solution is to focus on the process of experience by which all of our commitments, including those that address the relations among concepts, rationally and empirically develop. It is in terms of that historical process that we are to understand

(i) the conceptual form of facts and objects—what makes them *intelligible,* what makes *knowledge* of them possible, the reason that what they are can be *said* of them,

on the one hand, and

(ii) the objective content of claims and concepts—the way they answer to how things are and what there is as a standard of correctness, what makes it possible for them, when all goes right, to express genuine knowledge *of* something,

as two sides of one coin, each of which can only be understood in terms of the other. In the traditional (Verstand) conception, the distinction between appearances and reality, phenomena and noumena, is ontological, global, and absolute. In the conception Hegel is developing (Vernunft), the distinction is perspectival, local, and relativized. What it is (doubly) local and relativized to is a stage in the development of the whole constellation of discursive commitments, as retrospectively viewed from another such stage.

Within the scope of that unitary ontology of sense and reference, Hegel is addressing the question: what do we have to *do* thereby to be taking or treating the conceptual contents (senses), which we understand by grasping their material consequential and incompatibility relations to one another, *as* subjective *appearances of* some underlying objective *reality* to which they answer for their correctness *as* appearances of *it?* His answer is that the idea of *noumena,* of things as they are in themselves, the reality that appears in the form of *phenomena,* can be understood practically in terms of a distinctive role in a recollectively rationally reconstructed historical sequence of phenomena. One of the senses in which what he presents is a *phenomenology* is that he starts with an account of phenomena (what things are for consciousness) and seeks to reconstruct the notion of noumena (what things are in themselves) out of the resources it provides. The result of the most recent rational integration into the constellation of one's prior commitments of some new commitment (perhaps arrived at non-inferentially by observation, or inferentially by extracting new consequences from prior commitments) is intelligible as one's commitments as to how things really are, objectively, in themselves—as being what one takes to be not just an appearance of that reality, but a *veridical* appearance, one in which things appear as they really are—when it is accompanied by the right kind of rational recollection of the process of experience that produced it. The right kind of recollection is one that picks out a trajectory through the previous results of one's actual integrations that is *expressively progressive.* That is, it must exhibit a history that both culminates in one's current view and has the form of the gradual making *explicit* of what can now retrospectively be seen all along to have been *implicit.* Doing that is showing for each previous episode (of those that are selected as, as it were, precedential, as revelatory of what one now takes always already to have been there) how that set of commitments can be seen as a partial, and only partially correct revelation of things as they are now known (or at least taken) to be. That is, one must show how each of the recollectively privileged prior integrations made *progress* toward one's current constellation of commitments—both in the judgments that are endorsed and in the consequential and incompatibility relations taken to articulate the concepts applied in those judgments. In taking one's current commitments as the standard to judge what counts as expressive progress, one *is* taking them as the *reality* of which previous constellations of endorsements were ever more complete and accurate *appearances.* That is the lesson that the normative understanding of the representation relation teaches: what is represented is what serves as a standard for assessing what thereby, in this normative sense, counts as a representing (an appearance) of it.

Another way of putting the point is that the way the idea of <u>reference of *appearances* to an underlying *reality* that they represent</u>—the idea that they are appearances *of* some reality that was always already there, objectively (in the sense of being independent of the attitudes that are its appearances)—arises and is secured *for* consciousness itself is through the experience of *error:* through the realization of the untruth of appearances, as Hegel puts it. Prior error is acknowledged *internally* in each rational integration by engaging in the activity of repairing incompatible commitments (as prior ignorance is acknowledged by embracing a new consequence). And using one's current commitments as the *external* standard for assessing which such prior developments and adjustments were *successful* is treating it as presenting the reality, how things are in themselves, that all the others were more or less adequate appearances of. A successful recollective reconstruction of the tradition shows how previously endorsed constellations of commitments were unmasked, by internal instabilities, *as* appearances, representing how things really are only incompletely and partially incorrectly, but also how each such discovery contributed to filling in or correcting the picture they present of how it really is with what they were all along representing, by more closely approximating the actual consequential and incompatibility relations of the concepts and making more correct applications of them. So they were not *mere* appearances, in that they did genuinely reveal something of how things really are. Exhibiting a sequence of precedential concept applications-by-integration as *expressively progressive*—as the gradual, cumulative making explicit of reality as revealed by one's current commitments, recollectively made visible as having all along been implicit—shows the prior, defective commitments endorsed, and conceptual contents deployed, as nonetheless genuinely appearances representing, however inadequately, how things really are.

There is hard, concrete work involved in the retrospective semantic enterprise of recollectively turning a *past* into a *history* of this sort, just as there is in the prospective epistemic enterprise of integrating new commitments by extracting consequences and repairing incompatibilities.[8] For the provision of a rational genealogy vindicating one's current com-

---

8. As this formulation indicates (in the context of my prior claims), *both* retrospective *and* prospective perspectives are now visible as having *both* semantic *and* epistemic aspects. This structure is Hegel's successor-conception to the Kant-Carnap picture of an antecedent activity in which semantic contents are (fully) determined, followed by a separate, subsequent activity of epistemic activity in which those contents are confronted by and applied in the world.

mitments is constrained by the requirement that it suitably connect the judgments and conceptual relations previously endorsed with those currently endorsed. Hegel is trying to think through, as rigorously as the metaconceptual expressive tools he has managed to make available permit, the consequences of understanding meaning or conceptual content as articulated by non-monotonic, seriously multipremise material inferential and incompatibility relations, in the context of the realization (which we latecomers to the point associate with Quine, and he associated with Duhem) that those relations depend on the whole context of collateral discursive commitments. Because the material consequential and incompatibility relations both involve multiple premises and are non-monotonic, one can always take any such relation that was previously endorsed to have been all right in its context of collateral commitments, but to be infirmed by the addition of new information in later ones. Any such refinement of conceptual content itself involves a substantive commitment on the part of the one recapitulating the process of arriving at one's current constellation of commitments (including the conceptual contents that articulate them). And those commitments may themselves be found wanting by future recollecting assessors. A recollective rationalization of an integration is a petition for specific recognition, which like all such may or may not be successful in the eyes of those to whom it is addressed.

The retrospective, recollective form of reason (the owl of Minerva that flies only at dusk, reason's march through history) constructs a sunny, optimistic, Whiggish perspective that reveals, amid the random, contingent charnel house of our earlier discursive muddling, the emergence of an unbroken record of progress toward truth, understanding, and correct representation of how it is with the real world we turn out all along to have been thinking about and acting in. This is what Hegel means when he talks about "giving contingency the form of necessity." But it is important to remember that in the empirical case (whether we think of high theory, as when Newton's dynamics succeeds Descartes', and Einstein's Newton's, or simple cases of discovering the straight stick in the water only to appear bent), as in the juridical, a later recollective story may substantially disagree with an earlier one. It may treat some quite different episodes as progressive and precedential, quite different material inferences as good, different constellations of claims as incompatible. The moment of *finding*, discovering how things already were, which shows up from the perspective of each recollective reconstruction of a tradition is balanced by the moment of *making* that shows up when a new constellation of commitments must be integrated, and a new recollectively instituted tradition discovered to vindicate them. From the prospective perspective of new integrations driven by newly acknowledged commitments and consequences, and the emergence of new incompatibilities, the process of determining conceptual contents is characterized by discontinuities, caesurae, radical reassessment of old commitments, and the unraveling of previous progress. The open-endedness and determinability of conceptual contents lives in the spaces between successive recollective stories. Here we see the crookedness and zigzags that recollective rationality must then make straight: the creative *doings* that it must make look like *findings*.

At each stage, the author who retrospectively extracts an expressively progressive trajectory through past integrations as a vindication of the current synthesis of commitments as not only synchronically but diachronically rational exerts a distinctive kind of *authority* over the activity of past integrating recollectors, precisely by distinguishing some of them as correct and progressive, and rejecting others. But by the same token he makes himself *responsible* to the precedential authority of that previous activity, which supplies the only rationale available for his own. And that authority of the past over the present is administered on its behalf by future rational genealogists, who will pass judgment on the extent to which the current integration-and-recollection has fulfilled its responsibility to the prior tradition, and hence deserves to count as expressively progressive with respect to it. This structure of reciprocal authority and responsibility is the historical form of *recognition,* which institutes at once both a distinctive form of *community* (a *tradition*) and individuals exhibiting determinately conceptually contentful normative statuses: commitments representing how things objectively are. Recognition now shows up in its proper form, as a *process* providing the context within which we can understand the semantic *relations* that articulate the determinate conceptual contents of discursive commitments. This conception is recognizably a development of and a successor to Kant's story (retailed in Chapter One) about how the relations of material consequence and incompatibility function and become intelligible in the context of the *activity* of rational synthesis-by-integration of a transcendental unity of apperception.

Hegel thinks that each appearance, each actual constellation of commitments and conceptual contents, will eventually turn out to be inadequate. The inexhaustibility of concrete, sensuous immediacy guarantees that we will never achieve a set of conceptual contents articulated by relations of material inferential consequence and incompatibility that will not, when correctly applied, according to their own standards, at some point lead to commitments that are incompatible, according to those same standards.[9] No integration or recollection is final at the ground level. (Hegel does think a finally adequate set of philosophical and logical metaconcepts can be achieved. The *Phenomenology* and the *Science of Logic* each presents a kind of retrospective rational reconstructive recollection of what Hegel takes those narratives to vindicate as *the* set of metaconcepts that are necessary and sufficient to make explicit the process by which ordinary determinate empirical and practical concepts develop and are determined.) Still, one should not draw skeptical conclusions from the fallibilist metainduction this observation invites, should not see the course of empirical cognition as a "path of despair." To do that is to focus one-sidedly on just one of the reciprocal recognitive perspectives. It is to ignore the retrospective recollective perspective, which is *reason* imposing the form of *necessity* on *contingency, making* the process rational and expressively progressive by engaging in the practical labor of concretely *taking* it to be so. And it is the exhibition of the sequence of subjective appearances as a structured history comprising elements that function in that tradition not as not *mere* appearances, but as appearances that are genuinely, if only darkly, revelatory of objective reality. It is the

9. I expand on this point in my "Sketch of a Program for a Critical Reading of Hegel: Comparing Empirical and Logical Concepts" *Internationales Jahrbuch des Deutschen Idealismus* 3 (2005): 131–161.

*historical* dimension of consciousness that makes its *referential* dimension intelligible.[10]

**8.**   In Chapter One I introduced Kant's founding insight into the normative character of intentionality: his idea that what distinguishes judgments and intentional actions from the performances of merely natural creatures is that judging and acting are things we are in a distinctive sense normatively *responsible* for. I described his account of what one must *do* to take discursive responsibility (to acknowledge a commitment), as rationally integrating it with other such commitments, along both ampliative and critical dimensions. I attributed to him two additional large, orienting methodological commitments. One is to a pragmatist order of explanation, which moves from an account of *pragmatic force* to one of *semantic content,* understanding the conceptual contents one becomes committed to or responsible for in terms of what one becomes responsible for *doing* in judging. What one becomes responsible for doing, I said, is rational integration. That requires concepts to be articulated by the relations of material inferential consequence and incompatibility that they stand in to other such contents—corresponding respectively to the ampliative and critical dimensions of the activity of rational integration. The other methodological commitment is to a semantic order of explanation that moves

10. Hegel's diachronic approach also provides the raw materials for a genealogical-semantic account of a concept that is otherwise quite hard to understand: the Kantian notion of a *bare,* that is unconceptualized, sensuous intuition of a particular. For this concept can be made intelligible as what is supposed to be common to all the conceptual presentations of it—not just as presented in *one* retrospective rational reconstruction of an expressively progressive tradition, but *across all* the successive rational rewritings, both those so far produced and those yet to come. Within each rational genealogy of a currently integrated constellation of commitments, what is common to the sequence of conceptualizations presented as ever-more-adequate representations is what they are thereby taken to represent: what is implicit in them all, becoming ever more explicit over the course of the expressively progressive trajectory of thought that has been traced out. That is just the conceptualization in which the process (so far) culminates. As such, it is no bare intuition, but something fully conceptualized, presenting it as a "this-such." What gives us a grip on the concept of a bare, unconceptualized sensuous intuition (something *merely* immediate) is thinking of something as common and constant across *all* the *different* retrospective, expressively progressive rational genealogies, present and future. (I am grateful to Paul Redding for this thought.)

from this account of judgeable contents (what I called "expressive 'that'-intentionality) to an account of the representational dimension of conceptual content (what I called "'of'-intentionality"). Extracting these themes from Kant, and abstracting from his other collateral commitments, I tried to show how all these fit together.

I have ended by saying something about the form in which Hegel endorses all of these Kantian commitments, and showing how his in many ways quite different story grows out of and builds on Kant's. In Chapter Two, I described the recognitive model of the social institution of normative bindingness and normative statuses such as responsibility, authority, and commitment. This is what Hegel proposes as a successor to Kant's autonomy model of the attitude-dependence of normative statuses. The new theory is called for by appreciation of the complementary requirement of the relative *independence* of conceptual contents from the attitudes of endorsing or committing oneself to them. We saw how the social model of reciprocal recognition leads Hegel to a distinctive linguistic, expressive version of Kant's idea of freedom as consisting in constraint by discursive, which is to say rational, norms.

In this chapter, I have sketched how Hegel's way of working out the pragmatist order of explanation turns on complementing Kant's prospective notion of rational integration with a retrospective notion of rational recollection, and how that leads to a description of a distinctive *historical* process that exhibits the norm-instituting structure of reciprocal recognition. By offering a certain kind of rationally reconstructed genealogy, recollective activity in a distinctive way vindicates a set of determinate, ground-level commitments—in the sense of clarifying their contents, explaining the advent of those commitments as the outcome of a rational process, and justifying them.

I mentioned two other important structural moves that provide the context for Hegel's account of the *representational* dimension of conceptual content. He rejects the Kantian two-phase account, which requires that concepts be given determinate contents by some process distinct from and antecedent to the process of applying them in making ordinary empirical judgments. And he rejects the Kantian two-sorted ontology, which distinguishes how things are for consciousness (representings, phenomena) and how they are in themselves (representeds, noumena) as different *kinds* of things, the appearances conceptually articulated and the realities they represent not (a recipe, Hegel thinks, for epistemological and semantic skepticism). Finally, I closed by indicating how in the context of those further metatheoretic moves, the dual perspectival *historical* account of discursive practice—of what one must *do* in order to take rational responsibility for applications of concepts in judgment—makes sense of the representational dimension of conceptual content.[11] The new notion of *reason,* expanded to include both integration and recollection, is the centerpiece of an account of what discursive practitioners must *do* in order to be intelligible as granting authority over the correctness of what they say and think (in a sense of 'correct' corresponding to a distinctive normative dimension of assessment they institute by those very practical attitudes) to an objective reality they count thereby in this normative sense as representing or talking and thinking *about.*

The story I have told in these first three chapters aspires to be an exercise of reason in that sense. I have tried to show how some of Hegel's commitments can be understood as the result of rationally integrating some of Kant's commitments, by extracting consequences, and taking on new commitments so as to resolve incompatibilities. My highly selective engagement with the thought of both takes the form of a rational recollection: picking out an expressively progressive trajectory that takes us from Kant to Hegel. Further, we are now in a position to appreciate that the whole enterprise amounts to a more comprehensive retrospective, recollective rational reconstruction and reappropriation of the thought of both—one that aims at recovering and displaying (making explicit) a complex set of interlocking ideas, sometimes only implicit in their texts, which makes clear the relevance of this aspect of their thought to signifi-

---

11. Hegel's story retains the rational-integrative activity in terms of which (at the end of Chapter One) I explained the form of objective representational purport: what one has to *do* in order thereby to be purporting to represent objects. Added to that story about triangulating on objects by rejecting incompatibles and extracting consequences is the story about rational recollection, which explains what one needs to do to be treating commitments as appearances answering for their correctness to an underlying reality they represent: retrospectively carving out a trajectory that distinguishes some rational integrations as expressively progressive. We could say that the first account explains what it is to take or treat one's commitments as about *objects,* and the second what it is to take or treat them as *about* objects, in the sense of answering for their correctness to how it is with what there really is.

cant contemporary philosophical issues and debates. The tradition I have retrospectively picked out (and given a rationale for) by selectively privileging some ampliative and critical moves as precedential, expressively progressive developments has at its core a concern with how conceptual *content,* in various senses, can be understood in terms of its role in discursive *activity* more generally.[12] I think that a variety of specific lessons that are valuable for our own thinking about this topic today emerge when we carve out this line of thought from the myriad contingent collateral commitments with which it is entangled in the original presentations. And I think, hope, and trust that there are deeper and more general philosophical lessons we can find in the way this tradition embeds these relatively narrow and technical semantic concerns in the broader context of considerations provided by larger philosophical topics such as those I have indicated in the titles of these first three chapters: norms, selves, concepts, autonomy, community, freedom, history, reason, and reality.

12. I am encouraged by the extent to which important aspects of the tradition I have reconstructed here can also be found in the work of various influential neo-Kantians, particularly Cohen and the later Windelband. But that is another story.

# PART TWO

# Reason and Philosophy Today

# CHAPTER FOUR

# Reason, Expression, and the
# Philosophic Enterprise

**1.** In this chapter, I want to address the question "What is philosophy?" We might begin by acknowledging a distinction between things that have *natures* and things that have *histories*. Physical things such as electrons and aromatic compounds would be paradigmatic of the first class, while cultural formations such as English Romantic poetry and Ponzi schemes would be paradigmatic of the second. Applied to the case at hand, this distinction would surely place philosophy on the side of things that have histories. But now we might ask: does philosophy differ in this respect from physics, chemistry, or biology? Physical, chemical, and biological *things* have natures rather than histories, but what about the disciplines that define and study them? Should physics itself be thought of as something that has a nature, or as something that has a history? Concluding the latter is giving a certain kind of pride of place to the historical. For it is in effect treating the *distinction* between things that have natures and things that have histories, between things studied by the Naturwissenschaften and things studied by the Geisteswissenschaften, as itself a cultural formation: the sort of thing that itself has a history rather than a nature. And from here it is a short step (though not, to be sure, an obligatory one) to the thought that natures themselves are the sort of thing that have a history; certainly the *concepts* <u>electron</u> and <u>aromatic com-</u>

<u>pound</u> are that sort of thing. At this point the door is opened to a thoroughgoing historicism. It is often thought that this is the point to which Hegel—one of my particular heroes—brought us. I think that thought is correct, as far as it goes, but that we go very wrong if we think that that is where Hegel left us.

To say that philosophy is, at least to begin with, to be understood as the sort of thing that has a history rather than a nature is to foreground the way in which what deserves to be counted as distinctively philosophical activity answers to what has actually been done by those we recognize as precedential, tradition-transforming philosophers. One of Hegel's deepest and most important insights, I think, is indeed that the determinate contentfulness of any universal—in this case, the concept of <u>philosophy</u>— can only be understood in terms of the process by which it incorporates the contingencies of the particulars to which it has actually been applied. But he goes on from there to insist that it is in each case the responsibility of those of us who are heirs to such a conceptual tradition to see to it that it is a *rational* tradition—that the distinction it embodies and enforces between correct and incorrect applications of a concept can be *justified,* that applying it in one case and withholding application in another is something for which *reasons* can be given. It is only insofar as we can do that that we are entitled to understand what we are doing as applying *concepts.* We fulfill that obligation by rationally reconstructing the tradition, finding a coherent, cumulative trajectory through it that reveals it as expressively progressive—as the gradual unfolding into greater explicitness of commitments that can be seen retrospectively as always already having been implicit in it. That is, it is our job to rewrite the history so as to discover in it the revelation of what then retrospectively appears as an antecedent nature. Hegel balances the insight that even natures have histories by seeing rationality itself as imposing the obligation to construe histories as revelatory of natures.

The aim is to pick out a sequence of precedential instances or applications of a concept that amount to the delineation of a content for the concept, much as a judge at common law is obliged to do. *Making* the tradition rational is not independent of the labor of concretely *taking* it to be so. It is a criterion of adequacy of each such Whiggish rewriting of our disciplinary history that it create and display continuity and progress by its systematic inclusions and exclusions. The discontinuities that correspond to shifts of topic, the forgetting of lessons, and the degeneration of research programs are invisible from within each such telling; but those differences live on in the spaces between the tellings. Each generation redefines its subject by offering a new retrospective reading of its characteristic concerns and hard-won lessons.[1] But also, at any one time there will be diverse interpretations, complete with rival canons, competing designations of heroes, and accounts of their heroic feats. Making canons and baking traditions out of the rich ingredients bequeathed to us by our discursive predecessors is a game that all can play.

In this chapter, I am going to sketch one such perspective on what philosophers do—discern a nature as revealed by the history.

Ours is a broadly cognitive enterprise—I say "*broadly* cognitive" to indicate that I mean that philosophers aim at a kind of *understanding,* not, more narrowly, at a kind of *knowledge.* To specify the distinctive sort of understanding that is the characteristic goal of philosophers' writing is to say what distinguishes that enterprise from that of other sorts of constructive seekers of understanding, such as novelists and scientific theorists. I want to do so by focusing not on the peculiar genre of nonfiction creative writing by which philosophical understanding is typically conveyed (though I think that subject is worthy of consideration), but rather on what is distinctive about the understanding itself: both its particular topic and its characteristic goal. Philosophy is a reflexive enterprise: understanding is not only the *goal* of philosophical inquiry, but its *topic* as well. *We* are its topic; but it is us specifically as *understanding* creatures: *discursive* beings, makers and takers of *reasons,* seekers and speakers of *truth.* Seeing philosophy as addressing the nature and conditions of our rationality is, of course, a very traditional outlook—so traditional, indeed, that it is liable to seem quaint and old-fashioned. I'll address this issue later, remarking now only that rationalism is one thing and intellectualism another: pragmatists, too, are concerned with the practices of giving and asking for reasons.

---

1. I am describing, of course, for the concept philosophy an exercise of the sort of recollective rationality (Hegel's "Erinnerung") considered for ordinary determinate empirical concepts in Chapter Three.

I understand the task of philosophers to have as a central element the explication of concepts—or, put slightly more carefully, the development and application of expressive tools with which to make explicit what is implicit in the use of concepts. When I say "explication of concepts," it is hard not to hear "analysis of meanings." There are obviously affinities between my specification and that which defined the concern specifically of "analytic philosophy" in the middle years of the twentieth century. Indeed, I intend, *inter alia,* to be saying what was right about that conception. But what I have in mind is different in various ways. *Explication,* making explicit, is not the same as *analysis,* at least as that notion was classically conceived. As I use the term, for instance, we have no more privileged access to the contents of our concepts than we do to the facts we use them to state; the concepts and the facts are two sides of one coin.

But the most important difference is that where analysis of meanings is a fundamentally *conservative* enterprise (consider the paradox of analysis), I see the point of explicating concepts rather to be opening them up to rational *criticism.* The rational enterprise, the practice of giving and asking for reasons that lies at the heart of discursive activity, requires not only criticizing *beliefs,* as false or unwarranted, but also criticizing *concepts.* Defective concepts distort our thought and constrain us by limiting the propositions and plans we can entertain as candidates for endorsement in belief and intention. This constraint operates behind our backs, out of our sight, since it limits what we are so much as capable of being aware of. Philosophy, in developing and applying tools for the rational criticism of concepts, seeks to free us from these fetters, by bringing the distorting influences out into the light of conscious day, exposing the commitments implicit in our concepts as vulnerable to rational challenge and debate.

**2.** The first thing to understand about concepts is that <u>concept</u> is a *normative* concept. This is a lesson we owe ultimately to Kant—the great gray mother of us all. Kant saw us above all as traffickers in concepts. In fact, in a strict sense, *all* that Kantian rational creatures can do is to apply concepts. For that is the genus he took to comprise both *judgment* and *action,* our theoretical activity and our practical activity. One of Kant's great innovations was his view that what in the first instance distinguishes judgments and actions from the mere behavior of denizens of the realm of nature is that they are things that we are in a distinctive sense *responsible* for. They express *commitments* of ours. The norms or rules that determine what we have committed ourselves to, what we have made ourselves responsible for, by making a judgment or performing an action, Kant calls 'concepts'. Judging and acting involve undertaking commitments whose credentials are always potentially at issue. That is, the commitments embodied in judgments and actions are ones we may or may not be *entitled* to, so that the question of whether they are *correct*, whether they are commitments we *ought* to acknowledge and embrace, can always be raised. One of the forms taken by the responsibility we undertake in judging and acting is the responsibility to give reasons that justify the judgment or the action. And the rules that are the concepts we apply in judging and acting determine what would count as a reason for the judgment and the action.

Commitment, entitlement, responsibility—these are all normative notions. Kant replaces the *ontological* distinction between the physical and the mental with the *deontological* distinction between the realm of nature and the realm of freedom: the distinction between things that merely act regularly and things that are subject to distinctively normative sorts of assessment.

Thus for Kant the great philosophical questions are questions about the source and nature of normativity—of the bindingness or validity (Gültigkeit) of conceptual rules. Descartes had bequeathed to his successors a concern for *certainty:* a matter of our grip on concepts and ideas—paradigmatically, whether we have a hold on them that is clear and distinct. Kant bequeaths to his successors a concern rather for *necessity:* a matter of the grip concepts have on us, the way they bind or oblige us. 'Necessary' (notwendig) for Kant just means "according to a rule." (That is why he is willing to speak of moral and natural necessity as species of a genus.) The important lesson he takes Hume to have taught isn't about the threat of skepticism, but about how empirical knowledge is unintelligible if we insist on merely *describing* how things in fact *are,* without moving beyond that to *prescribing* how they *must* be, according to causal rules, and how empirical motivation (and so agency) is unintelligible if we stay at the level of *'is'* and eschew reference to the *'ought'*'s that outrun what merely is. Looking further back, Kant finds "the celebrated Mr. Locke" sidetracked into a mere "physiology of the understanding"—the tracing of causal antecedents of thought in place of its justificatory antecedents—through a failure to appreciate the essentially normative character of claims to knowledge. But Kant takes the whole Enlightenment to be animated by an at least implicit appreciation of this point. For mankind's coming into its intellectual and spiritual majority and maturity consists precisely in taking the sort of personal responsibility for its commitments, both doxastic and practical, insisted upon already by Descartes' meditator.

This placing of normativity at the center of philosophical concern is the reason behind another of Kant's signal innovations: the pride of place he accords to *judgment*. In a sharp break with tradition, he takes it that the smallest unit of experience, and hence of awareness, is the judgment. This is because judgments, applications of concepts, are the smallest unit for which knowers can be *responsible*. Concepts by themselves don't express commitments; they only determine what commitments would be undertaken if they were applied. (Frege will express this Kantian point by saying that judgeable contents are the smallest unit to which pragmatic force—paradigmatically the assertional force that consists in the assertor undertaking a special kind of commitment—can attach. Wittgenstein will distinguish sentences from terms and predicates as the smallest expressions whose freestanding utterance can be used to make a move in a language game.) The most general features of Kant's understanding of the form of judgment also derive from its role as a unit of responsibility. The "I think" that can accompany all representations (hence being, in its formality, the emptiest of all) is the formal shadow of the transcendental unity of apperception, the locus of responsibility determining a coresponsibility class of concept-applications (including actions), what is responsible *for* its judgments. The objective correlate of this subjective aspect of the form of judgment is the "object=X" to which the judgment is directed, the formal shadow of what the judgment makes the knower responsible *to*.

I think that philosophy is the study of us as creatures who judge and act, that is, as discursive, concept-using creatures. And I think that Kant is right to emphasize that understanding what we do in these terms is attributing to us various kinds of normative status, taking us to be subject to distinctive sorts of normative appraisal. So a central philosophical task is understanding this fundamental normative dimension within which we dwell. Kant's own approach to this issue, developing themes from Rousseau, is based on the thought that genuinely normative authority (constraint by norms) is distinguished from causal power (constraint by facts) in that it binds only those who *acknowledge* it as binding. Because one is subject only to that authority one subjects oneself to, the normative realm can be understood equally as the realm of *freedom.* So being constrained by norms is not only compatible with freedom—properly understood, it can be seen to be what freedom consists in. I don't know of a thought that is deeper, more difficult, or more important than this.

**3.**   Kant's most basic idea, I said, is that judgment and action are things we are in a distinctive way *responsible* for. What does it mean to be responsible for them? I think the kind of responsibility in question should be understood to be task responsibility: the responsibility to do something. What (else) do judging and acting oblige us to do? The commitments we undertake by applying concepts in particular circumstances— by judging and acting—are ones we may or may not be entitled to, according to the rules (norms) implicit in those concepts. Showing that we are entitled by the rules to apply the concept in a particular case is *justifying* the commitment we undertake thereby, offering *reasons* for it. That is what we are responsible for, the practical content of our conceptual commitments. In undertaking a conceptual commitment one renders oneself in principle liable to demands for reasons. The normative appraisal to which we subject ourselves in judging and acting is appraisal of our reasons. Further, offering a reason for the application of a concept is always applying another concept: making or rehearsing another judgment or undertaking or acknowledging another practical commitment (Kant's "adopting a maxim"). Conceptual commitments both serve as and stand in need of reasons. The normative realm inhabited by creatures who can judge and act is not only the realm of freedom, it is the realm of reason.[2]

Understanding the norms for correct application that are implicit in concepts requires understanding the role those concepts play in reasoning: what (applications of concepts) count as reasons for the application

2. This story is told in more detail in Chapter One.

of that concept, and what (applications of concepts) the application of that concept counts as a reason for. For apart from such understanding, one cannot fulfill the responsibility one undertakes by making a judgment or performing an action. So what distinguishes concept-using creatures from others is that we know our way around the *space of reasons.* Grasping or understanding a concept just is being able practically to place it in a network of inferential relations: to know what is evidence for or against its being properly applied to a particular case, and what its proper applicability to a particular case counts as evidence for or against. Our capacity to know (or believe) *that* something is the case depends on our having a certain kind of know-*how:* the ability to tell what is a reason for what.

The cost of losing sight of this point is to assimilate genuinely conceptual activity, judging and acting, too closely to the behavior of mere animals—creatures who do not live and move and have their being in the normative realm of freedom and reason. We share with other animals (and for that matter with bits of automatic machinery) the capacity reliably to respond differentially to various kinds of stimuli. We, like they, can be understood as classifying stimuli as being of certain kinds, insofar as we are disposed to produce different repeatable sorts of responses to those stimuli. We can respond differentially to red things by uttering the noise "That is red." A parrot could be trained to do this, as pigeons are trained to peck at a different button when shown a red figure than when shown a green one. The empiricist tradition is right to emphasize that our capacity to have empirical knowledge begins with and crucially depends on such reliable differential responsive dispositions. But though the story begins with this sort of classification, it does not end there. For the rationalist tradition is right to emphasize that our classificatory responses count as applications of concepts, and hence as so much as candidates for knowledge, only in virtue of their role in reasoning. The crucial difference between the parrot's utterance of the noise "That is red" and the (let us suppose physically indistinguishable) utterance of a human reporter is that for the latter, but not the former, the utterance has the practical significance of making a claim. Doing that is taking up a normative stance of a kind that can serve as a premise from which to draw conclusions. That is, it can serve as a reason for taking up other stances. And further, it is a stance that itself can stand in need of reasons, at least if challenged by the adoption of other, incompatible stances. Where the parrot is merely responsively sounding off, the human counts as applying a concept just insofar as she is understood as making a move in a game of giving and asking for reasons.

The most basic point of Sellars's rationalist critique of empiricism in his masterwork "Empiricism and the Philosophy of Mind" is that even the *non*-inferentially elicited perceptual judgments that the empiricist rightly appreciates as forming the empirical basis for our knowledge can count as judgments (applications of concepts) at all only insofar as they are *inferentially* articulated. Thus the idea that there could be an autonomous language game (a game one could play though one played no other) consisting entirely of non-inferentially elicited reports—whether of environing stimuli or of the present contents of one's own mind—is a radical mistake. To apply any concepts *non*-inferentially, one must be able also to apply concepts inferentially. For it is an essential feature of concepts that their applications can both serve as and stand in need of reasons. Making a report or a perceptual judgment is doing something that essentially, and not just accidentally, has the significance of making available a premise for reasoning. Learning to observe requires learning to infer. Experience and reasoning are two sides of one coin, two capacities presupposed by concept use that are in principle intelligible only in terms of their relations to each other.[3]

To claim that what distinguishes specifically conceptual classification from classification merely by differential responsive disposition is the inferential articulation of the response—that applications of concepts are essentially what can both serve as and stand in need of reasons—is to assign the game of giving and asking for reasons a preeminent place among discursive practices. For it is to say that what makes a practice *discursive* in the first place is that it incorporates reason-giving practices. Now of course there are many things one can do with concepts besides using them to argue and to justify. And it has seemed perverse to some post-Enlightenment thinkers in any way to privilege the rational, cognitive dimension of language use. But if the tradition I have been sketching is right, the capacity to use concepts in all the other ways explored and

3. Chapter Seven develops this theme further.

exploited by the artists and writers whose imaginative enterprises have rightly been admired by romantic opponents of logocentrism is parasitic on the prosaic inferential practices in virtue of which we are entitled to see concepts as in play in the first place. The game of giving and asking for reasons is not just one game among others one can play with language. It is the game in virtue of the playing of which what one has qualifies as *language* (or thought) at all. I am here disagreeing with Wittgenstein, when he claims that language has no downtown. On my view, it does, and that downtown (the region around which all the rest of discourse is arrayed as dependent suburbs) is the practices of giving and asking for reasons. This is a kind of linguistic *rationalism.* 'Rationalism' in this sense does not entail intellectualism, the doctrine that every *implicit* mastery of a propriety of practice is ultimately to be explained by appeal to a prior *explicit* grasp of a principle. It is entirely compatible with the sort of pragmatism that sees things the other way around.

**4.** As I am suggesting that we think of them, concepts are broadly inferential norms that implicitly govern practices of giving and asking for reasons. Dummett has suggested a useful model for thinking about the inferential articulation of conceptual contents. Generalizing from the model of meaning Gentzen introduces for sentential operators, Dummett suggests that we think of the use of any expression as involving two components: the circumstances in which it is appropriately used and the appropriate consequences of such use. Since our concern is with the application of the concepts expressed by using linguistic expressions, we can render this as the circumstances of appropriate application of the concept, and the appropriate consequences of such application—that is, what follows from the concept's being applicable.

Some of the circumstances and consequences of applicability of a concept may be inferential in nature. For instance, one of the circumstances of appropriate application of the concept <u>red</u> is that this concept is applicable wherever the concept <u>scarlet</u> is applicable. And to say that is just another way of saying that the inference from "X is scarlet" to "X is red" is a good one. And similarly, one of the consequences of the applicability of the concept <u>red</u> is the applicability of the concept <u>colored</u>. And to say that is just another way of saying that the inference from "X is red" to "X is colored" is a good one. But concepts like <u>red</u> also have *non*-inferential circumstances of applicability, such as the visible presence of red things. And concepts such as <u>unjust</u> have non-inferential consequences of application—that is, they can make it appropriate to *do* (or not do) something, to make another claim true, not just to *say* or judge that it is true.

Even the immediately empirical concepts of *observables,* which have non-inferential *circumstances* of application, and the immediately practical *evaluative* concepts, which have non-inferential *consequences* of application, however, can be understood to have contents that are inferentially articulated. For all concepts incorporate an implicit commitment to the propriety of the inference from their circumstances to their consequences of application. One cannot use the concept <u>red</u> as including the circumstances and consequences mentioned above without committing oneself to the correctness of the inference from "X is scarlet" to "X is colored." So we might decompose the norms that govern the use of concepts into three components: circumstances of appropriate application, appropriate consequences of application, and the propriety of an inference from the circumstances to the consequences. I would prefer to understand the inferential commitment expansively, as including the circumstances and consequences it relates, and so as comprising all three normative elements.

I suggested at the outset that we think of philosophy as charged with producing and deploying tools for the criticism of concepts. The key point here is that concepts may incorporate defective inferences. Dummett offers this suggestive example:

> A simple case would be that of a pejorative term, e.g. 'Boche'. The conditions for applying the term to someone is that he is of German nationality; the consequences of its application are that he is barbarous and more prone to cruelty than other Europeans. We should envisage the connections in both directions as sufficiently tight as to be involved in the very meaning of the word: neither could be severed without altering its meaning. Someone who rejects the word does so because he does not want to permit a transition from the grounds for applying the term to the consequences of doing so.[4]

4. *Frege: Philosophy of Language* (New York: Harper and Row, 1973), p. 454.

(It is useful to focus on a French epithet from World War I, because we are sufficiently removed from its practical effect to be able to get a theoretical grip on how it works. But the thought should go over *mutatis mutandis* for pejoratives in current circulation.) Dummett's idea is that if you do not accept as correct the inference from German nationality to an unusual disposition to barbarity and cruelty, you can only reject the word. You cannot deny that there are any Boches, for that is just denying that the circumstances of application are ever satisfied, that is, that there are any Germans. And you cannot admit that there are Boches but deny that they are disposed to barbarity and cruelty (this is the "Some of my best friends are Boches" ploy), since that is just taking back in one breath what one has asserted just before. Any use of the term commits the user to the inference that is curled up, implicitly, in it. (At Oscar Wilde's trial the prosecutor read out some passages from *The Importance of Being Earnest* and said, "I put it to you, Mr. Wilde, that this is blasphemy. Is it? Yes or no?" Wilde replied just as he ought on the account I am urging: "Sir, 'blasphemy' is not one of my words.")[5]

Although they are perhaps among the most dangerous, it is not just highly charged words, words that couple 'descriptive' circumstances of application with 'evaluative' consequences of application, that incorporate inferences of which we may need to be critical. The use of *any* expression involves commitment to the propriety of the inference from its circumstances to its consequences of application. These are almost never logically valid inferences. On the contrary, they are what Sellars called "material" inferences: inferences that articulate the content of the concept expressed. Classical disputes about the nature of personal identity, for instance, can be understood as taking the form of arguments about the propriety of such a material inference. We can agree, we may suppose, about the more or less forensic consequences of application of the concept <u>same person,</u> having in mind its significance for attributions of (co-) responsibility. When we disagree about the circumstances of application that should be paired with it—for instance whether bodily or neural continuity or the psychological continuity of memory counts for more—we

---

5. Of course, being right on this point didn't keep Wilde out of trouble, any more than it did Salman Rushdie.

are really disagreeing about the correctness of the inference from the obtaining of these conditions to the ascription of responsibility. The question about what is the correct concept is a question about which inferences to endorse. I think it is helpful to think about a great number of the questions we ask about other important concepts in these same terms: as having the form of queries about what inferences from circumstances to consequences of application we ought to acknowledge as correct, and why. Think in these terms about such very abstract concepts as <u>morally wrong</u>, <u>just</u>, <u>beautiful</u>, <u>true</u>, <u>explain</u>, <u>know</u>, or <u>prove</u>, and again about 'thicker' ones such as <u>unkind</u>, <u>cruel</u>, <u>elegant</u>, <u>justify</u>, and <u>understand</u>.

The use of any of these concepts involves a material inferential commitment: commitment to the propriety of a substantial inferential move from the circumstances in which it is appropriate to apply the concept to the consequences of doing so. The concepts are substantive just because the inferences they incorporate are. Exactly this commitment becomes invisible, however, if one conceives conceptual content in terms of *truth conditions*. For the idea of truth conditions is the idea of a single set of conditions that are at once necessary and sufficient for the application of the concept. The idea of individually necessary conditions that are also jointly sufficient is the idea of a set of consequences of application that can also serve as circumstances of application. Thus the circumstances of application are understood as already including the consequences of application, so that no endorsement of a substantive inference is involved in using the concept. The concept of concepts like this is not incoherent. It is the ideal of *logical* or *formal* concepts. Thus it is a criterion of adequacy for introducing logical connectives that they be inferentially conservative: that their introduction and elimination rules be so related that they permit no new inferences involving only the old vocabulary. But it is a bad idea to take this model of the relation between circumstances and consequences of application of logical vocabulary and extend it to encompass also the substantively contentful *non*-logical concepts that are the currency in which most of our cognitive and practical transactions are conducted.

It is a bad idea because of its built-in conservatism. Understanding meaning or conceptual content in terms of truth conditions—individually necessary and jointly sufficient conditions—squeezes out of the picture the substantive inferential commitment implicit in the use of any non-logical concept. But it is precisely those inferential commitments that are subject to *criticism* in the light of substantive collateral beliefs. If one does not believe that Germans are distinctively barbarous or prone to cruelty, then one must not use the concept <u>Boche</u>, just *because* one does not endorse the substantive material inference it incorporates. On the other model, this diagnosis is not available. The most one can say is that one does not know how to specify truth conditions for the concept. But just what is objectionable about it and why does not appear from this theoretical perspective. Criticism of concepts is always criticism of the inferential connections. For criticizing whether all the individually sufficient conditions (circumstances) "go together," i.e. are circumstances of application of one concept, just is wondering whether they all have the same consequences of application (and similarly for wondering whether the consequences of application all "go together").

**5.** When we think of conceptual contents in the way I am recommending, we can see not only how beliefs can be used to criticize concepts, but also how concepts can be used to criticize beliefs. For it is the material inferences incorporated in our concepts that we use to elaborate the antecedents and consequences of various candidates for belief—to tell what we would be committing ourselves to, what would entitle us to those commitments, what would be incompatible with them, and so on. Once it is accepted that the inferential norms implicit in our concepts are in principle as revisable in the light of evidence as particular beliefs, conceptual and empirical authority appear as two sides of one coin. Rationally justifying our concepts depends on finding out about how things are—about what actually follows from what—as is most evident in the case of massively defective concepts such as <u>Boche</u>.

Adjusting our beliefs in the light of the connections among them dictated by our concepts, and our concepts in the light of our evidence for the substantive beliefs presupposed by the inferences they incorporate, is the rationally reflective enterprise introduced to us by Socrates. It is what results when the rational, normative connections among claims that govern the practice of giving and asking for reasons are themselves brought into the game, as liable to demands for reasons and justification. Saying or thinking something, making it explicit, consists in applying concepts, thereby taking up a stance in the space of reasons, making a move in the game of giving and asking for reasons. The structure of that space, of that game, though, is not given in advance of our finding out how things are with what we are talking about. For what is *really* a reason for what depends on how things *actually* are. But that inferential structure itself can be the subject of claims and thoughts. It can itself be made explicit in the form of claims about what follows from what, what claims are evidence for or against what other claims, what else one would be committing oneself to by making a certain judgment or performing a certain action. So long as the commitment to the propriety of the inference from German nationality to barbarity and unusual cruelty remains merely implicit in the use of terms such as 'Boche', it is hidden from rational scrutiny. When it is made explicit in the form of the conditional claim "Anyone who is German is barbarous and unusually prone to cruelty," it is subject to rational challenge and assessment; it can, for instance, be confronted with such counterexamples as Bach and Goethe.

Discursive explicitness, the application of concepts, is Kantian apperception or consciousness. Bringing into discursive explicitness the inferentially articulated conceptual norms in virtue of which we can be conscious or discursively aware of anything at all is the task of reflection, or self-consciousness. This is the expressive task distinctive of philosophy. Of course, the practitioners of special disciplines, such as membrane physiology, are concerned to unpack and criticize the inferential commitments implicit in using concepts such as <u>lipid soluble</u> with a given set of circumstances and consequences of application, too. It is the emphasis on the "anything at all" that distinguishes philosophical reflection from the more focused reflection that goes on within such special disciplines. Earlier I pinned on Kant a view that identifies us as distinctively *rational* creatures, where that is understood as a matter of our being subject to a certain kind of *normative* assessment: we are creatures who can undertake *commitments* and *responsibilities* that are *conceptually* articulated in that their contents are articulated by what would count as *reasons* for them (as well as what other commitments and responsibilities they provide reasons for). One of philosophy's defining obligations is to supply and deploy an expressive toolbox, filled with concepts that help us make explicit various aspects of *rationality* and *normativity* in general. **The topic of philosophy is normativity in all its guises, and inference in all its forms.** And its task is an *expressive, explicative* one. So it is the job of practitioners of the various philosophical subfields to design and produce specialized expressive tools, and to hone and shape them with use. At the most general level, *inferential* connections are made explicit by *conditionals,* and their *normative* force is made explicit by *deontic* vocabulary. Different branches of philosophy can be distinguished by the different sorts of inference and normativity they address and explicate, the various special senses of "if . . . then___" or of 'ought' for which they care. Thus philosophers of science, for instance, develop and deploy conditionals codifying causal, functional, teleological, and other explanatory inferential relations, value theorists sharpen our appreciation of the significance of the differences in the endorsements expressed by prudential, legal, ethical, and aesthetic 'oughts', and so on.

**6.** I said at the outset that I thought of philosophy as defined by its history, rather than by its nature, but that, following Hegel, I think of our task as understanding it by finding or making a nature in or from its history. The gesture I have made in that direction today, though, could also be summarized in a different kind of definition, namely in the ostensive definition: philosophy is the kind of thing that Kant and Hegel did (one might immediately want to add Plato, Aristotle, Frege, and Wittgenstein to the list, and then we are embarked on the enterprise of turning a gesture into a story, indeed a history). So one might ask: why not just say that, and be done with it? While, as I've indicated, I think that specification is a fine place to start, I also think there is a point to trying to be somewhat more explicit about just what sort of thing it is that one takes it Kant and Hegel (and Frege and Wittgenstein) did. Doing that is not being satisfied just with a wave at philosophy as something that has a history. It is trying rationally to reconstruct that tradition, to recast it into a form in which a constellation of ideas can be seen to be emerging, being expressed, refined, and developed.

With those giants, I see philosophy as a discipline whose distinctive concern is with a certain kind of *self-consciousness:* awareness of ourselves as specifically *discursive* (that is, concept-mongering) creatures. Its task is understanding the conditions, nature, and consequences of conceptual norms and the activities—starting with the social practices of giving and asking for reasons—that they make possible and that make them possible. As concept users, we are beings who can make explicit how things are and what we are doing—even if always only in relief against a background of implicit circumstances, conditions, skills, and practices. Among the things on which we can bring our explicitating capacities to bear are those very concept-using capacities that make it possible to make anything at all explicit. Doing that, I am saying, is philosophizing.

It is easy to be misled by the homey familiarity of these sentiments, and correspondingly important to distinguish this characterization from some neighbors with which it is liable to be confused. There is a clear affinity between this view and Kant's coronation of philosophy as "queen of the sciences." For on this account philosophy does extend its view to encompass all activity that is discursive in a broad sense—that is, all activity that presupposes a capacity for judgment and agency, sapience in general. But in this sense, philosophy is at most *a* queen of the sciences, not *the* queen. For the magisterial sweep of its purview does not serve to distinguish it from, say, psychology, sociology, history, literary or cultural criticism, or even journalism. What distinguishes it is the *expressive* nature of its concern with discursiveness in general, rather than its inclusive scope. My sketch was aimed at introducing a specific difference pertaining to philosophy, not a unique privilege with respect to such other disciplines.

Again, as I have characterized it, philosophy does not play a *foundational* role with respect to other disciplines. Its claims do not stand prior to those of the special sciences in some order of ultimate justification. Nor does philosophy sit at the other end of the process as final judge over the propriety of judgments and actions—as though the warrant of ordinary theoretical and practical applications of concepts remained somehow provisional until certified by philosophical investigation. And philosophy as I have described it likewise asserts no methodological privilege or insight that potentially collides with the actual procedures of other disciplines.

Indeed, philosophy's own proper concerns with the nature of normativity in general, and with its conceptual species in particular, so on inference and justification in general, impinge on the other disciplines in a role that equally well deserves the characterization of "handmaiden." For what we do that has been misunderstood as having foundational or method-ological significance is provide and apply tools for unpacking the sub-stantive commitments that are implicit in the concepts deployed through-out the culture, including the specialized disciplines of the high culture. Making those norms and inferences explicit in the form of claims exposes them for the first time to reasoned assessment, challenge, and defense, and so to the sort of rational emendation that is the primary process of conceptual evolution. But once the implicit presuppositions and conse-quences have been brought out into the daylight of explicitness, the pro-cess of assessment, emendation, and so evolution is the business of those whose concepts they are—and not something philosophers have any par-ticular authority over or expertise regarding. Put another way, it is the business of philosophers to figure out ways to increase semantic and dis-cursive self-consciousness. What one does with that self-consciousness is not our business *qua* philosophers—though of course, *qua* intellectuals generally, it may well be.

Philosophy's *expressive* enterprise is grounded in its focus on us as a certain kind of thing, an expressing thing: as at once creatures and cre-ators of conceptual norms, producers and consumers of reasons, beings distinguished by being subject to the peculiar normative force of the bet-ter reason. Its concern with us as specifically *normative* creatures sets philosophy off from the empirical disciplines, both the natural and the social sciences. It is this normative character that binds together the currents of thought epitomized in Stanley Cavell's characteristically tren-chant aphorism that Kant de-psychologized epistemology, Frege de-psychologized logic, and Wittgenstein de-psychologized psychology. We might add that Hegel de-psychologized history. The de-psychologizing move in question is equally a de-sociologizing. For it is a refocusing on the *normative bindingness* of the concepts deployed in ground-level empirical knowledge, reasoning, and thought in general. This is a move beyond the narrowly *natural* (in the sense of the describable order of causes), toward what Hegel called the 'spiritual' (geistig), that is, the *nor-mative* order. That its concern is specifically with our *conceptual* norma-tivity sets philosophy off from the other humanistic disciplines, from the literary as well as the plastic arts. Conceptual commitments are distinguished by their inferential articulation, by the way they can serve as reasons for one another, and by the way they stand in need of reasons, their entitlement always potentially being at issue. Now in asserting the centrality and indispensability, indeed, the criterial role, of practices of giving and asking for reasons, I am far from saying that reasoning—or even thinking—is all anyone ought to do. I am saying that philosophers' distinctive concern is with what else those reason-mongering practices make possible, and how they do, on the one hand, and with what it is that makes them possible—what sort of doings count as sayings, how believing or saying that is founded on knowing how—on the other. It is this distinctive constellation of concerns that makes philosophy the party of reasons, and philosophers the friends of the norms, the ones who bring out into the light of discursive explicitness our capacity to make things discursively explicit.

# CHAPTER FIVE

# Philosophy and the Expressive Freedom of Thought

1.   In this chapter I address an ancient challenge: to present the virtues of a life devoted to the pursuit of philosophical wisdom, as contrasted with a life of sophisticated pleasure and a life of honorable political activity. One of the defining aims of philosophers is to address just such questions as how we ought to characterize, compare, and assess the worth of these different forms of life. My defense of a life of philosophical activity must include comparisons with these traditionally prominent alternatives. And it must be framed by a discussion of the conceptual basis that justifies a comparative evaluation. Although this topic is an ancient one—pursued most vigorously and memorably in Plato's *Republic* and Aristotle's *Nichomachean Ethics*—I want to say something about how things look from the here and now. For I don't just want to talk *about* philosophy here, I want to *do* some.

So it is part of my plan to illustrate how philosophers think. It is a distinctive intellectual approach with which any student of the high culture, anyone who seeks to understand contemporary understanding, should be familiar—should be able to lay alongside such other distinctive ways of thinking as those characteristic of the engineer, the lawyer, the economist, the politician, and the sociologist. At its best the philosopher's way involves working out deep, important metaphysical ideas by crafting, honing, and deploying concepts with immense sensitivity and critical attention to subtleties and details concerning their exact contents. Partly because my intent is in part pedagogical, I'm not going to be bashful about pausing for critical asides about the dangers—in the form of implicit, therefore in the first instance invisible, assumptions—involved in using certain concepts, terms, or ways of talking. In the end, I'm after big game; cleaning, oiling, and otherwise maintaining the critical equipment the hunt relies on is a critical element of the enterprise—but a means only, never to be mistaken for the end itself.

The aim is essentially *evaluative:* critically to assess the merit of various forms of life. (Here is the first conceptually fastidious aside: notice that I've said "forms of life." It would not do to substitute here the pop-speak term "life*styles*"—not because it is meaningless or trendy, but because of *what* it means. *Style* contrasts in the first instance with *substance,* and if we have to pick between these, our concern is with the latter. Even if there are cases where it is style all the way down—where there is nothing to assess *except* style—and even if pursuits of that character are not for that reason taken to be irretrievably trivial or light-minded, still one should not build into one's terminology at the very beginning the assumption or presumption that issues of the relative values of lives structured by devotion to different aims should be assimilated to these exceptional cases. Terminology matters, because commitments of various sorts are implicit in choice of vocabulary. End of quibble.) This comparative evaluative task already involves certain important conceptual obligations.

- One is to be clear and explicit about the kinds of lives being compared: what *are* lives of pleasure, political activity, or philosophical contemplation?
- Another, perhaps more fundamental one, is to be clear and explicit about the basis on which *normative* appraisals are to be made. What can justify assessments of *better* and *worse?* Where can one stand—on what ground—to *justify* such evaluations? What is one allowed to presuppose, if one is mindful of the danger of simply assuming at the outset the values that one hopes to justify at the end?

On this point we must be vigilant and critical, lest the rabbit later triumphantly produced be smuggled into the hat at this stage.

One of Plato's and Aristotle's big ideas concerns the form of an answer to that very basic question: it is to be found in an account of what *kind of creature* we are, an account of *human nature*. The thought is that if we understand what kind of beings we are, we will have the basis for an assessment of what better or worse lives are for *us*—that is, better or worse for *that* kind of being.

This is an important idea, and it is one that I'll be pursuing in what follows. But just for that reason it is important to go slowly at this point, examine it carefully from different sides, and think about how one can put it without taking on optional or objectionable collateral commitments— commitments that may deflect, deform, or dictate the course of the subsequent investigation.

- To illustrate the sort of pitfall one wants to avoid, let me pick a not very threatening example. One way I just characterized what is to justify assessments of lives as better or worse is an account of "what kind of creature" it is whose lives are being assessed. 'Creature' literally means "created thing," "part of God's creation." We clearly would not want that connotation of the term (in contemporary usage, a largely vestigial resonance—hence the non-threateningness) to tempt us (never mind somehow oblige us) to assume without further argument that the sort of normative assessment underwritten by knowing what kind of creature we are talking about must be "pleasingness to God," or "consilience with God's plan or providence." When I'm being careful about this, I'll talk about 'beings' instead of 'creatures'. (The German equivalent is 'Wesen', which means 'essence', and has all the problems that go with the hylomorphic metaphysics in which *that* term is embedded.)

- In order to avoid this possible slide, one might be tempted to go to a different extreme, by substituting the more scientific phrase "kind of organism." After all, whatever else we are, we surely are organisms—*that* is not a characterization that is controversial in the way that 'creature', when read literally, is. But what if on these same grounds we substituted 'oxygen-breathers'? We are, indeed, oxygen-breathers. But answering the question "What kind of oxygen-breathers are we?" does not seem to bear in the right way on the question of what the good life for beings of our sort is. The real issues might be just the same for nitrogen-breathers. By taking this path, we seem to be courting the danger of thinking of 'us' too narrowly, picking us out by contingent features, irrelevant to the issue at hand. In the same way "kind of organism" suggests that the notion of *kind* in question is specifically *biological* kind. Aristotle might have been happy enough with that, at least on some readings. But it is not *obvious* that biology is the right place to look for an account of *human* flourishing. This is a point I will return to.

- The other rough, initial characterization I offered of the metaphysical basis for normative evaluation of kinds of life according to the Plato-Aristotle line was "human nature." This is a very common, and so seemingly innocuous, phrase. But it, too, harbors potentially suspect implications. By exploring them we can begin to get into the philosophical meat of our issue.


We could call this general explanatory strategy Plato and Aristotle recommend the "metaphysical strategy" for grounding large-scale normative evaluations. It is predicated on the idea that if we know enough about what we in some deep (I've used the term 'metaphysical' without saying anything at all about what I mean by it) sense *are,* that will enable us to draw conclusions about how we *ought* to live, what kinds of activity are *proper,* or *fitting,* or at least *better* or *worse* for us. In some sense, the metaphysical strategy is the only game in town for justifying normative assessments. It is the form of almost *everyone's* theory, not only of traditional theistic and theological accounts of the good life, and of those due to heavy-duty metaphysicians such as Spinoza and Hegel, and to such different thinkers as Kant and Hobbes, but even of such avowedly anti-metaphysical thinkers as Nietzsche and Heidegger. But it is worth pointing out that Hume gave us the conceptual raw materials for a thoroughgoing critique of this way of thinking—of the very idea of a metaphysics of normativity. (And this in spite of the fact that his own naturalistic theory can itself be understood as employing a variant of the same general strategy.) For he denies that one can *ever* justify an inference from *is* to *ought*—from a mere *de*scription of how things in fact *are* to a *pre*scription of how they *ought* to be. That is a conceptual gap he says no theory can bridge. Of course, he may not be right—and if he *is* right, it is not clear what conclusion we should draw from the in-principle failure of any metaphysical grounding of normative claims. (Should we be nihilists, and deny that normative claims *can* be justified?) But his critique (which I have only stated, not pretended to explain or justify) presents a challenge that would have been absurd to the ancients, but which we cannot today simply ignore—that is one of the deep differences between then and now, them and us. It has been seconded and deepened more recently by pragmatists such as Dewey and Rorty.[1]

Although objections have been made to it, I want to take seriously the metaphysical strategy for grounding normative appraisals of different forms of life. The conclusions of any such argument are going to be quite sensitive to its starting point: the metaphysical characterization of the kind of beings we are. One characterization of us that seems to get at

---

1. Notice that these *sorts* of questions—just how one ought to distinguish the various kinds of life on offer, both the genus to which they belong (which is what I've been calling a "form of life") and the various species (devotion to pleasure, political activity, or philosophy, all in broad senses of the terms), and what could be a justifiable, non-question-begging basis for comparative evaluation of them—are ones the *philosopher* is in a better position to address (indeed, perhaps being in a position to address them *is* being a philosopher). Of course, that by itself is not *dispositive* of the question whether the philosophical is the *best* sort of life. And even claiming—as I, like Aristotle, eventually will—that it is *probative* requires a serious argument. (The jurisprudential conceptual distinction I'm employing here is between evidential considerations that are decisive and final, that *settle* an issue, and those that merely *bear* on it, that provide *some* evidence, but evidence which may turn out to be outweighed or defeated by other considerations.) Maybe what careful philosophical consideration of the relevant reasons will show is that the philosophical life is not *the* best, not *a* better nor even a good one. And of course we must be wary of special pleading. Is the fact that when philosophers address this issue philosophy often turns out to be a highly recommended way to direct one's energies best explained by those opinions reflecting a fact, which emerges after careful, dispassionate consideration? Or is it a reflection of the prejudices or interests of those undertaking an investigation whose conclusion is already—for them, given their commitments to that sort of life—foregone?

something central and important about us (by contrast, say, to our being oxygen-breathers) is that we are *conscious* creatures, creatures with *minds,* subjects of *awareness.* Only creatures of *that* general sort have even the theoretical option of leading lives of pleasure, political activity, or the pursuit of philosophical wisdom. So this much is common ground between them; starting with this characterization begs no questions against one or another of the forms of life.

If we look just a little bit closer at our consciousness or mindedness, we see that it comes in two importantly different flavors. We are *sentient* beings, and we are *sapient* beings—we *feel,* and we *think.* Sentience is *sensuous* awareness, of the generic sort also exhibited by at least our mammalian cousins. Paradigmatic states of sentience are feeling pain, seeing colors, and hearing sounds. Sentient awareness is what an organism has when it is *awake,* but, dreaming aside, not when it is *asleep.* Sapience is *conceptual* awareness—a kind of mindedness that is tied to *understanding* rather than *sensing.* Paradigmatic sapient states are thinking or believing *that* things are thus-and-so (or desiring or intending that they be thus-and-so)—*that* Vienna is the capital of Austria, *that* the Washington Monument is 555 feet high, *that* freedom is better than slavery. In order to be in these sapient states one must grasp the *concepts* that articulate their *content.* The content of sapient states is accordingly something that at least in principle can be *said:* specified by the use of declarative sentences ("The moon is round") or sentential 'that'-clauses ("Sam believes *that* the moon is round"). By contrast, the content of my sentient visual awareness of a red triangle is something particular—an *instance,* or perhaps an *image,* of a red triangle. For a sufficiently complex image, or a particular tactile sensation, we will not in general have words that let us exhaustively specify its content. (Can you *say* what a middle C played on a French horn sounds like—even if in some sense you know perfectly well?)

**2.**  Let us see what help the distinction between sentience and sapience can give us in thinking about the life of pleasure and the life of political activity (I will get to the philosophical life later on). At first blush, the relevance of the distinction to the life of pleasure may seem straightforward. There is such a thing as *sensuous pleasure,* paradigmatically associated with the satisfaction of various mammalian drives: for food, drink, and sex. Sensuous pleasure is a sentient state, which even non-sapient creatures such as dogs and cats can experience. And it has a sort of intrinsic *normative* significance: pleasure is sentiently experienced *as* good, and pain is experienced *as* bad. As sentient beings we know that normative character of the experiences as it were from the 'inside', that is, just from *having* pleasurable and painful experiences, from *being* sentient. And we can confirm it from the third-person rather than the first-person point of view by noting that pleasurable experiences *positively* reinforce the behavior that brings them about, while painful ones *negatively* reinforce it.[2] Here the move from 'is' to 'ought' is underwritten by the felt character of the experience: a sentient being that actually *is* in pain *feels* that it *ought not* to be.

These considerations motivate an argument of the following form:

(1) Pleasure is the natural good for sentient beings as such, and pain is the natural bad for sentient beings as such.

So:

(2) A life of pleasure is the best life for sentient beings.

(3) We are sentient beings.

So:

(4) A life of pleasure is the best life for us.

When it is thus baldly put, the fallacy in this voluptuary syllogism ought to be obvious. We are not only sentient beings, we are also sapient beings. If the as it were 'natural' good for *sapient* beings as such is something other than sensuous pleasure, the premises of this argument could

---

2. There are subtleties concerning how to characterize the repeatable behavior-kinds that are properly understood as the objects of such reinforcement, and those subtleties matter a great deal for disputes between behavioristic approaches to animal behavior and representationalist ones more characteristic of contemporary cognitive science. But for present purposes those subtleties can safely be ignored.

all be true without their settling that the conclusion is also true. For they do not provide grounds for adjudicating the claims between what is best for us *as* sentient beings and what is best for us *as* sapient beings.

There is also a subtler way in which the fact that we are not only sentient but sapient bears on this line of thought. For our sapience means that it would be a mistake to equate 'pleasure' with '*sensuous* pleasure' in our case, however much sense such an equation makes for the non-sapient beasts of forest and field. Our sapience is not just something added to our sentience, leaving that base undisturbed. Sapience fundamentally transforms our sentience, turning mere inchoate *sensation* into articulated *perception.* Our sentience is not that of the beasts. What we share with them is only the physiological raw materials for our conceptually articulated sensuous experiences. Our seeing starts off as seeing-as. Pigeons can in one straightforward sense see red triangles—but we see them *as* red triangles. And so it is with even the most sensual of our pleasures. They are—one wants to say, using a term already flagged as potentially dangerous—distinctively *human* pleasures. Food is for us a thoroughly cultural affair. And the more pleasure one takes in it, the more *knowledge* and *understanding,* the more carefully *cultivated* practices are involved. For cooking to be an art, eating must also be one. We don't just *eat,* we *dine.* (The German language marks this point with the distinction between 'essen' and 'fressen'.) And the same point holds for the pleasures of drink. Beyond the basic subsistence level of those dying in the desert, the most characteristic feature of this form of life is the seemingly ineluctable drive to *connoisseurship:* not just in wine, but in whiskey, beer, tequila, tea, coffee, even water. We don't just drink, we sip and savor, we compare, contrast, assess, develop, and articulate preferences. And the point is most obtrusively and ostentatiously manifest for the case of sexual pleasure. Since each of us can elaborate and illustrate it from our own experience, I will say about it only that it is not for nothing that the guiding precept and most important lesson of all those who study sexual phenomena—not just culturally, but just as much from the point of view of pure physiology—a slogan drummed into every student and emblazoned over the door of every research laboratory, is that overwhelmingly the most important human sexual organ is the *brain.*

So while we sapients *do* experience pleasures that have a significant sensual element, our pleasures are not for that reason to be identified with or understood on the model of the pleasures of *merely* sentient beings. Even our sensuous pleasures are never *merely* sensuous. Our sapience penetrates them to their core. As William James said: "The trail of the human serpent is over all." This is why no sophisticated defender of the life of pleasure as the good life for us ought to allow the identification of the pleasures in question with those that are displayed already in—as Aristotle puts it—the lives of grazing animals. Defending the life of pleasure does not require simply ignoring sapience in favor of sentience.

In fact, the distinction bears on our understanding of the life of pleasure in another way as well. For among the pleasures of sapients are to be found some that seem to owe little if anything to our sentience: distinctively *intellectual* pleasures. They are experienced in answering questions, satisfying curiosity, solving puzzles, unraveling mysteries, producing explanations, constructing theories, and in general achieving various kinds of *understanding.* Throwing pleasures of this sort into the mix motivates a famous line of thought—originating already in Aristotle, but perhaps most prominently defended by John Stuart Mill—that seeks to appeal to intellectual pleasures to undermine the distinction between a life of pleasure and a life of intellectual contemplation. The claim is that the pursuit of wisdom is not *not* a life of pleasure—it is just a life aiming at the *purely* sapient intellectual pleasures of *understanding,* rather than the hybrid sapient-sentient sensuous pleasures of *feeling.* If we then ask which of these sorts of pleasure is *better*—hence, which of the life of intellectual pleasure and that of sensual pleasure *ought* to be preferred—the thing to do is to look to the testimony of those who have thoroughly experienced *both.* And what one will find, the claim is, is that the *only* ones who doubt the superiority of the intellectual pleasures to the sensual are those who have only experienced the sensual, and know nothing of the joys of intellectual understanding. If and insofar as that empirical claim is right, it supports the conclusion that the intellectual pleasures are *experienced as* better than the sensual ones, in much the same sense that sensual pleasure is experienced as better than pain. In that sense, then, intellectual pleasures are *intrinsically,* that is, *as experiences,* better than sensual ones. And this is a reason to classify the pleasures of understanding as *higher* pleasures, and the pleasures of the senses as *lower* ones, without relying on the suspect identification of our sensual pleasures with those of the 'lower', i.e. non-sapient, animals.

There is certainly something to this celebrated line of thought—though the crucial empirical premise has been hotly contested by some. But it *not* the way I am going to argue in defense of the philosophical life. The argument I will offer turns on features of *sapience* that are independent of its relation to sentience.

We've seen how focusing on ourselves as sentient can provide raw materials that can serve as inputs to the metaphysical strategy for justifying normative assessments—including those that bear on the goodness of a form of life (though I've not attempted a comparison of forms of life along this dimension). For some sentient states are *felt as* good or bad. Indeed, we could use the terms 'pleasure' and 'pain', in very broad senses, as generic for *whatever* sentient states exhibit that sort of intrinsic positive or negative normative character, just *as* feelings—for whatever *feels good* or *feels bad*. So we can ask: does the fact that we are *sapients* provide any corresponding prospects for employing the metaphysical strategy for underwriting normative judgments about better and worse lives for us? Of course, the answer depends on how one unpacks the notion of sapience. I'll consider three ways of doing that, following out in more contemporary terms philosophical ideas we owe to Hume, Kant, and Hegel.

**3.**    The first may be called the *instrumental* model of normativity. According to it, what is in the most explanatorily basic sense *good* is getting what you *want:* satisfying desires and fulfilling intentions. What is *bad* is the frustration of desires and the failure of intentions. The metaphysical basis for normative assessments appealed to here is that intentional states such as desire and intention come with conditions of satisfaction, fulfillment, or success. Desires and intentions intrinsically, as the kind of sapient states they are, say how things *ought,* according to them, to be.

It is the *conceptual content* of sapient states of desire, intention, and also belief that determines what *counts* as success or satisfaction. If I desire that the ball go through the hoop, or intend that the international monetary system be reformed, my desire is satisfied and my intention fulfilled just in case the ball goes through the hoop and the international

monetary system is reformed—and those facts can be the intentional contents of my beliefs about those matters.

What makes the content determining these conditions of satisfaction
*conceptual* content, and so qualifies the states exhibiting it as *sapient*
states and distinguishes them from merely sentient states such as pleasure
and pain, which are devoid of specifically conceptual content, is the way
desires, intentions, and beliefs interdigitate in practical *reasoning*. To be
conceptually contentful is in the most basic sense to be the sort of thing
that can serve as or stand in need of *reasons*—that is, to be able to serve as
premise or conclusion in an *inference*. In the paradigmatic case of practical reasoning, beliefs and desires together serve as *premises* providing reasons for an intention, which serves as *conclusion*. A sample bit of practical
reasoning might go like this:

I want to stay dry. (Desire)

Only opening my umbrella will keep me dry. (Belief)

So:

I shall open my umbrella. (Intention)

The primitively *good* case, in this instrumental sense, is where I *succeed*
in opening the umbrella, *fulfilling* the intention, and that *does* keep me
dry, *satisfying* the desire. The primitive instrumental normative *bad* is
failure to fulfill the intention or frustration of the desire. The conceptual
contents of the intentional sapient states are what make the beliefs, desires, and intentions fit together *rationally*, in the sense that beliefs and
desires can provide *reasons* for intentions.

On the instrumental conception, rationality is intelligence in the sense
of a generalized capacity for getting what one wants. The most sophisticated contemporary way of working out the instrumental picture of rationality and sapience is rational choice theory, based on the mathematical
formulations of decision theory (in the one-agent case) and game theory
(in the multiple-agent case). It is one of the dominant conceptual frame-
works of contemporary social science—not just economics (which is in
some sense its home), but also in such other disciplines as political theory
and even sociology.

Whatever the merits of this framework may be when put to work in a social-scientific context, I do not think it will do as a way of understanding the sort of normativity that is most fundamental for rational (that is, sapient) creatures as such. For it takes for granted at the outset intentional states understood as conceptually contentful, as part of the explanatory raw materials from which is to be elaborated a notion of rationality as effectiveness at satisfying desires and fulfilling intentions—or, in the full-blown rational choice version, maximizing probabilistically expected utility (where utility is the measure of preference). And I think that one needs to appeal to the role of intentional states in *inference,* hence in reasoning, in order to see them as conceptually contentful at all.[3] If that is right, the normativity distinctive of reasoning must come into the explanatory story already in understanding the conceptual contents of sapient states, and is not itself to be explained later in terms of them, as on the instrumental model. But I'm not going to try to argue for that claim here.[4] Instead, I want to sketch a different approach.

**4.**   Sapient creatures are knowers and agents. They make judgments and perform intentional actions. Perhaps Kant's most basic idea is that what distinguishes judgments and intentional actions from the responsive behavior of merely sentient creatures is that judgments and actions are things that we are in a distinctive sense *responsible* for. They express *commitments* of ours; they are exercises of *authority,* stands we authorize. Responsibility, commitment, authority—these are all *normative* statuses. We sapients are at base *normative* beings.

Further, Kant understands the *contents* of our normatively significant sapient states to be *rules* that determine *what* we have made ourselves responsible for, *what* we have committed ourselves to, *what* we have autho-

---

3. This point is developed further in Chapter Seven.

4. *Making It Explicit* (Cambridge, MA: Harvard University Press, 1994) is an extended argument for that claim. More compact arguments for the conclusion that one cannot underwrite conceptual content in purely instrumental terms can be found in "Unsuccessful Semantics," *Analysis* 54, no. 3 (1994): 175–178, and "When Philosophy Paints Its Blue on Grey," *boundary 2* 29, no. 2 (2002): 1–28. A more focused critique of rational choice theory is offered in "What Do Expressions of Preference Express?" in *Practical Rationality and Preference: Essays for David Gauthier,* ed. Christopher Morris and Arthur Ripstein (Cambridge: Cambridge University Press, 2001), pp. 11–36.

rized. And his name for those content-articulating rules is *'concepts'*. So he understands what one is doing in judging as applying a concept: a concept that determines how one is *taking* things to be, how one is committing oneself to things being, how they must be if the commitment one has authorized and made oneself responsible for is to count as *correct*. And he understands what one is doing in acting intentionally also as applying a concept: a concept that in the case of this sort of act determines how one is committing oneself to *make* things be, how they must turn out if the practical commitment one has authorized and made oneself responsible for is to count as *successful*. In a strict sense, *all* Kantian sapient beings can do *as such* is to apply concepts, in judgment and action. Understanding concepts as rules that determine what we have committed ourselves to by applying them is a radically *non-psychological* concept of concepts. For Kant, what matters is not our grip on concepts—how well or clearly we understand them—but their grip on us, how they bind us by articulating our commitments and responsibilities.

Part of what one is committing oneself to, part of what one is responsible for, in applying a concept is having *reasons* for doing so. Indeed, the way concepts settle *what* one is committing oneself to by applying them in judgment or action is by articulating what is a *reason* for what: what follows from applying the concept and what is a reason for or against applying it. Conceptual content is *rational* content, in the sense that it determines the *role in reasoning*—whether theoretical, in judgment, or practical, in agency—of concept-applications. So where on the instrumental model of sapience one appeals to a notion of conceptual content as an explanatory primitive, and then builds out of it notions of instrumental rationality and normative appraisal of satisfaction and success, on the kantian[5] model of sapience, normative notions of rationally articulated commitment and responsibility are appealed to at the ground level, to explain what it is to be conceptually contentful.

Sapient beings are beings that are sensitive to conceptual norms, which is to say beings that can act for *reasons*. Being sensitive to the normative

5. I use 'Kantian' when attributing views to Kant himself and 'kantian' when discussing a more generic kind of view inspired by, or associated with, that figure. I adopt the corresponding policy for such terms as 'Platonist'/'platonist', 'Cartesian'/'cartesian', and so on.

force of the better reason—the phenomenon that so puzzled and fascinated the ancient Greek philosophers—is what kantian *freedom* consists in. Understood in this way, freedom is the capacity constitutive of sapience: the capacity to undertake conceptually articulated responsibilities, to make commitments, the capacity to respond not just to *natural properties,* but to *normative proprieties.* Real freedom comes not from the *absence* of an externally imposed *cause,* but from the *presence* of an internally endorsed *reason.* Becoming the subject of normative statuses such as responsibility, commitment, and authority is, for Kant, moving from being a *denizen* of the *realm of nature* to being a *citizen* of the *realm of freedom.*

Kant's conception of the freedom that consists in the capacity to *bind* oneself by conceptual norms, to undertake responsibility, to make commitments, to exercise and acknowledge authority, was a radically original one. The tradition had thought of freedom as *negative* freedom: freedom *from* constraints of various sorts. Kant focuses instead on *positive* freedom: freedom *to* do something. It is the freedom *to* act for *reasons.* Freedom in that sense is freedom *to* bind or constrain oneself by norms, to commit oneself, to make oneself responsible. For sapient beings, the relevant and essential contrast between freedom and unfreedom is not that between lack of constraint and constraint, but that between *normative* and merely *natural* constraint—the difference between constraint by *reasons* and by *causes.* This constellation of ideas about normativity in the form of responsibility and commitment, reasons and concepts, and a positive conception of freedom is what Heidegger is talking about when he refers to "the dignity and spiritual greatness of German Idealism."[6]

These Kantian ideas are deep and important ones. One way to see that is to think about the significance of this way of thinking about the essential metaphysics of sapience for assessing the two strands of irrationalism whose twentieth-century advocates are Foucault and Derrida. The first develops ideas championed already by Nietzsche in the second half of the nineteenth century. It sees the practice of giving and asking for *reasons* as just the distinctively modern form of *power.* Instead of controlling people by threatening them with violence, one systematically manipulates the language they use to understand and interpret themselves and their

6. Chapter One develops this line of thought more fully.

world. And the thought is that that is *all* reason is. (At the end of his life, even Foucault admitted that doing it that way at least represented an improvement over threatening to hurt or kill people, but he still insisted that the concept of rational persuasion—moving someone by the special normative force of reasons—was a mere ploy by the powerful.) The second line of thought has its roots in the Romanticism of the early nineteenth century. It claims that giving and asking for reasons is just *one* game one can play with words, and that only a self-serving conspiracy of philosophers and scientists has convinced people that it deserves any privilege at all over all the other playful and artistically creative things one can do with language.

It is natural and easy to respond to these challenges to what they denominate as the "hegemony" of reason simply by recoiling from their anti-intellectualism and irrationalism. But I would argue that these criticisms deserve to be taken seriously—and that they should then be contested on their own ground and in their own terms. Since the Enlightenment, *reason* has tended to be identified with *science* (*thought* with *scientific* thought). So in rejecting the intellectual hegemony of natural science, the Romantics tended to reject the claims of *reason* more generally. The importance of idealism was the disentangling of these two: the realization that the rejection of *scientism* need not be a form of *irrationalism.* If Kant is right, the practice of giving and asking for reasons is not just one optional strategy among others for controlling our fellow citizens, nor is it one optional game among others we can play with words. It is what makes it so much as possible for us to think and act, to entertain determinately contentful plans, to commit ourselves, to exercise authority, to undertake responsibility—in short, to be sapient *persons* at all. It provides the conceptual basis on which exercises of power and the playing of games rest, and cannot properly be understood in terms of those latecoming possibilities. The picture of us as creatures of our own rational commitments provides a positive response to the irrationalist challenges that are so characteristic of our times.

**5.**   Hegel transforms these Kantian ideas by combining them with three others. First, he understands *normative* statuses such as responsibility, commitment, and authority as essentially *social* statuses. There were no such normative statuses until people adopted practical normative *attitudes* toward each other—that is, until they started *holding* each other responsible, *treating* each other as committed, *acknowledging* each other's authority. Adopting those attitudes toward one another is what he calls '*recognition*'. On his view, adopting normative statuses—being a free kantian agent, able to judge and act intentionally—is in principle possible only in the context of a community. Those communities form the social substance in which we normative creatures live and move and have our being—what Hegel calls 'Geist', Spirit. Normative communities are synthesized by reciprocal recognition. Sapience is not a wholly individual achievement: it takes a village.

The second of Hegel's contributions is an *expressive* account of positive freedom. The aspect of sapient life that exhibits the normative structure of Geist in its purest, clearest form is *language*—the ultimate medium of expression.[7] Language is a social practice. Performing speech acts such as asserting, promising, and commanding should be understood as doing things that have the social significance of undertaking commitments, taking on responsibilities, exerting authority. Engaging in discursive practices is accordingly the paradigmatic exercise of Kantian positive freedom. In doing so, we bind ourselves by norms articulated by the contents of the concepts we apply. If I claim that the coin is copper, I have said something that, whether I know it or not, is *correct* only if the coin would melt at 1084°C and would *not* melt at 1083°C. If you promise to drive me to the airport at three tomorrow, it is not up to you what would count as fulfilling that promise. The positive freedom to adopt these normative statuses requires and partly consists in constraining oneself by conceptual norms. As I discuss in Chapter Two, the conceptual normativity implicit in linguistic practice provides a model of a kind of loss of negative freedom (freedom from constraint) that is more than balanced by an outpouring of positive expressive freedom.

Hegel's third idea is that sapient beings are the subjects of developmental processes that exhibit a distinctive structure. Sapience is a kind of consciousness. Concept users are beings things can in a distinctive sense

7. As Hegel says: "Language is the Dasein of Geist." *Phenomenology of Spirit*, trans. A. W. Miller (Oxford: Oxford University Press), sec. 652.

be something *for*. And concept use allows a kind of *self*-consciousness not available to mere sentients: being something *for* oneself. (Since this is one of the payoffs of sapience, of being a concept user, for Hegel it is fundamentally a *social* achievement.) The selves of self-conscious creatures exhibit a distinctive structure: what they *really* are—as Hegel says, what they are *in* themselves—depends on what they *take* themselves to be—in Hegel-speak, what they are *for* themselves. And that means that a self-conscious being can change what it is *in* itself by changing what it is *for* itself. Self-conscious creatures accordingly enjoy the possibility of a distinctive kind of self-*transformation: making* themselves be different by *taking* themselves to be different. Because what they are in themselves is at any point the outcome of such a developmental process depending on their attitudes, essentially self-conscious beings don't have *natures,* they have *histories.*[8] Or, put differently, it is their nature to have not just a *past,* but a *history:* a sequence of partially self-constituting self-transformations, mediated at every stage by their self-conceptions, and culminating in their being what they currently are. Understanding what they are requires looking retrospectively at the process of sequential reciprocal influences of what they at each stage were for themselves and what they at each stage were in themselves, by which they came to be what they now are. Rehearsing such a historical narrative (Hegel's 'Erinnerung') is a distinctive way of understanding oneself *as* an essentially historical, because essentially self-conscious, sort of being.[9] (The twentieth-century existentialist slogan "Existence precedes essence" is an attempt to express a weak, watered-down version of this Hegelian conception.)

**6.**    I want now to use the conceptual raw materials I've assembled so far to say something briefly about the life of political activity, and then about the philosophical life. The first thing to notice is that ways of thinking about what the good life consists in for creatures like us—rooted in ways of thinking about what kind of beings we are—come into play *twice* in thinking about the life of political activity. It is itself, of course, one of the

8. Chapter Four opens by introducing this contrast between things that have natures and things that have histories.

9. Chapter Three develops this line of thought more fully.

forms of life to be assessed. But it is also true that one of the central *aims* of political activity is to *enable* and *promote* the freedom of one's fellow citizens (*our* freedom) to live the best lives possible. Here *enabling* is increasing *negative* freedom, freedom *from* constraints that hinder living normatively good lives, and *promoting* is increasing *positive* freedom, freedom *to* live those lives, by making available resources that can be deployed in the service of living *well,* living *better,* and living the *best* lives possible. So devoting oneself to a life of political activity requires practically endorsing a view about how to address the normative question of what makes better lives for beings like us. Since that is a principal question that philosophers must address, the *content* of *political* life depends on the answer to a distinctively *philosophical* question.

What difference does it make for the understanding of the aims of political life which of the three metaphysical conceptions of us discussed above one adopts as the basis for this sort of normative assessment? The three are

- a conception of us as essentially *sentient* beings whose good is *pleasure,*

- a conception of us as essentially *sapient* beings in the Humean-instrumental sense, whose good is satisfying our desires or maximizing utility, and

- a conception of us as essentially *sapient* beings in the Kantian sense as elaborated by Hegel: expressive beings whose good consists in exercising their capacity for self-conscious self-constitution and self-transformation.

My main concern, however, is with the last of these, since I think the metaphysical views of us that ground the first two are ultimately unsustainable. But I can here only gesture at the reasons.

One *can* lead a life of political activity premised on an understanding of us as essentially *sentients,* so of the good life for us as one of sensuous pleasure. Doing that is taking as one of one's principal aims enabling and promoting the pursuit of pleasure and the avoidance of pain. I'm not going to say a lot about this. From the point of view of those of us who think what matters is not biology but sapience, discursivity, Hegelian Geist, this way of thinking about us is too narrow. It is a kind of biological chauvinism—a morally objectionable parochialism. Sentience is merely a *medium;* the *message* lies in sapience. The point of *feeling* is not its mere *intensity,* positive or negative. It is that its modulations can articulate *thoughts,* which turn us from mere *animals* into *selves.*

But this biological way of picking *us* out is also too *wide.* Here the debate over whether embryos are *persons* is a good case in point. Here the question is: should moral respect go with *sapience* or with *biology?* Sentience-utilitarians such as Singer say the latter because they see *morality* as normatively driven by the intrinsic *sensuous* evaluation implicit in the phenomena of *pain* and *pleasure.* But we kantians see the normative basis of morality as derived from the *positive freedom* of giving and asking for *reasons.* Mammalian sensuousness, sentience, is at best a *necessary* condition of that, not a *sufficient* one. According to this line of thought, it is the capacity to engage in *conceptual* activity, being a subject of *sapience,* not of *sentience,* that is in the first instance *morally* significant. This does not, of course, *settle* it that we should not accord *respect* and *rights* to embryos, as *potential* moral persons, or for that matter, to non-human *animals.* But in each case the argument appeals to an *indirect* connection to the *primary* subjects of moral respect and (so) rights: discursive creatures. Kant certainly thought it was wrong to cause pain to animals for no reason—but that is not in the first instance because of what it does to *them,* but because of what doing that to *them* does to *us.*

In any case, since the political life itself is a life of sapient activity, there is something odd about devoting it to enabling and promoting *sensuous* self-indulgence on the part of one's fellows—a vision of the politician as civic designated driver, or as the only adult in a community of children.

By contrast, it certainly makes sense as a public political aim to enable and promote the pursuit of *happiness* by one's fellows, where happiness is thought of instrumentally, as a matter of their getting whatever it is that they privately want, of their succeeding in the pursuit of whatever projects they have taken on. But a devotee of the political life who consulted *this* philosopher would be told that the instrumental conception of the rationality that structures sapience is radically defective. I can't pursue here the reasons for this assessment, but I'll register one familiar source of discontent. At a practical level, this model of sapient rationality puts the endorsement of ends or goals ultimately beyond rational assessment, except as some serve as sub-goals to others. Reason is understood as *exclusively* concerned with means to already-adopted ends. But this seems wrong: the formation of preferences should also be subject to rational assessment.

What I do want to discuss is the relations between political and philosophical activity according to the richer, more interesting conception of sapience that Hegel develops out of Kant's insights. I've already indicated how thinking of us as *expressive,* self-constituting, and self-transforming beings provides a linguistic model for the *political* justification of constraint by communal norms—how sufficient gains in the positive expressive freedom that is the good for sapients on this metaphysical understanding can justifiably be seen to compensate for a corresponding loss of negative freedom. That line of thought is one of the conceptual gifts the philosopher can give the politician. But on this line of thought, philosophers have a still more important role to play. We sapients are self-constituting beings because what we are *for* ourselves is an essential element of what we are *in* ourselves. One of the central tasks of philosophy is to craft vocabularies we can use to interpret, understand, constitute, and ultimately transform ourselves. The production of potentially self- and community-transforming vocabularies is not, to be sure, the exclusive province of philosophers. For instance, filmmakers and novelists (imagers and imaginers of lives and projects), poets (sculptors of language and linguistic images), and such hard-to-classify thinkers as Marx and Freud are all practitioners of this arcane, human-alchemical art.

But philosophers not only craft vocabularies rich with the possibility of redescribing, reconceiving, and (so) reconstituting ourselves, they are also the ones whose province within the high culture is to study and theorize *about* the vocabularies that enable and promote sapient self-development. It is the philosophers' job to come to *understand* the process by which expressive, self-interpreting, self-constituting historical creatures produce and consume those vocabularies so as to become what they (then) are. This is what the philosophers I have been talking about— Aristotle, Hume, Kant, and Hegel—do. They produce new vocabularies in which we can understand ourselves and each other, and they do that by

thinking about the kinds of being we are, and about the role of such vocabularies in instituting and constituting the conceptual normativity that
is the medium in which beings like us live our lives. Specifically philosophical vocabularies are the principal organs of self-consciousness for
expressive beings.

On the Hegelian conception of us, then, one of the great goods for us
is the availability of an inexhaustible supply of new vocabularies in which
to express, develop, constitute, and transform ourselves and our institutions, and for understanding the process by which we do that. This is the
great positive, expressive freedom that makes us what we are. As the part
of the good for us, it is also a *telos* of political activity—that which those
who take *our* good as *their* practical aim are thereby obliged to enable and
promote. And that is to say that a central aim of a *political* life must be to
enable and promote the living of specifically *philosophical* lives—as well
as those of the other, less self-conscious, conceptual sculptors of vocabularies for self-redescription. That conclusion expresses the metaphysical
basis of a division of labor between these two sorts of paradigmatically
sapient forms of life.

7.   What of the life of philosophical activity itself? I've taken what may
have seemed a somewhat roundabout path to this question. But I've done
that because the best way to see what goods are secured by philosophical
activity is not to talk *about* it, but to *do* a bit of it. The ideas I've put on
the table let us pick out distinctively *philosophical* activity by a series of
nested characterizations. On the conception of us as sapients I have been
suggesting, we are to be understood to begin with as *normative* creatures,
hence as essentially *social* ones. Because those norms are *conceptual*
norms, which is to say norms governing inferential practices of giving and
asking for reasons, we are *rational, discursive* beings. Binding ourselves
by conceptual norms that go beyond mere causal constraint makes possible the positive *expressive freedom* to think new thoughts, to make new
claims, and to describe and understand ourselves and our recognitive
communities in new ways, achieving a new sort of self-consciousness.
With that expressive freedom and self-consciousness comes the possibility of *transforming* ourselves by adopting new vocabularies, redescribing and so reconstituting our selves and discursive institutions. While all

of us are in some sense *consumers* of such new vocabularies, it is the special calling of some to *produce* them. And among those producers some take the construction of unique, potentially transformative vocabularies as the project by commitment to which they understand and define themselves. Among that group, some seek to produce those new vocabularies precisely by trying to understand the phenomena of sapience, normativity, conceptuality, reason, freedom, expression, self-consciousness, self-constitution, and historical transformation by subversive, empowering vocabularies.[10] Those are the philosophers. They are charged neither with simply understanding human nature (human history), nor with simply changing it, but with changing it *by* understanding it.

All the goods of sapient life flow from participation in the great human conversation. Producing the vocabularies that, as the medium in which that conversation is conducted, are the discursive, expressive organs of self-consciousness, self-constitution, and self-development for sapients is accordingly an especially important sort of contribution one can make to that conversation. And sculpting conceptual tools for *understanding* the nature, history, and potential for such self-conscious expressive self-transformation enables and promotes the deepest, grandest form of self-consciousness of which we are capable.

Doing that is exercising a unique kind of expressive freedom—the kind characteristic of the philosophical life. And the goods distinctive of that life flow from that sort of positive freedom. The philosopher is responsible for and committed to digesting the most profound thoughts and mastering the most intricate and powerful vocabularies that have been developed for articulating our sapience, and for producing from them new such thoughts and vocabularies—new forms of self-consciousness—for our own times.

It does not go without saying that societies provide environmental and institutional niches within which those doing the sort of work I am talking about can flourish. That depends, after all, on the vision and abilities of the politicians who—I've urged—are specially charged with enabling and promoting it. For instance, medieval Muslim culture provided ample institutional opportunities—and nourished many good and some great

10. That is pretty much the aim of this book.

philosophers and other transformative thinkers—while contemporary Muslim culture has apparently so far provided only stony ground for such seeds. Courtly patronage from Renaissance Italy to the France of the *ancien régime* was one institution that made room for and even supported philosophical work, even if fitfully and unevenly. But the principal institutional locus of environmental niches suitable for philosophical lives in the modern world is the *university*. In its contemporary form, as independent of the Church, it is largely a nineteenth-century development—owing a surprisingly extensive debt to the intellectual vision of Hegel and the institutional genius of Humboldt. Even in developed Western countries, its role as a haven for the most abstract sort of speculation and vocabulary construction—as opposed to an engine for applied technological progress—is always fragile and often threatened.

But in that favored environment, academic philosophers enjoy to an unusual extent the peculiar individual positive freedom of the intellectual. Prime among these is control over one's own time and problems. Almost anyone who can do this work could make lots more money doing something else; this is what we've gotten in return for forgoing that. What we think about and work on is wholly up to us: the *only* consideration is what we find most interesting and promising, what we think we can use, can make something important of. Equally smart and well-educated people in other professions—think of law, medicine, business, politics—are almost exclusively obliged to think about problems and issues that are important to *other* people, that are made pressing by the passing demands of events or institutions over which they have little control. The resources at our command are not massive; we don't supervise large teams of eager subordinates, can't bring to bear large capital investments. But we are free to deploy our own time and efforts as we see fit—free to waste them if we make bad judgments. Though one is always uncomfortably aware of the ultimately weightier judgments of one's work that will eventually be made by colleagues as yet unborn, on a day-to-day and year-to-year basis, academics are free to work on what *they* care about.

Almost uniquely, academics are also granted the positive freedom to take whatever time, invest whatever energy, they deem necessary for the task to which they are committed: paradigmatically, digesting or producing a text, a contribution to the great Conversation in which one is but a link connecting the mighty dead to the mighty to come. If one asks capable and committed people across modern culture generally what they find most objectionable about their professional situations, a great number will say that it is that their institutions do not, for one reason or another, allow them to do their work properly—to take the time to get it right. Everything is a rush, a compromise, a make-do solution that could be vastly improved were one only allowed to. We are allowed and even encouraged to agonize, to hone, to polish—to take the time and make the effort to make the work the best it can be. I spent eighteen years writing my big book *Making It Explicit,* for instance—though that was not *all* I was doing, it was my principal project. And I've been at my nearly finished (I think) Hegel book for more than twenty-five. I'm not working under journalistic constraints—the remarkable thing is that it can be done at all. Our projects are ones that can be undertaken without depending on the acquiescence or cooperation of others. (Compare the frustration of an architect with a compelling idea who is not allowed even to work it out in detail, never mind to see it constructed, until and unless a client can be persuaded to pay for it.) And how good our products turn out to be is wholly a matter of how good *we* make them. There is no one else on whom to blame flaws of conception or execution. (Compare the frustration of a film writer or director, whose vision must be distorted in many ways in order to be implemented, since it depends in so many ways on the efforts of so many other people.) Of course, having no excuses can be difficult, too. As Nietzsche said, "Hard is it to be alone with one's own judge and executioner." But having the positive freedom to find out what one is really capable of—in a way that the journalist, architect, or director may never be able to—is still a substantial satisfaction.

These forms of the public freedom of the philosopher are institutional reflections of a kind of private freedom that is harder to characterize: the freedom of thought itself, the medium in which we sapients live and move and have our being. It is the freedom exercised by the theoretical mathematician. When she says, "Let $y$ be a function of $x$," God and all his angels cannot say, "Let it not." It may be a foolish, pointless, or fruitless stipulation; it may lead to any number of difficulties. But the capacity to bind oneself by that sort of discursive commitment, to explore its consequences (what one has thereby made oneself responsible for) and possible ways of justifying it (what authority one could claim for it) is the normative, discursive freedom constitutive of thought itself. That realm of freedom is our ownmost domain. And it is the philosophers who are most self-consciously and explicitly at home in that freedom.

**8.**    I started my story with the question of how one might ground normative characterizations and comparative assessments of different forms of life. The answer that comes down to us from Plato and Aristotle is what I called the "metaphysical strategy": start with an account of the kind of beings we most deeply are. Focusing on consciousness or awareness in the broadest possible sense as what is characteristic of us, I then distinguished two fundamentally different dimensions of mindedness: sentience and sapience. Identifying ourselves as sentients valorizes a life of sensuous pleasure. I then marked out three ways in which we can instead describe and demarcate ourselves in terms of the sapience that distinguishes us from the beasts of forest and field.

- With Hume, we can think of ourselves as choosing, goal-pursuing beings, whose good consists in satisfying conceptually contentful desires and preferences. Reason, which articulates concepts, is understood as *practical,* instrumental intelligence—the capacity to deploy means deliberately and successfully to achieve ends. This sort of self-description underwrites a life primarily devoted, not to procuring more or less fleeting episodes of sensual pleasure, but to enjoying longer-term states of *satisfaction* of articulated, consciously endorsed desires, plans, and projects.

- Kant offers a still richer picture of sapience as a *normative* achievement—the positive ability to commit oneself, to take on responsibilities, to acknowledge and exercise authority. The conceptual contents of those commitments and entitlements are a matter of what counts as good *reasons* for adopting them—on a much broader conception of reason than the Humean-instrumental.

- The third, most sophisticated conception of sapience is Hegel's account of us as creatures of our positive expressive freedom—beings whose essence it is to have no essence, no nature, but only a history structured and driven by the description of ourselves that we endorse at each stage in our development—hence self-creating beings, who can change what we are *in* ourselves by changing what we are *for* ourselves, by identifying with new descriptions of ourselves, by adopting new vocabularies.

Each of these metaphysical meta-vocabularies for describing ourselves—as sentients, and as sapients thought of in the three different ways I've sketched—offers a different view of the kind of flourishing that we should seek, and that it should be a principal aim of the political life to enable and promote. It is up to the philosopher, however, to assess the merits of the competing claims of these ways of thinking about ourselves. According to the metaphysical strategy, that requires deciding which is the best metaphysical vocabulary to use in describing us. It is *true* of us that that we are sentient, and that we are sapient in all three of the senses considered: Humean, Kantian, and Hegelian. But which best characterizes what is *essential* about us—which makes us *us?* Note that the Hegelian offers a special kind of answer to this question: there is no once-and-for-all, matter-of-factual answer to that question, privileging one of the vocabularies for describing us. For what we really, essentially are, *in* ourselves, depends on what we are *for* ourselves. It depends on which vocabulary for self-description we adopt, endorse, interpret ourselves in terms of, and so identify with. Fans of sentience, Hume, Kant, and Hegel himself have done their philosophical work well, and offered us candidate vocabularies whose adoption *makes* us into different sorts of beings. The lesson we should learn from studying their efforts is *not* a decision about who is *right,* but one concerning the importance of coming up with new, ever-more-interesting such vocabularies as candidates to identify with, as expressive tools allowing us to *take* ourselves to be new kinds of being, and so to *make* ourselves into something new and different, preserving and accumulating previously disclosed possibilities and projects while transforming and adding to them. That is the job of the philosophers. As Henry James said on behalf of all those who devote themselves to this sort of metasapient labor:

We do what we can. We give what we have. We work in the dark. Our doubt is our passion, and our passion is our task. The rest is the madness of art.

# CHAPTER SIX

# Why Truth Is Not Important
# in Philosophy

**1.** John Austin said that any philosophical claim consists of the bit where you say it and the bit where you take it back. I am going to explicate the claim made in my inflammatory title in the reverse order.

The claim is not that *truthfulness* is not an important virtue. For it is a species of *honesty* or *sincerity:* honesty or sincerity in expressing one's beliefs. A truthful person does not assert what she does not believe. We *can* describe this virtue in terms of truth—"Don't put forward *as* true what you don't believe *is* true"—but the appeal to truth in expressing it is optional, not essential, as my previous formulation shows. So I am not saying that philosophers can forget about telling the truth (as Plato thought poets do).

The claim is not that *epistemic conscientiousness* is not an important virtue. We should not be heedless, reckless, or careless in forming or adopting our beliefs. Once again, we *can* put this point in terms of truth: we should work hard to see to it that our beliefs are true. But once again, expressing this point in terms of truth is optional. For what doing that consists in is paying critical attention to our *evidence,* to the *justification* we have for endorsing various claims that we consider. What is incumbent on us as conscientious believers is not to be *credulous,* that is, not to acquire beliefs on the basis of insufficient evidence. It is not to be *preju-*

*diced* or biased, that is, not to allow our preferences or desires—how we would *like* things to be—to suborn our assessment of the reasons there are to think that things actually are that way. It is to be *critical*, that is, actively to seek out and honestly to assess possibly countervailing reasons: carefully to consider what justifications there might be for claims incompatible with the one we are assessing. So long as we pay sufficiently close attention to the *reasons* that can be offered for and against various claims, their *truth* will take care of itself—or at least, we will have done everything we can do about it.

The claim is not that *knowledge* is not important. Since Plato we have been told that knowledge is not just *belief,* but belief that can be *justified;* and not just justified belief, but *true* justified belief. And that is a perfectly good way of picking out a centrally important cognitive status.[1] But I think it is a fundamental mistake to think that what is important is the possession by beliefs of a certain metaphysically weighty *property:* being *true.* I think the beginning of wisdom in assessing the significance of the justified true belief analysis of knowledge is to think about what one is *doing* when one *attributes* knowledge to another, or *assesses* the credentials of another as a knower. For me to take you to know, for instance, that the Washington Monument is 555 feet tall, I must do three things. First, I must *attribute* to you a *belief* that the Washington Monument is 555 feet tall. You can't know what you don't believe. (Notice that we *could* say "believe to be *true,*" but that doing so adds nothing.) Second, I must take it that you are *entitled* to that belief or commitment, that you have *reasons* for it, that you can *justify* it. An accidentally acquired belief is not yet knowledge. If you just picked some number out of the air, even if your lucky guess was right, you don't *know* that it is. Third, I must *myself* endorse the belief, that is, believe that the Washington Monument is 555 feet tall. That is, besides *attributing* to you both a *commitment* (corresponding to the *belief* condition) and an *entitlement* to that commitment (corresponding to the *justification* condition), I must myself *undertake* the corresponding commitment. That is what corresponds to the *truth*

---

1. Edmund Gettier famously argues that *more* is required for our ordinary conception of knowledge. But his arguments don't tell against the claim that justified true belief is still an important cognitive status.

condition on knowledge. But *all* that condition is doing is marking the coincidence of belief across social perspectives: I only count as knowledge beliefs that I *share*.

Suppose you are standing in a darkened room and seem to see a candle ten feet in front of you. I attribute to you the belief that there is a candle ten feet in front of you. And so long as you have no reason to think anything funny is going on, I take you to be justified in that belief, since you can see it. So I take you to be committed to there being a candle ten feet in front of you, and entitled to that commitment: to have a justified belief. Nonetheless, I will not take it that you *know* that there is a candle ten feet in front of you if *I* don't believe that—if, for instance, I, but not you, can see that there is an angled mirror five feet in front of you, and that the candle you see is actually quite close to you, hidden from you by a curtain. My assessment that your justified belief is not *true* is a way of expressing the fact that under the circumstances described, I am not willing myself to *undertake* commitment to the claim I *attribute* to you. Assigning some belief the honorific status of *knowledge* is important, because in doing that I am classifying it as being of the kind that I think *everyone* should employ as premises in their own inferences, should appeal to in their own reasoning. These are the beliefs that I take to be eligible to serve as reasons on the basis of which to form further beliefs. For I take it that any good inference in which they figure as premises is one whose conclusions I should endorse, and I take it that good reasons can be given to believe them, in turn. Thus, these are the beliefs that I take it deserve to spread.

**2.** So far, in "the bit where I take it back," I've said that my claim that truth is not important in philosophy should *not* be understood as denying the importance of truthfulness, epistemic conscientiousness, or assessments of knowledge. But I've also said that in each of those cases, though we may if we like talk about the phenomena in question in terms of truth, we need not do so, and lose nothing essential if we do not. That last claim points toward a more positive characterization of the view I want to defend: *truth* is not a concept that has an important *explanatory* role to play in philosophy. Appearances to the contrary are the result of *mis*understanding its distinctive *expressive* role. The word 'true' does indeed let us *say* things that in many cases we could not say without it. But when we understand *what* it lets us say, and *how* it does that, we will see that the very features that make it *expressively* useful make it completely unsuitable to do the sort of theoretical *explanatory* work for which philosophers have typically enlisted its aid.

The expression "... is true" looks like a predicate that ascribes a property. If it were, it would be a very special kind of immediately and unconditionally normatively significant property: a kind of "to-be-believed-ness" property. No wonder metaphysicians, ethicists, and especially epistemologists have regarded it with fascination. Nor is its normative weight exclusively of an abstract, disinterested, ethical sort—a high ideal that is a suitable object of selfless commitment by those of good character, lofty aspiration, and sufficient leisure. For, we are assured by the philosophical tradition, the *truth* of our beliefs is the touchstone and sole possible guarantor of the *success* of our practical endeavors—including the lowest and most narrowly self-interested. Having *beliefs* with the special, desirable property of being *true* is the only reliable way to get what you want—to imbue your *desires* with the most important and desirable property *they* can aspire to: being *satisfied.* So truth is of supreme *practical* importance.

Besides its central significance for both the most ethereal principles and the most egoistical practices, truth has also seemed to hold the key to our inmost, ownmost nature. For (as Chapter Five emphasized) we are not merely *sentient* creatures, but also *sapient* ones. That is, in addition to consciousness in the sense of having *feelings* and *sensations*—awareness in the sense that underwrites a distinction between being *awake* and *asleep*—as our mammalian cousins such as cats do, we have states with conceptually articulated contents that can be expressed in *sentences.* We can believe *that* the international monetary system needs to be reformed and desire *that* it be reformed. These are the *propositional attitudes* that can constitute *knowledge.* And the standard way to understand the *propositional contents* that distinguish these states from the images and raw feels that are the contents of merely sentient states is that they can be assessed as to their *truth.* The *meaning* of a declarative sentence, expressing the *content* of a possible belief (or desire, or intention), consists in the circumstances under which it would be *true.* To grasp or understand that meaning or content just is to know its truth conditions: how the world would have to be for it to be true. So the sort of mindedness that distinguishes us from the beasts of the field—the sapience that gives our species its very name—consists in the relations we stand in to the very special property of truth: that we can think things that could be true, desire and intend that they be true. Take away that relationship to truth and you take away our sapience, relegate us to the cognitive torpor of mere sentience. This sapience- constituting directedness at *truth* is the essence and the motor of our ascent out of that primeval sea into the broad highlands of thought. Philosophical concern with us, our nature and our spirit, *is* philosophical concern with truth.

**3.** This familiar philosophical scene, with truth at center stage and in the leading role, is no doubt uplifting and inspiring. But I think it is deeply confused and almost totally wrong. Consider to begin with the idea that truth is the property of beliefs that conduces to the *success* of practical projects based on those beliefs. This thought is so deeply entrenched that some pragmatists have even sought to *define* truth as the success-producing property of beliefs.[2] But even those not inclined to endorse such an order of definition have felt free to appeal to the intimate connection between the truth of beliefs and the satisfaction of desires for other philosophical projects—for instance when scientific realists argue that the at least approximate truth of our scientific theories is the only possible explanation for the practical success of our technologies: the extent to which they provide powerful instruments for getting what we want (at least, for some kinds of things we want).

The idea is that it is the truth of my belief that there are cookies in the cupboard that explains the fulfillment of my desire for cookies. This is an intuitively compelling thought, but we need to be careful with it. The truth of that belief will not lead to satisfaction of my desire in the context of the collateral *false* belief that the cupboard is in the kitchen, rather than in the pantry. And, to vary the example, the *false* belief that one can tan

---

2. For a sophisticated contemporary example, see J. T. Whyte's "Success Semantics," *Analysis* 50, no. 3 (1990): 149–157, followed up by "The Normal Rewards of Success," *Analysis* 51, no. 2 (1991): 65–73. I present a more detailed version of the argument that follows in my commentary "Unsuccessful Semantics," *Analysis* 54, no. 3 (1994): 175–178.

leather by boiling it with birch bark will result in practical success if it is combined with the false collateral belief that the oak in front of me is really a birch. So the practical utility of a belief's being true is wholly hostage to the truth or falsity of the collateral beliefs with which it is combined.

Well then, perhaps one should only talk about the truth of a whole *set* of beliefs—indeed, of *all* one's beliefs. The requirement that we banish *all error* from our beliefs is a tall order, and probably not very realistic. But surely *that* would reliably produce successful, desire-satisfying actions? Not really. For the effects of collateral *ignorance* are just as bad as those of collateral *error*. If I am unaware that wet weather has swelled the cupboard door so that it cannot be opened, all my true beliefs about the location of the cookies and of the cupboard will be of no practical avail. But banishing *ignorance* as well as *error* seems over the top: is truth really only of practical use to the omniscient?

At this point one might be tempted to assimilate ignorance to error, by claiming that in the case where the swelling shut of the cupboard thwarted the good practical effects of my believing the cookies were in there, I really did believe that the door had *not* swelled and stuck, and so was in fact done in by my false belief. But there are not just an infinite, but, worse, an *indefinite* number of ways in which my plan could go awry through circumstances of which I am unaware. Is it at all plausible that I have beliefs about them all? That the cupboard has not been nailed shut, moved, mined, infested with voracious beetles, encased in glass, shrunk to microscopic size, and so on? As a last, desperate attempt, one might stipulate that I had a collateral belief that there were no impediments to my opening the cupboard and eating the cookies. Insisting that *that* collateral belief be present and true will indeed ensure that my true belief that there are cookies in the cupboard will lead to practical success in satisfying my cookie desire. But it does so only by trivializing the original claim. For it is, in effect, the demand that the original true belief be accompanied by a *true* belief that it will lead to practical success. And *that* would hold also for my *false* belief that boiling with birch bark will tan leather, in all those cases in which I have a *true* collateral belief that there are no impediments to my tanning leather by boiling it with birch bark. I think that when one looks closely at the claim, one finds that there is no way to make sense of the idea that true beliefs produce successful actions so that it is both true and non-trivial. This sort of explanatory appeal to truth, at any rate, collapses when weight is put upon it.

4. What about the role of truth in *semantic* explanation, via a definition of propositional content in terms of truth conditions? We certainly do use 'true' to *say* what the content of a claim is. If you don't understand the sentence "The surgeon performed a cholecystectomy," I can explain it to you by telling you that it is true just in case the surgeon removed the patient's gallbladder. And we can say more general things, such as: Any claim of the form $\sim p$ is true just in case $p$ is not true. But it would be a mistake to infer from this sort of appeal to truth conditions to *express* propositional contents that one can *explain* what propositional contents *are* by appeal to the conditions under which sentences are true. That would be a possible order of explanation *only* if one could make sense of the notion of *truth* prior to and independently of making sense of the notion of *propositional content*. And there is good reason to think that that cannot be done.

What is the expressive role of 'true'? Let us start by drawing a lesson from our discussion of the JTB (justified true belief) account of knowledge. What is one *doing* when one *says* that some claim is true? The answer offered there is that one is *endorsing* it, undertaking or acknowledging a *commitment* with that same content. So here is a first try: Saying or believing that "Snow is white" is true—that it is true that snow is white— is just saying or believing that snow is white. This, however, by itself, won't do. For it only covers some of the cases. When I say "If it is true that $p$, then $q$," I have *not* said that $p$ is true, and have not asserted $p$. We need something more general, something that applies to freestanding, assertional uses of 'true', but also to embedded, non-assertional uses of 'true', in which its use just contributes to the *content* of what is said, without being itself invested with assertional *force*.

So here is a try. "It is true that $p$" is in *all* cases, *both* freestanding, force-bearing, *and* embedded uses, equivalent to $p$.[3] This is, roughly, Tarski's famous "Convention T." It defines 'true' by the principle that the quoted-or-named sentence $\ulcorner p \urcorner$ is true just in case $p$, where '$p$' is any claim that has

---

3. For a powerful exposition and defense of this view, see Paul Horwich, *Truth* (Oxford: Oxford University Press, 1998).

the same *content* as is expressed by the expression ⌜*p*⌝. This can be called a "content-redundancy" theory of truth.[4] This is plausible. But notice that it *uses* the notion content, or at least same-content (co-contentful), to *define* 'true'. If *that* is how we define truth—Tarski-wise—then truth cannot be appealed to in explaining the notion of content, since that notion is rather defined by appeal to the notion of content, and accordingly presupposes it.

I think that the theory that best captures the insight behind the intuitive thought that "It is true that *p*" just *means* the same (expresses the same content as) ⌜*p*⌝, is the *prosentential* account.[5] The basic idea behind this theory is to exploit the analogy between identity of content within the category of *sentences* (which is what the content-redundancy theory appeals to in defining 'true') and identity of content within the category of *singular terms.* For in that case, there are *two* ways that one can commit oneself to the identity of content of two term-tokenings. One can explicitly assert an *identity.* So in the context of the claim "Benjamin Franklin was a printer," the explicit identity statement "Benjamin Franklin was (=) the inventor of the lightning rod" licenses the conclusion: "The inventor of the lightning rod was a printer." But one also might use a *pronoun* to achieve the same effect, by implicitly *stipulating* the relevant content-identity. Thus one can derive the very *same* conclusion from the claim "Benjamin Franklin was a printer" by appending the auxiliary hypothesis "And *he* was the inventor of the lightning rod." For the fact that the anaphoric *antecedent* of the pronoun 'he' is the term "Benjamin Franklin" licenses the very same substitution as the explicit identity. The prosentential theory of truth is what you get if you transform the content-redundancy view by assimilating it to the second paradigm rather than the first. On this view, when Hegel says "History is the progress of the consciousness of freedom" and I say "That is true," I have made myself a same-sayer with Hegel in exactly the same way that I have managed to refer to the same person when he says "Hamann was a great philosopher" and I say "But he was an incredibly strange human being." In both cases

4. It is usually associated with Frank P. Ramsey, on the basis of his article "Facts and Propositions (1927)," reprinted in *F. P. Ramsey: Philosophical Papers,* ed. D. H. Mellor (Cambridge: Cambridge University Press, 1990), pp. 34–51.

5. First put forward in Dorothy Grover, Joseph Camp, and Nuel Belnap, "A Prosentential Theory of Truth," *Philosophical Studies* 27 (1975): 73–74.

the content of my remark inherits its content—respectively what I say and who I am talking about—from the antecedent provided by Hegel.

The anaphoric account of the identity (redundancy) of content of "It is true that $p$" and $\ulcorner p \urcorner$ has many technical advantages. In the most sophisticated version of the theory, ". . . is true" is understood as a prosentence-forming operator. It applies to a singular term, which specifies the sentence that is the anaphoric antecedent of the prosentence, from which, accordingly, it inherits its content, in the same way a pronoun like 'he' or 'it' inherits its content from its antecedent. There are as many ways of using 'true' as there are ways of specifying sentences that can serve as the anaphoric antecedents. There are quote-names, such as "Snow is white," yielding prosentences such as "'Snow is white' is true," which inherit their content from the named-by-being-quoted sentence. But there are also descriptions of sentences, such as "Fermat's last theorem" and "The first full sentence on page 37 of Quine's *Word and Object*," and prosentences that inherit their content from the sentences so indicated, such as "Fermat's last theorem is true" and "The first full sentence on page 37 of Quine's *Word and Object* is true." The rule for applying sentential operators such as 'not' and 'probably' in prosentences such as "What the policeman said is not true" and "Tarski's favorite sentence is probably true" is that the resulting prosentence is equivalent to the result of applying the operator to the sentence (or sentences) picked out as an antecedent by the phrase the prosentence-forming operator applies to. So if the policeman said "The suspect fell down," the prosentence-user is claiming something equivalent to "The suspect did not fall down" and, in the other case, something equivalent to "Snow is probably white." And notice that all of these equivalences work equally well for embedded uses. If I say "If what Hegel said is not true, then I don't know what history is," I've committed myself to the conditional claim that if history is not the progress of the consciousness of freedom, then I don't know what it is.

I assert, though I certainly cannot pretend to be able adequately to justify the claim here,[6] that the prosentential theory offers a complete, adequate, and satisfactory account of the use of the term 'true'. If that is

---

6. I try to do that in Chapter Five of *Making It Explicit* (Cambridge, MA: Harvard University Press, 1994) and "Expressive vs. Explanatory Deflationism About Truth," in *What Is Truth?*, ed. Richard Schantz (New York: de Gruyter, 2002), pp. 103–119.

so, two consequences are worthy of note. First of all, one can use 'true' to *express* conceptual or propositional contents, since claims formed using 'true' inherit their contents from their antecedents. But the pronominal or prosentential relation is one of content-*inheritance:* one must *already* have a good grip on the notion of the content that is inherited in order to understand it. Second, on this account there is no more a *property* expressed by 'true' than there is a kind of *object* picked out by 'it'. After all, "that is so" (which I used just above) is *also* a prosentence, and one ought not be (though some have been, are, and will be) tempted to look for a property of so-ness that claims could have. And surely, even if one succumbed to that temptation, one would have to admit that one needed an *antecedent* grasp of the content that was a *candidate* for being ˢsoˢ. There is no go at all to the idea that one could *explain* those contents (the things that could be so) in terms of a *prior* notion of so-ness or being so (what, exactly, being so?). If we are going to explain one in terms of the other, surely the right way to go about things is to make sense first of the notion of a proposition—of something that *can* be true (as, for instance, the doorknob on my office cannot).

Prosentences, like pronouns, do let us say things we could not say otherwise. Besides the lazy or redundant uses of pronouns, there are quantificational ones. Using pronouns, I can say not only "If John thinks that, then he is being foolish," but also "If anyone beats his donkey, then he is mean." And using prosentences, I can say not only "What John said is true," but "Everything the policeman said is true." Our language would be expressively impoverished without pronouns, and it would be expressively impoverished without prosentences. But that important fact has no bearing on the suitability of the ˢconceptˢ <u>it</u> to serve to explain the notion of <u>object</u>,[7] nor, correspondingly, on the suitability of the ˢconceptˢ <u>so</u>, or <u>true</u> to explain the notion of a <u>proposition</u>.

**5.** So far, my aim has been relentlessly critical. I've claimed that one should no more think of truth as a philosophically weighty property that

7. Not such a quixotic enterprise that it has never been attempted. Think of Quine's slogan: "To be is to be the value of a variable." But Quine uncritically took for granted the availability of a *metalanguage* in which one *could* pick out the domain elements over which his variables (a kind of pronoun) ranged. Though that is unobjectionable for certain *formal* purposes, it does not support a corresponding order of *philosophical* explanation.

can be wheeled in to perform various sorts of crucial explanatory labor than one should think of no one as a particularly spooky kind of person: the one who is in your room even when *no one* is in your room. (Think here of crafty Ulysses, telling the Cyclops that his name was "Noman," so that when he escaped, blinding the Cyclops, the Cyclops' neighbors responded to his cries "Noman is killing me!" by saying: "If no man is killing you, shut up and let us sleep!") But it is fair enough to ask: if truth is not important in philosophy, what is? What *does* articulate our sapience and so constitute the difference that makes a difference in distinguishing us from the beasts of the field? What *does* matter in epistemology, in semantics, and in the philosophy of mind? It is no use deflating truth unless there is some candidate available to replace it. And after all, the anaphoric, prosentential account, it was insisted, *presupposes* a notion of the propositional contents that truth-claims inherit from their antecedents. How *are* we to understand and explain propositional content, if not in terms of truth conditions? And what *is* the overarching cognitive goal we are supposed to be pursuing, if not truth?

The slogan that expresses the view I want to recommend as an answer to these reasonable questions is: from *knowledge* to *understanding;* from *truth* to *inference.* On the first point, we may paraphrase T. S. Eliot: "Where is the understanding we have lost in knowledge? Where is the knowledge we have lost in information?" But it is by thinking about propositional and conceptual content—and thereby our sapience—in terms of *inference* rather than *truth* that we will find a way through and forward from the confusions I have been diagnosing and criticizing.

Frege, the founder of modern logic, explicitly codified a semantic principle relating truth to inference: good inferences never take premises that are true into conclusions that are not true. The traditional way of exploiting this principle is to use it to underwrite an explanation of the goodness of inference in terms of truth: any inference is good, so long as it does not have true premises and a false conclusion. This is a very weak notion of good inference: the inference from "Snow is white" to "Grass is green" is a good one in this sense, even though the premise has nothing to do with the conclusion. It is, of course, a good feature of an inference that it does not have true premises and a false conclusion—at least, it would be a bad feature if it did. Surprisingly, Frege was able to show that this weak notion of good inference suffices for many purposes in mathematics. But we could exploit Frege's semantic principle to underwrite an explanation going the other way around: truth is what is preserved by good inferences. Of course, to do that, we would need an antecedent, independent grip on the notion of good inference.

In the very same work in which he puts forward his semantic principle—his seminal *Begriffsschrift* of 1879—Frege suggests how we could think about propositional content in terms of inference. His avowed aim is to explicate the notion of "conceptual content" (begrifflicher Inhalt). The qualification "conceptual" is explicitly construed in inferential terms:

> ... there are two ways in which the content of two judgments may differ; it may, or it may not, be the case that all inferences that can be drawn from the first judgment when combined with certain other ones can always also be drawn from the second when combined with the same other judgments. The two propositions 'the Greeks defeated the Persians at Plataea' and 'the Persians were defeated by the Greeks at Plataea' differ in the former way; even if a slight difference of sense is discernible, the agreement in sense is preponderant. Now I call that part of the content that is the same in both the conceptual content. Only this has significance for our concept language [Begriffsschrift] ... In my formalized language [*BGS*] ... only that part of judgments which affects the possible inferences is taken into consideration. Whatever is needed for a correct ['richtig', usually misleadingly translated as 'valid'] inference is fully expressed; what is not needed is ... not.[8]

Two claims have the same conceptual content iff they have the same inferential role: a good inference is never turned into a bad one by substituting one for the other.

Frege's idea is that we think of conceptual content in terms of its role in reasoning. To be *propositionally* contentful is to be able to play the role

---

8. Frege, *Begriffsschrift*, sec. 3. The 1879 *Begriffsschrift* is translated in *From Frege to Gödel: A Source Book in Mathematical Logic, 1879–1931*, ed. Jean van Heijenoort (Cambridge, MA: Harvard University Press, 2002).

both of *premise* and of *conclusion* in an inference. (We have to insist on both, since one common way of thinking about *practical* reasoning is in terms of inferences whose conclusions are *doings* rather than *sayings.*) Frege's semantic principle relating truth to inference tells us that anything that can play the role both of premise and conclusion in an inference will be the right sort of thing to be evaluated as to its *truth.* So we can pick out declarative *sentences,* as the linguistic items that express *propositions,* in terms of their role in *inference.*

An order of semantic explanation that approaches the notion of <u>conceptual content</u>, paradigmatically *<u>propositional</u>* <u>content</u>, through that of *<u>inference</u>* rather than through that of <u>truth</u> has the advantage of establishing at the outset of the enterprise a connection between the *contents* possessed or expressed by sentences, on the one hand, and what language users actually *do,* on the other. For *inferring* is something that thinkers and speakers *do.* It is, in Wittgenstein's phrase, making a *move* in the language game. So, of course, is asserting. Asserting *can* be thought of as putting a sentence forward *as true.* But then we need to ask what doing that consists in: putting it forward as *what,* exactly? Following out Frege's strategy of focusing on inference suggests that putting something forward as true just is putting it forward as an appropriate *premise* from which to make *inferences.* That is putting it forward as something that is appropriately responded to practically by *doing* something: making an inference. It is not possible to make sense of the notion of <u>inference</u> apart from that of <u>assertion</u>, since assertions are the termini of inferential moves. But it may be possible to make sense of these two kinds of doing together, without having to appeal to the notion of <u>truth</u> at the outset, and then get a grip on the notion of truth as what is both preserved by good inferences and what one is putting something forward *as* when one asserts it.

**6.** Consider how the notion of *understanding* looks from the two different semantic perspectives being considered. From the point of view of *truth,* understanding a sentence, associating a propositional content with it, is knowing its truth conditions: knowing how the world would have to be for it to be true. Here *understanding* is explained in terms of a special kind of *knowledge.* But what does this kind of knowledge consist in? Is it a justified true belief? If so, *what* belief? I understand the content of the sentence "Snow is white." I know that it is true just in case snow is white. Is *that* the justified true belief that my knowledge of the truth conditions of "Snow is white" consists in? If so, how do I understand *that* content? We seem to be moving in a very small circle, and not really explaining the content or what understanding it consists in. From the point of view of *inference*, understanding a sentence, associating a propositional content with it, is having practical mastery of its inferential role: knowing what follows from it, and what would be evidence for or against it. The talk of 'knowledge' here is very different from that involved in knowledge of truth conditions. For it is a kind of knowing *how* rather than knowing *that:* knowing how to *do* something, namely distinguish in practice between good inference and bad inference in which the sentence appears as a premise or conclusion, rather than knowing *that* the truth conditions are such-and-such. Understanding shows up on this account as a practical ability, a kind of skill: sorting possible inferences into good ones and bad ones, endorsing or being disposed to make some of them, and rejecting or being disposed not to make some others.

Of course, one might try to understand the knowledge of truth conditions that understanding consists in on the traditional approach also as a kind of practical know-how, rather than as a kind of theoretical knowing that—that is, as not consisting in an explicit (hence itself propositionally contentful true and justified) *belief,* which is what gets us into circularity problems. But what kind of know-how or practical ability *is* knowing the truth conditions of a sentence? The standard answer—that of Michael Dummett, for instance—is that it is the capacity to *recognize* the truth of the sentence: to sort situations into those in which it is true and those in which it is not. This is a practical *classificatory* ability: the ability reliably to respond differentially to situations in which the claim is true. The case where this proposal has the most intuitive appeal is that of *observational* concepts. One who understands the concept <u>red</u> can respond differentially to the visible presence of red things: paradigmatically, by saying "That's red." But we need to be careful here. After all, a parrot could learn to do that. Do we want to say that a parrot that reliably responds to red things by uttering the noise "Rrawk—that's red!" shows that it grasps or understands the concept <u>red</u>? What about a photocell hooked up to a tape recorder? A chunk of iron reliably responds differentially to wet environments by rusting. Should we therefore credit it with understanding the concept <u>wet</u>, and treat its rusting as the utterance of a sentence whose truth conditions are that it is true just in case something is wet?

Something has gone wrong here. The parrot, the photocell, and the chunk of iron can serve as *instruments* for the detection of red things or wet things, because they respond differentially to them. But those responses are *not* claims *that* things are red or wet, precisely because they do *not understand* those responses *as* having that meaning or content. By contrast, when *you* respond to red things or wet things by saying, "That's red" or "That's wet," you *do* understand what you are saying, you *do* grasp the content, and you *are* applying the *concepts* <u>red</u> and <u>wet</u>. What is the difference that makes the difference here? What practical know-how have you got that the parrot, the photocell, and the chunk of iron do not? I think the answer is that *you*, but *not* they, can use your response as the premise in *inferences*. For *you*, but *not* for them, your response is situated in a network of connections to other sentences, connections that underwrite inferential *moves* to it and from it. You are disposed to accept the inference from "That's red" to "That's colored," to reject the move to "That's green," and to accept the move to it from "That's a stoplight." You are willing to make the move from "It's wet" to "There is water about," to infer it from "It is raining," to take it as ruling out the claim "We are in a desert," and so on. Because you have the practical ability to sort inferences in which it appears as a premise or conclusion into good ones and bad ones, *your* response "That's red" or "It's wet" is the making of a *move* in a language game, the staking of a claim, the taking of a stand that commits you to other such claims, precludes some others, and could be justified by still others. Having practical mastery of that inferentially articulated space—what Wilfrid Sellars calls "the space of reasons"—is what *understanding* the concepts <u>red</u> and <u>wet</u> consists in. The responsive, merely classificatory, *non*-inferential ability to respond differentially to red and wet things is at most a necessary condition of exercising that understanding, not a sufficient one.[9]

We can come to the same conclusion from another direction. We were considering a semantic theorist who claims that understanding the prop-

9. This line of thought is pursued further in Chapter Seven.

ositional content expressed by a sentence consists in knowledge of its truth conditions. This claim faces the objection that if that knowledge is understood as knowing *that* things are thus-and-so, that is, as having some justified true *belief,* that the account is going to be objectionably circular or fatally incomplete, since we will not have an account of what understanding the content of *that* belief consists in. The response was then that one might instead construe knowledge of truth conditions as a kind of know-how, as practical mastery of inferential roles is. In particular, it could be thought of as a *recognitional* capacity. We've seen that this will work in the central cases that motivate the idea, namely *observational* concepts, concepts that have *non*-inferential, responsive uses, *only* if we supplement it with an appeal to practical mastery of *inferences.* But what about the contents of other kinds of sentences, sentences that do *not* have observational uses? How am I supposed to manifest the practical ability to recognize the truth conditions of sentences such as "The Washington Monument is 555 feet tall" or "The international monetary system needs to be reformed"? It is hard to avoid the conclusion that this practical ability would itself have to be understood in *inferential* terms. I could manifest my capacity to recognize the truth conditions of the first sentence for instance by endorsing the inference to the claim about the height of the Washington Monument from a picture of it next to a giant ruler, or from a measurement of the length of its shadow and a simultaneous measurement of the length of the shadow of a stick of known length. And I could manifest my practical capacity to recognize the truth conditions of the second sentence by accepting an argument to that conclusion from a claim about the tendency of currency fluctuations to further impoverish the poorest of the poor countries, while rejecting an argument to that conclusion from the claim that international trade is growing by great leaps and bounds.

So it looks as though, whether we think about observational concepts or theoretical ones, the practical abilities associated with the grasp of truth conditions turn out to be inferential ones. And there seem to be a large number of other philosophically interesting kinds of concepts whose contents are *only* going to be intelligible in terms of their roles in reasoning: for instance, modal, normative, and probabilistic concepts, and those having to do with the past or the future. At the very least, approaching these potentially puzzling kinds of concepts by asking about their role in reasoning promises to avoid the sort of spooky metaphysical questions that would arise were we to ask instead about the truth-makers of claims formulated in those vocabularies: about the metaphysical status of *past* (hence no longer existent) facts, or merely *possible* fat men stuck in the doorway, or of that famous 10 percent chance of rain on a day when it does not in fact rain. So, for instance, the difference between merely accidental regularities, such as "all the coins in my pocket are copper," and genuinely lawlike regularities, such as "the melting point of copper is 1083.4°C," is that the latter, but not the former, support *counterfactual* inferences. It does *not* follow from the first claim that if this nickel *were* in my pocket, it *would be* copper, but it *does* follow from the second that if I *were* to heat this penny to 1083.4°C, it *would* melt. Again, you will think much more usefully about the content of claims such as "Freedom is better than slavery" and "Blake is a better poet of the imagination than Milton" by thinking in terms of their inferential roles—what follows from such claims, what do they preclude, what would be evidence for or against them?—than if you try to think in terms of their truth conditions.

**7.** Thinking of conceptual content in terms of inferential role, and of understanding correspondingly as practical mastery of such an inferential role—as the ability to sort into good and bad the inferences in which the concept appears in the premises or conclusions—has other advantages as well. It is a powerful corrective to the philosophically unilluminating and pedagogically damaging cartesian picture of the achievement of understanding as the turning on of some kind of inner light, which permits one then to see clearly. This is what the elementary-school kid thinks happens in math class when the girl next to him "gets it" and he doesn't. He is waiting for the light to go on in his head, too, so that he'll understand fractions. In fact, he's just got to practice making the moves, and distinguishing which ones are okay and which ones are not, until he masters the practical inferential abilities in question. It is not unusual for teachers of technical material to have students who can do all the problem sets and proofs, can tell what does and doesn't follow from some situation described using the concepts being taught, but still think that they don't understand those concepts. A feeling of familiarity and confidence in knowing one's way around in an inferential network often lags behind one's actual mastery of it. The important thing is to realize that the understanding *is* that practical mastery, and the feeling (the cartesian light) is at best an indicator of it—often an unreliable one.

We professors tell our students that it is important to think and write *clearly*. No doubt it is. But this can be frustrating advice to receive. After all, presumably no students think that fuzzy thinking and fuzzy writing are better than the alternative. The hard thing is to tell the difference. What, exactly, is one supposed to *do* in order think or write more clearly? Thinking about meaning and understanding in terms of inference provides some more definite guidance in this area. Thinking clearly is a matter of knowing, for each claim that you make, what else you are committing yourself to by making it, what you are ruling out, and what would be evidence for or against it. You can test the clarity of your thinking by rehearsing sample inferences, so as to test your practical mastery of the inferential vicinity of your thoughts. Of course, you may be mistaken about what really does follow from your claims. But that is *just* a mistake. So long as you are sure what you *take* to follow from and be evidence for your claim, your mistaken thought is at least *clear*. And writing clearly is giving your reader enough clues that *she* can tell what you *mean* to be committing yourself to by the claims you make, what *you* would take to be evidence for or against them, what follows from them, and what they preclude. And once again, this is something you can check for yourself when writing, by asking yourself, for each important consequence you take to follow from one of your claims, how your reader is supposed to *know* that you take it to be a consequence: what clues have you given to that effect?

The prosentential approach to truth-talk not only supports the claim that the use of 'true' presupposes a notion of *semantic content,* and so cannot be the basis of an *explanation* of that notion, but also shows how to build an account of truth-talk out of an account of semantic content. Since we now have in view the possibility of explaining semantic content in terms of role in reasoning, we have in place the raw materials the prosentential theory needs to elaborate the important *expressive* (not explanatory) role that 'true' plays. The resulting account will, as desired, underwrite Frege's semantic principle relating truth and goodness of inference.

**8.**   One might ask whether the inferentialist approach does not require overestimating the extent to which we are rational. Are we really very good at telling what is a reason for what? How often do we act for reasons—and in particular, for *good* reasons? The question betrays a misunderstanding. We are rational creatures in the sense that our claims and aims are always liable to *assessment* as to our reasons for them. How good we are at satisfying those demands doesn't change our status as rational. And it must be kept in mind that on this way of thinking about the nature of semantic content, it makes no sense to think of us *first* having a bunch of sentences expressing definite propositions, which accordingly stand in inferential relations to one another, and only *then* having there be a question about how many of those inferences we *get right*. For it is our practices of treating what is expressed by some noises as *reasons for* what is expressed by other noises that makes those noises express conceptual contents in the first place. Once the enterprise is up and running, we can certainly make mistakes about what follows from the commitments we have undertaken, and what would justify them. But there is no possibility of us *massively* or *globally* getting the inferences wrong (for very much the same Quinean reasons that Davidson has emphasized).

I have been arguing that it is better to think in terms of understanding than knowledge, and better to think of meaning and understanding (which on this approach are two sides of one coin) in terms of inference than in terms of truth. So far, I have approached this issue largely from the point of view of semantics and the philosophy of language. But there is more at stake here. For this way of thinking about semantic content goes to the heart of the question of what it is to be sapient—to be the kind of creature we most fundamentally are. It says that we are beings that live and move and have our being in the space of *reasons*. We are, at base, creatures who give and ask for reasons—who are sensitive to that "force of the better reason," persuasive rather than coercive, which so mystified and fascinated the ancient Greek philosophers. Crossing that all-important line from mere sentience to sapience is participating in practices of giving and asking for reasons: practices in which some performances have the pragmatic significance of *claims* or *assertions,* which accordingly, as both standing in need of reasons and capable of serving as reasons (that is, of playing the role both of conclusion and of premise in inference), count as expressing *propositional* semantic content.

This *semantic rationalism*—which goes with thinking of content in the first instance in terms of *inference* rather than *reference, reason* rather than *truth*—flies in the face of many famous movements in twentieth-century philosophical thought. The American pragmatists, above all John Dewey, used the possibility of explaining knowing *that* in terms of knowing *how* not only to assimilate our sapient intellectual activity to the skillful doings of merely sentient animals, but at the same time to blur the sharp, bright line I am trying to draw between sapience and sentience. Wittgenstein famously said that language does not have a 'downtown': a core set of practices on which the rest depend, and around which they are arrayed, like suburbs. But inferentialism says that practices of giving and asking for *reasons are* the 'downtown' of language. For it is only by incorporating such practices that practices put in play propositional and other conceptual contents at all—and hence count as *discursive* practices, practices in which it is possible to *say* anything. The first 'Sprachspiel', language game, Wittgenstein introduces in the *Philosophical Investigations* has a builder issuing ˢordersˢ to an assistant. When he says "Slab!" the assistant has been trained to respond by bringing a slab. When he says "Block!" the assistant has been trained to respond by bringing a block. From the inferentialist point of view, this does not qualify as a *Sprach*spiel at all; it is a *vocal,* but not a *verbal,* game. For the assistant is just a practical version of the parrot I considered earlier: he has been trained reliably to respond differentially to stimuli. But he grasps no concepts, and if this is the whole game, the builder expresses none. An *order* or command is not just any signal that is appropriately responded to in one way rather than another. It is something that determines *what is* an appropriate response by *saying* what one is to do, by *describing* it, specifying what *concepts* are to apply to a doing in order for it to count as *obeying* the order. Derrida's crusade against what he calls the 'logocentrism' of the Western philosophical tradition has brilliantly and inventively emphasized all the *other* things one can do with language, besides *arguing, inferring, explaining, theorizing,* and *asserting.* Thus we get the playful essays in which the key to his reading of Hegel is that his name in French rhymes with 'eagle', his reading of Nietzsche that turns on what Derrida claims is the most important of his philosophical writings (a slip of paper that turned up in his belongings after his death, reading only "I have forgotten my umbrella"), and the unforgettable meditation on the significance of the width of the margins of the page for the meaning of the text printed there. But if inferentialism is the right way to think about contentfulness, then the game of giving and asking for reasons *is* privileged among the games we play with words. For it is the one in virtue of which they mean anything at all—the one presupposed and built upon by all the other uses we can then put those meanings to, once they are available. Again, the master idea of Foucault's critique of modernity is that *reason* is just one more historically conditioned form of *power,* in principle no better (and, in its pervasive institutionalization, in many ways worse) than any other form of oppression. But if giving and asking for reasons is the practice that institutes *meanings* in the first place, then it does *not* belong in a box with violence and intimidation, which show up rather in the contrast class precisely insofar as they *constrain* what we do by something *other* than reasons.

**9.** My initial claim was that truth is not important in philosophy. I offered some reasons for that critical assessment, culminating in the more specific claim that when we properly understand the *expressive* role of 'true', we see that that role precisely disqualifies it from doing the sort of important *explanatory* work in various areas of philosophy, beginning with semantics, for which it has often been pressed into service. But rather than leaving it at that—content, as it were, with the bit where one takes it back—in the second half of this chapter I have sketched an alternative constructive account of some of the most important phenomena that one *might* have thought one needed an oomphy concept of *truth* to address. On this view, we are seekers and speakers of *truth because* we are makers and takers of *reasons.* I think this way of thinking about ourselves can be as edifying and inspiring as the one it seeks to supplant.

# CHAPTER SEVEN

# Three Problems with the
# Empiricist Conception of Concepts

**1.**   Systems properly described as *understanding* something about their environment, for instance that it contains red things or water, must be able to apply empirical concepts, such as <u>red</u> and <u>water</u>. What must be true of a system for its going into a certain kind of state or producing a certain kind of performance properly to count as the application of such concepts?

There seem to be three ways in which conceptual contents might be attached to states and performances. First, they might be attached *intentionally* to independently specifiable vehicles by the *stipulation* of some interpreter who is antecedently able to deploy the concepts involved. This is how the sign-designs of artificial formal languages come to express the contents they do: what *makes* an expression in such a language mean <u>successor,</u> <u>between</u>, or <u>is red</u> is just that the theorist who uses the language explicitly *takes* it to express those concepts. There is also a familiar line of thought according to which it is in this broadly instrumental fashion that meanings are associated with the expressions of *natural* languages as well: words and sentences mean what they do because linguistic practitioners who are antecedently capable of thought *use* them, by a combination of intention and convention, to convey their concepts and beliefs.

Second, conceptual contents might be attached to states and performances *functionally*, in virtue of their relations to one another and to elements of the environment to which they apply. This approach construes conceptual contents as consisting in the significance states and performances have within the behavioral economy of a system because of their interactions with each other and with the environment. According to this sort of account, it is the activity of the system itself that establishes the conceptual contentfulness of the states it exhibits, the performances it produces, and the expressions it uses.[1] In this way it is distinguished from the first sort of account, according to which conceptual contents are conferred by the activity of an external interpreter. The functional picture does not require that conceptual contentfulness derive from the antecedently conceptually articulated intentions and beliefs of another. Rather, in some sense the system itself implicitly takes or treats its own states as contentful, and thereby makes them so.

The stipulative and the functional stories are alike in addressing the question of how conceptual contents might be attached to some vehicle that is describable independently of its having the content it has: for instance sign-designs as marks or noises, performances as bodily movements, states as voltage distributions or neurophysiological conditions. It is these vehicles that the interpreter intentionally invests with meaning by stipulation or convention, on the first approach, and that play the functional roles by virtue of which they implicitly acquire such meanings, on the second. A third possibility is that for some items, conceptual contentfulness is *intrinsic*, in that it makes no sense to talk about its being attached to such a vehicle. The conceptual contents of states such as belief, desire, and intention, it might be thought, are *essential* to them. They differ from linguistic expressions such as sentences precisely in that there is nothing that plays the role for them that physically describable sign-designs do for sentences, as something independently characterizable to which conceptual content is *attached* (by anyone's activity).[2]

1. Notice that this abstract characterization allows the possibility that the system whose doings one must consider as conferring genuine conceptual content may have to be a whole linguistic community rather than a single agent.

2. John Searle, in *Intentionality* (Cambridge: Cambridge University Press, 1982), puts forward a view of this sort. Although sentences (in the sense of marks and noises) play an essential role for Davidson, his account of intentional states such as beliefs also has this vehicleless character. Only the whole human subject is the vehicle, and is the identical vehicle of *all* its intentional states.

The issues discussed in this chapter arise in connection with pursuit of the second or functionalist explanatory strategy. The stipulative approach is not in principle available as a candidate for explaining the conceptual contentfulness of our thought—or that, if any, of chimps, dolphins, or Martians. And if it describes the only way in which conceptual contents can be understood to attach to the states and performances of machines we build, then we will never be able to make them do what we would like them to do, what we can do. For we are semantically autonomous—one need not look to the activity of anyone outside of us in order to make sense of the conceptual contentfulness of our thought and talk.[3] The sort of conceptual contentfulness the stipulative strategy addresses is parasitic on or *derivative* from the more basic sort possessed by the stipulator or interpreter. By contrast, the other two approaches address the sort of *original* conceptual contentfulness our own thought might be taken to have.

The third way of thinking about conceptual contentfulness is put to one side for a different reason: it is not clear how to follow out its consequences for the project of diagnosing or producing concept use in other creatures, such as chimps, dolphins, and various sorts of hypothetical aliens, nor for the project of artificially constructing genuine concept users. Methodologically, it makes sense to try to specify—in non-semantic, non-intentional terms—what one has to be *doing* in order to be applying concepts (and hence *understanding*) in an original or non-derivative way. Success would provide the critical criteria of adequacy needed to make progress on the diagnostic, pedagogic, and engineering projects regarding non-human understanders.[4] And attention to the particular ways in which our attempts fall short can in their own way be equally instructive. The rest of this chapter is accordingly addressed to some of the aspects of our activity that have been thought to be of particular significance for the

3. Again, notice that to say this is not to insist that each of us is individually semantically autonomous in this sense. Insofar as language use is essential to the genesis of genuinely conceptual content, it is only the whole linguistic community—all of us—that exhibits this sort of autonomy. According to such an account, our interpretation of each other might be an essential part of the story; but it will not be interpretation of the sort involved in stipulating, say, that '→' is to be understood as expressing strict implication.

4. This is the topic of Chapter Eight.

functional conferral of conceptual content on states, performances, and expressions playing suitable roles in that activity.

**2.**    Historically there have been four different approaches to the question of what sort of functional involvements should be understood as conferring conceptual contents:

(1) *Empiricism,* of the sort associated with Locke, takes it that the contents of the concepts applied by knowers are a function of their *origin in experience.* This tradition counsels us to look to the *causal antecedents* of concept use, to the empirical circumstances in which concepts are applied, in order to understand the nature of their contentfulness. The content of a concept is to be read off what its application is typically or correctly a response to. One grasps the concept <u>red</u>, and so has it available to apply to things, only because one has had experiences of red things.

(2) *Pragmatism,* of the sort associated with Peirce or James, takes it that the contents of the concepts applied by knowers are a function of *their significance for action.* This tradition counsels us to look to the *causal effects* of concept use, to the *practical consequences* of applying concepts, in order to understand the nature of their contentfulness. The content of a concept is to be read off what the typical or correct response is to its application. One applies the concept <u>food</u> to something by being disposed to eat it when hungry.

(3) *Rationalism,* of the sort associated with Leibniz, takes it that the contents of the concepts applied by knowers are a function of their *role in reasoning.* This tradition counsels us to look to the antecedents and consequents of concept use, not in the order of *causation,* but in the order *of justification.* The content of a concept is to be read off the good inferences in which it serves as premise or conclusion. Grasping a concept is mastering its inferential role—knowing for instance that being a trilateral rectilinear plane figure is a sufficient condition for the applicability of the concept <u>triangle</u>, and that having angles adding up to a straight line is a necessary condition of its applicability.

(4) Finally, the *synthetic or combined* view, which may be associated with Kant, takes it that the contents of concepts involve all of these dimensions. According to this approach, the challenging theoretical question is not which of these to focus on—the causal or the inferential,

circumstances or consequences of application—but rather how these various aspects of concept use should be understood to be related to one another. What is the nature of the relation between causal and inferential grounds of application of an empirical concept, or between its causal and inferential consequences? What underwrites the transition from its circumstances of application (of either sort) to its consequences of application (whether practical or theoretical)?[5]

The synthetic view has the familiar agreeable virtues of a position that resolves a dispute by allowing the participants to have their cake and eat it too. There are all sorts of concepts, and no doubt all sorts of functional relations are involved in their articulation—both inferential relations to other concepts and non-inferential causal relations with elements of the environment, through both perception and action. Important insights concerning the contributions of these different sorts of functional relations are in danger of being obscured, however, if we rush to embrace an eclectic approach without looking at what each of the more partial views it embraces can and cannot illuminate. In particular, I believe that the rationalists are right to the extent that to talk about a state, performance, or expression as *conceptually* contentful is to talk about it as playing a distinctively *inferential* role. It is its inferential articulation that is distinctive of the conceptual as such. It is only within the framework of specifically inferential involvements that *causal* interactions with the environment—whether upstream, as in perception, or downstream, as in action—can contribute to specifically conceptual contents. Our ordinary concepts do involve both empirical and practical dimensions, but no amount of empirical or practical functional articulation can take the place of the inferential functional relations characteristic of concepts.

This point is not always appreciated, and in order to reinforce it, I want in the rest of this chapter to consider three systematic sorts of explanatory failings to which attempts to specify conceptual contents purely in terms of causal inputs and outputs are subject. I will start with empiricist attempts to elaborate conceptual contents on the basis of a system's reliable

5. I am here suppressing some issues that are important in other contexts. For one can separate the question of whether one should focus on perceptual experience, inference, or action from whether one construes those aspects of concept use in causal or normative terms.

dispositions to respond differentially to various sorts of stimuli, since I think this remains the most tempting sort of reductionist ploy. But I will indicate in each case why supplementing the empirical inputs with practical outputs does not obviate the difficulties being considered.

**3.** We may start with a very simple question. What more is there to grasping the empirical concept <u>red</u> than being able to respond differentially to red things? The empiricist intuition is that what makes something a representation of red is its status as a response that is reliably differentially elicited by red stimuli. A suitably frequency-sensitive photocell can do that, or a well-trained pigeon. It seems, however, that a distinction ought to be made between the capacity merely to respond differentially to red stimuli and the capacity to respond differentially to them by applying the *concept* <u>red</u>. After all, a chunk of iron responds differentially to its environment by rusting in, and only in, the presence of water and accelerating in, and only in, the presence of forces. Indeed, every actual object produces behavior of different kinds in response to stimuli of different kinds.

Although such differential responsiveness is no doubt a *necessary* condition for mastery of empirical concepts, it is not at all plausible to take it as a *sufficient* condition. Stones and photocells certainly do not apply concepts when they respond differentially to impressed forces or energetic photons. And although much of the psychological literature whose topic is labeled "concept formation" in fact addresses little else than this sort of reliable differential recognitive capacity, it requires quite a stretch to say that pigeons acquire the *concept* <u>red</u> simply by learning to peck at a round button when presented with a red stimulus.[6] The empiricist is not in a position to say what discriminates specifically *conceptual* responses or representations from simpler *non*-conceptual discriminations.

At this point it is tempting to invoke *complexity*. There is a sliding scale, it will be claimed, with stones and photocells at the bottom, simply trained pigeons somewhat further up, more complexly trained chimps further up, barely linguistically capable human children above them, and

6. And it is only in the context of the stipulative paradigm for attaching conceptual content to performances that it makes any difference whether the round button bears the sign design 'red', or the photocell is wired up to produce a tokening of that type on a VDT.

linguistically sophisticated human adult reporters of the colors of stop-lights and stop signs at the top. Our resistance to taking the discrimina-tive capacities exhibited at the lower end of the scale as involving the ap-plication of concepts is just a matter of their insufficient complexity.

In some sense this suggestion must be correct. But it is nonetheless almost completely unhelpful with respect to the point at issue. For there is complexity and complexity. Pigeons are not *biologically* substantially less complex than we are. Everything turns on just what *sort* of complex-ity of differential response is sufficient for genuine concept use. It is pretty clear that neither increasing the fineness of discrimination nor the sheer numbers of stimulus-response connections can by themselves suffice to turn the individual responses into applications of concepts. Intuitively what is missing in these cases is *understanding*. The responses of a genu-ine concept-using reporter of red *mean* something to that reporter in a way that the responses of photocells and pigeons do not. (The responses of the photocell and the pigeon can mean something to *us*, who can at-tach conceptual significance to them—but this is relevant to the stipula-tive strategy, not the functionalist one.) What sort of 'complexity' of dif-ferential responsive disposition corresponds to *understanding* (hence to sapience)? The empiricist intuition about contentfulness does not supply the resources for an answer.[7]

Nor is it clear what sort of additional help is offered by adding the con-siderations advanced by the pragmatist concerning practical activity—looking at outputs rather than just inputs. There is a sense in which an animal treats something as food by eating it. For what it produces is not just any differentially elicited response, but one that is appropriate to it as food. And this is a proper functional matter of the role the stimulus plays in the activities of the animal itself, not simply a matter of our stipulation or interpretation. But doesn't the stone also respond to an impressed force as an impressed force by producing the response that is appropriate to it as such, namely accelerating? And doesn't the pigeon's training sim-ply create an environment in which the appropriate response for the pi-

---

7. This issue is discussed in more detail in Chapter Eight, where a specific, four-leveled hierarchy of semantic complexity of concepts is described.

geon to something *as* red is to peck at the round button? Again, nothing seems to mark off the distinctively conceptual.

One could at this point throw up one's hands, jettison the functionalist project, and concede that what is missing can only be supplied by invoking *intrinsically* conceptually contentful states of understanding—something that we concept-mongering sapients have, but that mere sentients such as pigeons do not. But there is an alternative. The rationalist's idea is that what is distinctive of the conceptual is its specifically inferential articulation. For a response reliably differentially elicited by red things to qualify as the application of a concept, it must have the significance of a move in the game of giving and asking for reasons. It must be available as a premise for drawing further conclusions, and be liable to challenge by inferences from premises with incompatible consequences. Grasping the concept red requires practical mastery of its *inferential role,* as well as its *non*-inferential role as an appropriate response to certain sorts of stimuli. This means being able to discriminate what follows from it, what it follows from, and what is incompatible with it—endorsing in practice the moves from red to colored and from scarlet to red, and treating red as ruling out green. (Indeed, the considerations advanced by the pragmatist can be seen to be subsumed by those advanced by the rationalist, for the inferential role of a claim or concept includes its service as a premise in *practical* inferences: those whose conclusions are intentional actions.)

When we say that the reliable differential responses elicited by red things don't *mean* anything to the photocell or the pigeon—that they don't *understand* anything by those responses, and hence are not grasping or applying concepts—we are pointing to the fact that they don't treat those responses as *inferentially* significant, as premises providing potential evidence for further conclusions and as potentially confirmed by or clashing with the conclusions that follow from other evidence. When we say that in spite of the conceptual incapacity of photocells and pigeons it is nonetheless possible for *us* to interpret their responses conceptually— *to attach* conceptual content to their otherwise non-conceptual differential responses—we are saying that *we* can use the fact that they responded in a particular way as a premise for inference, confront it with incompatible evidence, and so on. This is in effect using them as measuring instruments, exploiting their reliability by endorsing inferences from claims about their responses ("The pigeon pecked the round button") to claims about the stimuli that elicited those responses ("So the ball it was looking at was probably red"). Thus the rationalist insight—that conceptual content is attached to states, performances, and expressions by the role they play in *reasoning*—provides an answer to the demarcational question that empiricism and pragmatism cannot answer. It potentially offers the missing ingredient needed to turn into *sufficient* conditions the *necessary* conditions for grasp of empirical concepts that they provide.[8]

**4.** A second dimension along which the empiricist construal of concept use can be seen to be in need of supplementation by considerations of the sort forwarded by the rationalists concerns the notion of *reliability*. According to the empiricist, being able to apply a concept such as <u>red</u> consists in being able reliably to respond differentially to red things, for instance by saying, "That's red." Systems that cannot do this reliably don't count as grasping the concept. The reliability of discriminative capacities, the criterion of concept use, is understood as an objective matter of fact. In particular, it consists in the objective probability of a correct response. With respect to the dispositions of the system at a given time, this probability can be identified with the relative frequency of correct responses, the proportion of circumstances in which the system is disposed to respond correctly. In this way the sort of understanding involved in taking something as something by applying a concept to it is *naturalized*, by identifying it with an aspect of the purely causal order.

The difficulty with this aspect of the empiricist approach is, briefly, this. The responsive dispositions of a system determine the objective probability of, say, producing the response appropriate to the presence

8. Notice that to say this much is not yet to say what is required for specifically inferential articulation. It might be understood simply as more conditioned stimulus-response connections among states and performances—a matter of being disposed to make one move in response to others. At the least such a story must include an account of what it is for such a 'move' to have the status of a claim or judgment, taking a stand, undertaking a commitment, that one can come to be entitled to in various ways and that can commit and entitle one to other such stands. What can in this way both serve as a reason for other stands and is itself liable to demands for reasons will be recognizable in virtue of that role as having a specifically propositional content, the fundamental sort of conceptual content.

of a red barn when (or only when) stimulated by a red barn, only relative to a reference class of possible situations. No matter what its dispositions, any system will count as reliable relative to some reference classes and as unreliable relative to others. But the causal order itself does not privilege any of these reference classes over any other; there is no objective way to pick out one or some of them as correct. Thus there is no objective fact of the matter as to whether a given system is a reliable discriminator of red things. Accordingly, whether or not a system counts for the empiricist as grasping and applying concepts such as <u>red barn</u> is not—as the empiricist wants it to be—settled by its responsive dispositions.

To see this, consider a version of an example put forward in another context by Goldman.[9] Consider Barney, whom we would intuitively take to be a reliable reporter of red barns. Barney is looking at a red barn in good light, and he reports "There's a red barn." What Barney doesn't know, however, is that he is in Barn-Façade County. The local hobby in that county is building incredibly lifelike trompe l'oeil façades of red barns. Ninety-nine percent of what appear to be red barns in this county are actually such façades. Barney is not capable of discriminating real barns from these façades. It is just dumb luck that he happens to be looking at one of the few real red barns in the county. Thus, as he wanders around the county, Barney will be wrong ninety-nine times out of a hundred in his barn reports. However, these façades are the *only* thing that Barney can't tell from real red barns, and the county is small enough that those amount to only 1 percent of the apparent barns in the whole state— the rest of whose inhabitants spend their time more productively than the façade-fanciers. Within the state as a whole, as a consequence, Barney's reports are right ninety-nine times out of a hundred.

According to the empiricist criterion, Barney has the concept of red barns just in case he has a reliable disposition to respond differentially to them with a red-barn report. Does he or doesn't he? If we draw the boundaries around the relevant reference class narrowly enough, then he is reliable. For in the case described he is looking at an actual barn, and so with respect to *that* situation he is 100 percent reliable. Broadening the

9. Alvin Goldman, "Discrimination and Perceptual Knowledge," *Journal of Philosophy* 73, no. 20 (1976): 771–791.

boundaries to include the whole county reveals him as unreliable, however. But if the boundaries of the reference class are broadened still further, to the whole state, his reliability is, so to speak, reinstated. Clearly
cases could be described in which such oscillations are repeated indefi-
nitely. Equally clearly, no simple rules about always using the narrowest
or the widest available reference class will resolve the difficulty.

It would be bad enough if we had to say that Barney gains and loses
his mastery of the concept <u>red barn</u> as he moves in and out of Barn-Façade
County. But Barney isn't even moving. Contradictory verdicts on his
grasp of that concept right now result from assessing his reliability with
respect to different reference classes. Yet his place in the causal order,
which includes all his responsive dispositions, doesn't settle the question
of which is the correct reference class, and so doesn't settle whether or
not he is reliable. Reliability is not an objective matter of fact; for it depends on the choice of a reference class, and that choice is not determined
by objective matters of fact.

Again the rationalist emphasis on the essential role played by mastery
of *inferential* roles in the grasp of concepts supplies what is missing from
the empiricist account. First, wherever Barney is, and no matter how a
reference class is chosen in accordance with which to assess the reliability
of his non-inferential responsive dispositions, he can count as grasping
the concept <u>red barn</u> in virtue of his knowing what follows from applying
that concept—e.g. that it is a structure the color of stop signs and sunsets,
in which farm animals can live—and what other claims would be evidence
for or against something qualifying as a red barn. Indeed, it is precisely
his mastery of these aspects of the inferential articulation of the concept
that could lead him to discover that his non-inferential responsive dispositions were leading him astray in Barn-Façade County.

This possibility of Barney's using his mastery of the concept to discover his local *un*reliability as a non-inferential reporter points to the second way in which the rationalist perspective sheds light on the intuition
that underlies the empiricist appeal to reliability. For to take Barney to be
a reliable reporter just is to endorse an *inference*—the inference, namely,
from Barney's responding to something *as* a red barn to its *being* a red
barn. To take a certain instrument to be a reliable indicator of the current
in a wire is to endorse the inference from its meter-needle indicating a

current of 5 amps to there being a 5 amp current running through the wire. Indeed, if Barney discovers his plight, he will himself cease to endorse the inference from "I am in Barn-Façade County and am non-inferentially disposed to report the presence of a red barn" to "There is a red barn in front of me." (As Sellars has taught us, at this point Barney can express his responsive disposition while withholding his endorsement of the claim he is tempted to make by his unreflective dispositions by saying "It *looks* as though there is a red barn in front of me.")[10]

The fact that assessments of reliability are relative to choice of reference class finds straightforward accommodation in this rationalist picture. It simply reflects the fact that endorsement of the reliability inference—from a system's responding to something as a **K** to its being a **K**—is sensitive to auxiliary hypotheses. The inference from "Barney is looking at a red barn and is non-inferentially disposed to report the presence of a red barn" to "There is a red barn in front of Barney" is a good one. The inference from "Barney is in Barn-Façade County and is non-inferentially disposed to report the presence of a red barn" to "There is a red barn in front of Barney" is not a good one. The inference from "Barney is somewhere in the state and is non-inferentially disposed to report the presence of a red barn" to "There is a red barn in front of Barney" is a good one. The fact that in the situation originally described the premises of each of these three inferences are true is why his reliability can be variously assessed, depending on how his situation is specified. The difference between the two approaches is that the rationalist can, as the empiricist cannot, accommodate these different assessments of reliability without being obliged to make mysterious and even contradictory claims about Barney's mastery of the empirical concept <u>red barn</u>.

**5.**  Another area in which the empiricist construal of concept use can be seen to be in need of supplementation by considerations of the sort forwarded by the rationalists has to do with the identification of what is reported, what a concept is being responsively applied *to*. The stimulus-response model of empirical conceptual content faces a fundamental

10. *Empiricism and the Philosophy of Mind,* ed. Robert B. Brandom (Cambridge, MA: Harvard University Press, 1997).

problem concerning the discrimination of the *stimulus.* In his discussion, Davidson introduces the familiar point this way:

> The location of a stimulus is, of course, notoriously ambiguous. We can place it almost anywhere in the causal chain that leads from far outside to various parts of the central nervous system. Quine offers us a choice between two of the possible locations: at the sensory receptors, or at the object and events our observations are traditionally about . . . it makes a vast difference whether meaning or evidence are tied to the proximal or the distal stimulus. Mindful of a certain tradition, let us call the two resulting theories of meaning and evidence the *proximal* and the *distal* theory.[11]

In another place, this difficulty is explained further:

> . . . why say the stimulus is the ringing of the bell? Why not the motion of the air close to the ears of the dog—or even the stimulation of its nerve endings? Certainly if the air were made to vibrate in just the way the bell makes it vibrate it would make no difference to the behavior of the dog. And if the right nerve endings were activated in the right way, there still would be no difference. And in fact if we must choose, it seems that the proximal cause of the behavior has the best claim to be called the stimulus, since the more distant an event is causally the more chance there is that the causal chain will be broken.[12]

Typically, there is a whole causal chain of covarying events culminating in a response. In the standard case, the occurrence of one is accompanied by the occurrence of all the rest. Under these circumstances, the response being keyed to one of the event kinds is being keyed to all the rest. How is one element of the chain to be singled out as the stimulus? What is the

---

11. "Meaning, Truth, and Evidence" (hereafter *MTE*), in *Perspectives on Quine,* ed. R. Barrett and R. Gibson (Oxford: Basil Blackwell, 1990), pp. 68–79.

12. "The Conditions of Thought," *Le Cahier du College International de Philosophie* (Paris: Editions Osiris, 1989), pp. 165–171, reprinted in *The Mind of Donald Davidson,* ed. J. Brandl and W. Gombocz (Amsterdam: Rodopi, 1990), pp. 193–200.

nature and source of the privilege that distinguishes one element from another?

One strategy for assigning such privilege, and therefore picking out as the stimulus one element from the whole chain of covarying event types that culminates in a response of the specified type, is, as Davidson suggests, to look to *proximity* to the eventual response. Such a proximal theory of stimuli will always yield the result that the stimuli being responded to are at the sensory surfaces or within the nervous system of the responding organism. The justification for seizing on causal proximity of stimulating event to the response as what matters is, as Davidson suggests, maximizing the relative *reliability* of the connection between the occurrence of events of the distinguished stimulus type and the occurrence of events of the distinguished response type. The proximal element of the chain is the one that most reliably brings about the response, since prior occurrences in the chain elicit the response only in the cases where they succeed in bringing about an event of the proximal type, while events of that type can elicit the response regardless of whether they have themselves been brought about in the standard way.

In the context of the project of using reliable differential responsive dispositions as a model to understand the application of the most basic empirical concepts, the adoption of such a policy for the discrimination of stimuli is the continuation of cartesianism by other means.[13] The clearest evidence of this is the room that proximal theories leave for global skepticism. Discriminating stimuli by proximity inevitably raises the possibility of skepticism about anything outside the responding organism, since the stimuli being responded to could, on the proximal reading, be just as they are regardless of variations in, or even the total absence of, the world of environing objects. The attempt to maximize reliability in responsive classification of stimuli (the primitive empiricist version of the application of concepts of observables) by contracting to the most proximal stimuli taken to be responded to ends by making the correctness of such classification bear only an ultimately accidental relation to anything happening outside the responding organism.

13. *MTE:* "Proximal theories, no matter how decked out, are Cartesian in spirit and consequence."

Thus proximal approaches to distinguishing stimuli are disastrous for the project of understanding the contents of fundamental empirical concepts from the way in which their application in observation depends on the exercise of reliable differential responsive dispositions. For the stimuli that are classified by responses do not extend out to the world, but remain in the organism, or at best at its functional surface. Thus what is classified by the proto-concepts that repeatable responses are going proxy for is not bells and tables and rabbits, but only states of the responding organism. Nothing that looks like one of our ordinary empirical concepts, applying to ordinary observable objects, is within reach of such an approach. A distal strategy is required in order to get the proto-concepts represented by reliably differentially elicited non-inferential response types to be intelligible as classifying, and so applying to, ordinary observable objects and properties. Understanding them this way involves respecting the language-learning situation in which these reliable differential responsive dispositions are established.

The most popular approach to identifying distal stimuli as what is classified by the exercise of reliable differential responsive dispositions is to appeal to *triangulation.* This is a strategy for picking out or privileging one bit of the causal chain of covarying event types that reliably culminates in a response of a distinguished type, by looking at the *intersection* of *two* such chains. The insight it develops is that the best way to pick a single *point* (the stimulus) out of a *line* (the causal chain of covarying event-types that reliably elicit a response of the relevant type) is to *intersect* it with another line—another causal chain corresponding to another reliable differential responsive disposition.

One writer who employs such a triangulation strategy to address the problem of picking out distal stimuli as what a response is about is Fred Dretske, in *Knowledge and the Flow of Information.*[14] He looks to the upstream intersection of two distinct "flows of information," or causal chains of reliably covarying event-types, that reliably culminate in responses of the same type, in order to pick out the distal stimulus. A simple example of the sort of system he has in mind would be a thermostat that keeps the temperature of a room within a certain range by turning a fur-

14. Cambridge, MA: MIT Press, 1981.

nace on and off. If the thermostat has only one way of measuring temperature, for instance by the bending of a bimetallic strip until it touches either the left electrical contact (too cold) or the right one (too warm), there
is no way, Dretske acknowledges, to say that what the system is responding to is the temperature of the room, rather than the temperature of the
bimetallic strip, or the curvature of the bimetallic strip, or the closing of
the circuit between the bimetallic strip and one or the other of the contacts. Notice that a pragmatist appeal to *consequences* of the response in
question is of no help here; for turning the furnace on affects not only the
temperature of the room, but also that of the bimetallic strip, its curvature,
and so its relation to the electrical contacts.

One can be entitled to such a description, however, if the thermostat
is slightly more complicated, and has another causal route to the same
response (turning the furnace on or off). If the thermostat has a second
sensor, for instance a column of mercury supporting a float with an electrical contact that completes one circuit to turn the furnace on whenever
the float is below one point (too cold) and turns it off whenever the float
is above another point (too warm), then the system has two ways of responding to the change in temperature in the room.[15] Although for this
second route by itself, just as for the first by itself, there is no feature of the
system that entitles one to say it is responding to changes in the temperature of the room rather than to the temperature of the mercury, or the
length of the mercury column, or the closing of the switches, when the
two routes are considered together, they intersect in just two places—upstream at the change of temperature in a room which is included in the
'flow' or causal chain corresponding to each route, and downstream in
the response of turning the furnace on or off. (Since the two routes intersect in two places, it is necessary to think of arcs rather than lines as inter-

---

15. For the purposes of the illustration, one need not worry about how the system deals
with conflicts arising when the two subsystems disagree. The range of response of one could
be set wider than the other (permitting a lower temperature before a 'too cold' message is processed and a higher one before a 'too warm' message is processed), so that the wider one
counts as an overriding fail-safe or backup, or the control could pass randomly from one to the
other in case of disagreement. The exact arrangement would matter a lot for how well the
thermostat maintained a steady-state temperature within its specified range, but does not seem
to affect the triangulation strategy in play.

secting, and the term 'triangulation' may be less happy.) But Dretske shows how the general strategy of looking to the *intersection* of two reliable differential responsive dispositions might be funded from the resources of the responding system itself.

One might worry that Dretske has not in fact succeeded in responding to the general worry about how to justify describing the system as responding to a distal stimulus rather than a proximal one. For there is an objection available to his strategy that seems to reinstate the original worry. Why, it might be asked, ought we not conclude that even in the two-subsystem case, what is responded to is not a proximal stimulus, but a *disjunctive* one? The system turns on the furnace just in case *either* the temperature of the bimetallic strip is low enough *or* that of the mercury column is low enough, or, alternatively, in case the curvature of the bimetallic strip is far enough to the left *or* the mercury column is short enough. (Again, pragmatic appeal to consequences of entering this state won't solve the problem.)

This worry is connected to the complaint voiced earlier, to the effect that mere differential responsiveness is not sufficient for identifying the responses in question as applications of *concepts*. The rationalist supplementation suggested there—that what is distinctive of the conceptual is the *inferential* role played by the responses that stimuli differentially elicit—is also what is required to exploit the triangulation strategy in connection with genuine concepts in a way that responds to the worry about disjunctive proximal stimuli.

Consider an individual who reliably responds, as one wants to say, to the visible presence of rabbits by saying 'gavagai'. Suppose further that he is reliably differentially responding not just to rabbits, but to the presence of the distinctive (according to him) rabbit flies that are for him decisive evidence of the presence of rabbits, or that the visual cue he is using, as determined by a physiologist of perception, is a glimpse of the fluff around the tail of the rabbit. What is it about the situation in virtue of which he can be said nonetheless to be reporting not the presence of the rabbit flies, or of the fluffy tail, but the presence of a rabbit? The rationalist response is that the difference is not to be found in the reliable differential responsive dispositions, not in the causal chain of covarying events that reliably culminates in the response 'gavagai', to which not only the rabbit but the flies or the fluffy tail belong, but rather in the inferential role of the response 'gavagai'. For instance, does the commitment undertaken by that response include a commitment to the claim that what is reported can fly? Or is the claim expressed by 'gavagai' incompatible with the further characterization of the item reported as flying? If it is incompatible, then it is not the flies that are being reported. What determines which element of the causal chain of covarying events that reliably elicit the report is being reported is the *inferential* role of the report, what it *entails*, what is *evidence* for it, what it is *incompatible* with.

Assuming that the observable predicate corresponding to 'flying' has already picked out the things that fly, noticing that the report 'gavagai' could mean rabbit flies in case its applicability entails the applicability of 'flying' and could not mean rabbit flies in case its applicability is incompatible with the applicability of 'flying' is just what is wanted to pick out the distal stimulus the concept expressed by 'gavagai' is being applied to or is classifying. But the appeal to inference and incompatibility may seem just to put off the issue. How does 'flying' get to apply properly to flying things, and not to whatever cues we in fact use in discriminating flying things, in short to one element of the causal chain of covarying event types that reliably culminate in its application? The answer must be that what the appeal to inferential role does is establish a sort of *triangulation,* or intersection of flows of information or reliable differential responsive dispositions. If 'gavagai' is used so as to entail 'flying', then whatever is properly responded to by the one expression must be properly responded to by the other, so what is classified as gavagai must also be classified as flying, so 'gavagai' must apply to rabbit flies, and not to the rabbits that are their invariable (we are supposing) concomitants. In short, the rationalist appeal to inferential role, in addition to reliable differential responsive dispositions, involves triangulation of the sort that Dretske invokes, where two (or more) different reliable responsive dispositions of the system are invoked, so that their intersection can pick out a unique element of the causal chain of covarying events as the stimulus being classified by a response of a certain type. Because 'flying' will *not* be taken to apply to lots of things that merely hop, we can be sure that it does not mean <u>flying or hopping</u>, and so that 'gavagai' does not mean something disjunctive like <u>rabbit or rabbit fly</u>.

Thus the rationalist view can incorporate Dretske-style triangulation, by using the inferential articulation of the response to connect one observable, with its chain of 'upstream' antecedents, with another chain, with its different but intersecting set of antecedents. It is in this way that concepts such as <u>red</u> and <u>colored</u> work, where each has non-inferential circumstances of appropriate application, as well as an inferential link to the other. In languages without purely theoretical claims (that is, claims whose only circumstances and consequences of application are inferential), all concepts in this way answer to two masters: their own non-inferential circumstances of appropriate application and their inferential links to the non-inferential circumstances of application of other concepts. Dretske could keep his basic insight, while avoiding the embarrassment of not being able to distinguish fancy thermostats from genuine concept-deploying believers, if he insisted on inferential articulation along with the intersecting chain move.

Thus, to make the triangulation approach to distinguishing distal stimuli work, one needs to look further 'downstream' from the response, as well as 'upstream'—just as orthodox functionalism would lead one to expect. What picks out one kind of thing as what is being *reported* out of all those that are being differentially *responded* to is a matter of the inferential commitments that response is involved in. These inferential consequences of going into a state make it clear that what is being classified is something outside the system. They are what determine that a physicist is reporting the presence of a mu meson in a bubble chamber, and not simply a large hook-shaped pattern. For the consequences of classifying something as a microscopic mu meson are quite different from those of classifying something as a macroscopic hook-shaped trace. It is the lack of such consequences that makes Dretske's dual thermometer liable to a disjunctive proximal interpretation.

**6.** At the outset, I distinguished four different ways in which a functionalist approach to the conferral of conceptual content might be pursued: the empiricist strategy, which looks exclusively to the causal antecedents that reliably elicit a (therefore) contentful state; the pragmatist strategy, which looks exclusively to the causal consequences reliably elicited by a (therefore) contentful state; the rationalist strategy, which looks to the role in reasoning of a (therefore) contentful state; and the combined strategy, which appeals to all these sorts of functional involvements, both causal and inferential. I don't take it to be surprising that the combined strategy is the most promising of these, and demonstrating that point has not been my primary goal here. My aim has been rather to show some of the ways in which the rationalist criterion of demarcation of the *conceptual* in terms of specifically *inferential* articulation remedies specific shortcomings of empiricist and pragmatist accounts of conceptual content, which appeal only to causal inputs (in perception) and outputs (in action). To that end, I have considered three difficulties that confront such non-inferential conceptions of conceptual content: inability to distinguish the sort of complexity distinctive of the *conceptual* as such, failure to make sense of the crucial notion of responsive *reliability,* and liability to *proximal* (including *disjunctive*) interpretations of what empirical concepts are applied to. In each case, I have claimed, the rationalist insight supplies what is missing from the empiricist approach.

# CHAPTER EIGHT

# How Analytic Philosophy Has Failed
# Cognitive Science

**1.** We analytic philosophers have signally failed our colleagues in cognitive science. We have done that by not sharing central lessons about the nature of concepts, concept use, and conceptual content that have been entrusted to our care and feeding for more than a century.

I take it that analytic philosophy began with the birth of the new logic that Gottlob Frege introduced in his seminal 1879 *Begriffsschrift*. The idea, taken up and championed to begin with by Bertrand Russell, was that the fundamental insights and tools Frege made available there, and developed and deployed through the 1890s, could be applied throughout philosophy to advance our understanding of understanding and of thought in general, by advancing our understanding of concepts—including the particular concepts with which the philosophical tradition had wrestled since its inception. For Frege brought about a revolution not just in *logic*, but in *semantics*. He made possible for the first time a *mathematical* characterization of meaning and conceptual content, and so of the structure of sapience itself. Henceforth it was to be the business of the new movement of analytic philosophy to explore and amplify those ideas, to exploit and apply them wherever they could do the most good. Those ideas are the cultural birthright, heritage, and responsibility of analytic philosophers. But we have not done right by them. For we have failed to communicate some of the most basic of those ideas, failed to explain their significance, failed to make them available in forms usable by those working in allied disciplines who are also professionally concerned to understand the nature of thought, minds, and reason.

Contemporary cognitive science is a house with many mansions. The provinces I mean particularly to be addressing are cognitive psychology, developmental psychology, animal psychology (especially primatology), and artificial intelligence. (To be sure, this is not all of cognitive science. But the points I will be making in this chapter are not of similarly immediate significance for such other subfields as neurophysiology, linguistics, perceptual psychology, learning theory, and the study of the mechanisms of memory.) Cognitive psychology aims at reverse-engineering the human mind: figuring out how we do what we do, what more basic abilities are recruited and deployed (and how) so as to result in the higher cognitive abilities we actually display. Developmental psychology investigates the sequence of stages by which those abilities emerge from more primitive versions as individual humans mature. Animal psychology, as I am construing it, is a sort of combination of cognitive psychology of non-human intelligences and a phylogenetic version of ontogenetic human developmental psychology. By contrast to all these empirical inquiries into actual cognition, artificial intelligence swings free of questions about how any actual organisms do what they do, and asks instead what constellation of abilities of the sort we know how to implement in artifacts might in principle yield sapience.

Each of these disciplines is in its own way concerned with the broadly empirical question of how the trick of cognition is or might be done. Philosophers are concerned with the normative question of what counts as doing it—with what understanding (particularly discursive, conceptual understanding) consists in—rather than how creatures with a particular contingent constitution, history, and armamentarium of basic abilities come to exhibit it. I think Frege taught us three fundamental lessons about the structure of concepts, and hence about all possible abilities that deserve to count as concept-using abilities.[1] The conclusion we should draw from his discoveries is that concept use is intrinsically stratified. It exhibits at least four basic layers, with each capacity to deploy concepts in a more sophisticated sense of 'concept' structurally presupposing the capacities to use concepts in all of the more primitive senses. The three lessons that generate the structural hierarchy oblige us to distinguish between

- concepts that only *label* and concepts that *describe,*
- *ingredient* and *freestanding* conceptual contents, making explicit the distinction between the *content* of concepts and the *force* of applying them, and
- concepts expressible already by *simple* predicates and concepts expressible only by *complex* predicates.

AI researchers and cognitive, developmental, and animal psychologists need to take account of the different grades of conceptual content made visible by these distinctions, both in order to be clear about the topic they are investigating (if they are to tell us how the trick is done, they must be clear about exactly which trick it is) and because the empirical and in-principle possibilities are constrained by the way the abilities to deploy concepts in these various senses structurally presuppose the others that appear earlier in the sequence. This is a point they have long appreciated on the side of basic *syntactic* complexity.[2] But the at least equally important—and I would argue more conceptually fundamental—hierarchy of *semantic* complexity has been largely ignored.

---

1. It ought to be uncontroversial that the last two of the three lessons are due to Frege. Whether he is responsible also for the first is more contentious. Further, I think both it and a version of the second can be found already in Kant, as I argue in Part One of this book. But my aims here are not principally hermeneutical or exegetical—those issues don't affect the question of what we philosophers ought to be teaching cognitive scientists—so I will not be concerned to justify these attributions.

2. I have in mind the Chomsky hierarchy, which associates regular, context-free, context-sensitive, and recursively enumerable languages with the increasingly complex kinds of grammars needed to specify them and automata needed to compute them.

**2.**   The early modern philosophical tradition was built around a *classifi-catory* theory of consciousness and (hence) of concepts, in part the result of what its scholastic predecessors had made of their central notion of Aristotelian forms. The paradigmatic cognitive act is understood as classifying: taking something particular *as* being of some general kind. Concepts are identified with those general kinds.

This conception was enshrined in the order of logical explanation (originating in Aristotle's *Prior Analytics*) that was common to *everyone* thinking about concepts and consciousness in the period leading up to Kant. At its base is a doctrine of *terms* or *concepts,* particular and general. The next layer, erected on that base, is a doctrine of *judgments,* describing the kinds of classificatory relations that are possible among such terms. For instance, besides classifying Socrates as human, humans can be classified as mortal. Finally, in terms of those metaclassifications grouping judgments into kinds according to the sorts of terms they relate, a doctrine of *consequences* or *syllogisms* is propounded, classifying valid inferences into kinds, depending on which classes of classificatory judgments their premises and conclusions fall under.

It is the master idea of *classification* that gives this traditional order of explanation its distinctive shape. That idea defines its base, the relation between its layers, and the theoretical aspiration that animates the whole line of thought: finding suitable ways of classifying terms and judgments (classifiers and classifications) so as to be able to classify inferences as good or bad solely in virtue of the kinds of classifications they involve. The fundamental metaconceptual role it plays in structuring philosophical thought about thought evidently made understanding the concept of *classifying* itself a particularly urgent philosophical task. Besides asking what differentiates various kinds of classifying, we can ask what they have in common. What is it one must *do* in order thereby to count as *classifying* something as being of some kind?

In the most general sense, one classifies something simply by responding to it differentially. Stimuli are grouped into kinds by the response-kinds they tend to elicit. In this sense, a chunk of iron classifies its environments into kinds by rusting in some of them and not others, increasing or decreasing its temperature, shattering or remaining intact. As is evident from this example, if classifying is just exercising a reliable differential responsive disposition, it is a ubiquitous feature of the inanimate world. For that very reason, classifying in this generic sense is not an attractive candidate for identification with conceptual, cognitive, or conscious activity. It doesn't draw the right line between thinking and all sorts of thoughtless activities. Pan-psychism is too high a price to pay for cognitive naturalism.

That need not mean that taking *differential responsiveness* as the genus of which *conceptual classification* is a species is a bad idea, however. A favorite idea of the classical British empiricists was to require that the classifying response be entering a *sentient* state. The intrinsic characters of these sentient states are supposed to sort them immediately into repeatable kinds. These are called on to function as the *particular* terms in the base level of the neo-Aristotelian logical hierarchy. *General* terms or concepts are then thought of as sentient state-kinds derived from the particular sentient state-kinds by a process of *abstraction:* grouping the base-level sentient state-repeatables into higher-level sentient state-repeatables by some sort of perceived *similarity.* This abstractive grouping by similarity is itself a kind of classification. The result is a path from one sort of consciousness, sentience, to a conception of another sort of consciousness, sapience, or conceptual consciousness.

A standing felt difficulty with this empiricist strategy is the problem of giving a suitably naturalistic account of the notion of *sentient awareness* on which it relies. Recent information-theoretic accounts of representation (under which heading I include not just Fred Dretske's theory, which actually goes by that name, but others such as Jerry Fodor's asymmetric counterfactual dependence and nomological locking models)[3] develop the same basic differential responsiveness version of the classic classificatory idea in wholly naturalistic modal terms. They focus on the information conveyed about stimuli—the way they are grouped into repeatables—by their reliably eliciting a response of one rather than another repeatable response-kind from some system. In this setting, unpalatable pan-psychism can be avoided, not, as with traditional empiricism, by insisting

---

3. Fred Dretske, *Knowledge and the Flow of Information* (Cambridge, MA: MIT Press, 1981); Jerry Fodor, *A Theory of Content* (Cambridge, MA: MIT Press, 1990). I discuss some aspects of such theories in Chapter Seven.

that the responses be sentient states, but for instance by restricting attention to flexible systems, capable in principle of coming to encode many different groupings of stimuli, with a process of *learning* determining what classificatory dispositions each one actually acquires. (The classical American pragmatists' program for a naturalistic empiricism had at its core the idea that the structure common to evolutionary development and individual learning is a Test-Operate-Test-Exit negative feedback process of acquiring practical habits, including discriminative ones.)[4]

Classification as the exercise of reliable differential responsive dispositions (however acquired) is not by itself yet a good candidate for *conceptual* classification, in the basic sense in which applying a concept to something is *describing* it. Why not? Suppose one were given a wand, and told that the light on the handle would go on if and only if what the wand was pointed at had the property of being *grivey*. One might then determine empirically that speakers are grivey but microphones are not, doorknobs are but windowshades are not, cats are and dogs are not, and so on. One is then in a position reliably, perhaps even infallibly, to apply the *label* 'grivey'. Is one also in a position to *describe* things *as* grivey? Ought what one is doing to qualify as applying the *concept* grivey to things? Intuitively, the trouble is that one does not know what one has found out when one has found out that something is grivey, does not know what one is taking it to be when one takes it to be grivey, does not know what one is describing it *as*. The label is, we want to say, uninformative.[5]

What more is required? Wilfrid Sellars gives this succinct, and I believe correct, answer:

> It is only because the expressions in terms of which we describe objects, even such basic expressions as words for the perceptible characteristics of molar objects, locate these objects in a space of implications, that they describe at all, rather than merely label.[6]

---

4. I sketch this program in the opening section of "The Pragmatist Enlightenment (and Its Problematic Semantics)," *European Journal of Philosophy* 12, no. 1 (2004): 1–16.

5. This point is explored in greater detail in Chapter Seven.

6. "Counterfactuals, Dispositions, and the Causal Modalities," in *Minnesota Studies in the Philosophy of Science,* vol. 2, ed. H. Feigl, M. Scriven, and G. Maxwell (Minneapolis: University of Minnesota Press, 1957), sec. 107.

The reason 'grivey' is merely a *label,* that it classifies without informing, is that nothing *follows* from so classifying an object. If I discover that all the boxes in the attic I am charged with cleaning out have been labeled with red, yellow, or green stickers, all I learn is that those labeled with the same color share *some* property. To learn what they *mean* is to learn, for instance, that the owner put a red label on boxes to be discarded, green on those to be retained, and yellow on those that needed further sorting and decision. Once I know what *follows* from affixing one rather than another label, I can understand them not as *mere* labels, but as *descriptions* of the boxes to which they are applied. Description is classification with *consequences,* either immediately practical ("to be discarded/examined/kept") or for further classifications.

Michael Dummett argues generally that to be understood as conceptually contentful, expressions must have not only *circumstances* of appropriate application, but also appropriate *consequences* of application.[7] That is, one must look not only *upstream,* to the circumstances (inferential and non-inferential) in which it is appropriate to apply the expression, but also *downstream* to the consequences (inferential and non-inferential) of doing so, in order to grasp the content it expresses. One-sided theories of meaning, which seize on one aspect to the exclusion of the other, are bound to be defective, for they omit aspects of the use that are essential to meaning. For instance, expressions can have the same circumstances of application and different consequences of application. When they do, they will have different descriptive content.

[1]  I will write a book about Hegel

and

[2]  I foresee that I will write a book about Hegel

---

7. I discuss this view of Dummett's, from his *Frege: Philosophy of Language* (Cambridge, MA: Harvard University Press, 1974), at greater length in Chapter Two of *Making It Explicit* (Cambridge, MA: Harvard University Press, 1994), and Chapter Three of *Articulating Reasons* (Cambridge, MA: Harvard University Press, 2000).

say different things about the world, describe it as being different ways. The first describes my future activity and accomplishment, the second my present aspiration. Yet the circumstances under which it is appropriate or warranted to assert them—the situations to which I ought reliably to respond by endorsing them—are the same (or at least, can be made so by light regimentation of a prediction-expressing use of 'foresee'). Here, to say that they have different descriptive content can be put by saying that they have different truth conditions. (That they have the same assertibility conditions just shows how assertibility theories of meaning, as one-sided in Dummett's sense, go wrong.) But that same fact shows up in the different positions they occupy in the "space of implications." For from the former it follows that I will not be immediately struck by lightning, that I will write some book, and, indeed, that I will write a book about Hegel. None of these is in the same sense a consequence of the second claim.

We might train a parrot reliably to respond differentially to the visible presence of red things by squawking "That's red." It would not yet be *describing* things as red, would not be applying the concept <u>red</u> to them, because the noise it makes has no significance for it. It does not know that it follows from something's being red that it is colored, that it cannot be wholly green, and so on. Ignorant as it is of those inferential consequences, the parrot does not grasp the concept (any more than we express a concept by 'grivey'). The lesson is that even observational concepts, whose principal circumstances of appropriate application are non-inferential (a matter of reliable dispositions to respond differentially to non-linguistic stimuli), must have inferential consequences in order to make possible description, as opposed to the sort of classification effected by non-conceptual labels.

The rationalist idea that the inferential significance of a state or expression is essential to its *conceptual* contentfulness is one of the central insights of Frege's 1879 *Begriffsschrift* ("concept script") and is appealed to by him in the opening paragraphs to define his topic:

> ... there are two ways in which the content of two judgments may differ; it may, or it may not, be the case that all inferences that can be drawn from the first judgment when combined with certain other

ones can always also be drawn from the second when combined with
the same other judgments . . . I call that part of the content that is the
same in both the conceptual content [begrifflicher Inhalt].[8]

Here, then, is the first lesson that analytic philosophy ought to have
taught cognitive science: there is a fundamental metaconceptual distinction between classification in the sense of *labeling* and classification in
the sense of *describing,* and it consists in the *inferential* consequences of
the classification: its capacity to serve as a premise in inferences (practical
or theoretical) to further conclusions. (Indeed, there are descriptive concepts that are purely *theoretical*—such as <u>gene</u> and <u>quark</u>—in the sense
that in addition to their inferential consequences of application, they have
*only* inferential *circumstances* of application.) There is probably no point
in fighting over the minimal circumstances of application of the concepts
<u>concept</u> and <u>conceptual</u>. Those who wish to lower the bar sufficiently are
welcome to consider purely classificatory labels as a kind of concept (perhaps so as not to be beastly to the beasts, or disqualify human infants, bits
of our brains, or even some relatively complex computer programs wholly
from engaging in conceptually articulated activities). But *if* they do so,
they must *not* combine those circumstances of application with the consequences of application appropriate to genuinely *descriptive* concepts—
those that *do* come with inferential significances downstream from their
application.

Notice that this distinction between labeling and describing is un-
touched by two sorts of elaborations of the notion of labeling that have
often been taken to be of great significance in thinking about concepts
from the classical classificatory point of view. One does not cross the
boundary from labeling to describing just because the reliable capacity to
respond differentially is *learned,* and in that sense flexible, rather than *innate,* and in that sense rigid. And one is likewise developing the classical
model in an orthogonal direction insofar as one focuses on the metaca-

---

8. Frege, *Begriffsschrift,* sec. 3. The passage continues: "In my formalized language [Beg-
riffsschrift] . . . only that part of judgments which affects the possible inferences is taken into
consideration. Whatever is needed for a correct inference is fully expressed; what is not
needed is . . . not."

pacity to learn to distinguish arbitrary Boolean combinations of micro-features one can already reliably discriminate. From the point of view of the distinction between labeling and describing, that is not yet the capacity to form *concepts,* but only the mastery of *compound* labels. That sort of structural articulation upstream has no *semantic* import at the level of description until and unless it is accorded a corresponding inferential significance downstream.

**3.**    Once our attention has been directed at the significance of applying a classifying concept—downstream, at the consequences of applying it, rather than just upstream, at the repeatable it discriminates, the grouping it institutes—so that *mere* classification is properly distinguished from *descriptive* classification, the necessity of distinguishing different *kinds* of consequence becomes apparent. One distinction in the vicinity, which has already been mentioned in passing, is that between *practical* and *theoretical* (or, better, *cognitive*) consequences of application of a concept. The significance of classifying an object by responding to it one way rather than another may be to make it appropriate to *do* something else with or to it—to keep it, examine it, or throw it away, to flee or pursue or consume it, for example. This is still a matter of inference; in this case, it is *practical* inferences that are at issue. But an initial classification may also contribute to further classifications: that what is in my hand falls under both the classifications *raspberry* and *red* makes it appropriate to classify it also as *ripe*—which in turn has practical consequences of application (such as, under the right circumstances, "falling to without further ado and eating it up," as Hegel says in another connection) that neither of the other classifications has individually. Important as the distinction between practical and cognitive inferential consequences is, in the present context there is reason to emphasize a different one.

Discursive intentional phenomena (and their associated concepts), such as assertion, inference, judgment, experience, representation, perception, action, endorsement, and imagination, typically involve what Sellars calls "the notorious 'ing'/'ed' ambiguity." For under these headings we may be talking about the *act* of asserting, inferring, judging, experiencing, representing, perceiving, doing, endorsing, and imagining, or we may be talking about the *content* that is asserted, inferred, judged, experienced, represented, perceived, done, endorsed, or imagined. 'Description' is one of these ambiguous terms (as is 'classification'). We ought to be aware of the distinction between the act of describing (or classifying), applying a concept, on the one hand, and the content of the description (classification, concept)—*how* things are described (classified, conceived)—on the other. And the distinction is not merely of theoretical importance for those of us thinking systematically about concept use. A distinctive level of conceptual sophistication is achieved by concept users that themselves distinguish between the contents of their concepts and their activity of applying them. So one thing we might want to know about a system being studied, a non-human animal, a prelinguistic human, an artifact we are building, is whether *it* distinguishes between the *concept* it applies and what it *does* by applying it.

We can see a basic version of the distinction between semantic content and pragmatic force as in play wherever *different* kinds of practical significance can be invested in the *same* descriptive content (different sorts of speech act or mental act performed using that content). Thus, if a creature can not only say or think that the door is shut, but also ask or wonder whether the door is shut, or order or request that it be shut, we can see it as distinguishing in practice between the content being expressed and the pragmatic force being attached to it. In effect, it can use descriptive contents to do more than merely describe. But this sort of practical distinguishing of pragmatic from semantic components matters for the semantic hierarchy I am describing only when it is incorporated or reflected in the *concepts* (that is, the *contents*) a creature can deploy. The capacity to attach different sorts of pragmatic force to the same semantic content is not sufficient for *this* advance in structural semantic complexity. (Whether it is a necessary condition is a question I will not address—though I am inclined to think that in principle the answer is "No.")

For the inferential consequences of applying a classificatory concept, when doing that is describing and not merely labeling, can be either *semantic* consequences, which turn on the *content* of the concept being applied, or *pragmatic* consequences, which turn on the *act* one is performing in applying it. Suppose John issues an observation report: "The traffic light is red." You may infer that it is operating and illuminated, and that traffic ought to stop in the direction it governs. You may also infer that

John has a visually unobstructed line of sight to the light, notices what color it is, and believes that it is red. Unlike the former inferences, these are not inferences from what John *said,* from the *content* of his utterance, from the concepts he has applied. They are inferences from his *saying* it, from the pragmatic force or significance of his *uttering* it, from the fact of his *applying* those concepts. For what he has *said,* that the traffic light is red, could be true even if John had not been in a position to notice it or form any beliefs about it. Nothing about John follows just from the color of the traffic light.[9]

It can be controversial whether a particular consequence follows from how something is described or from describing it that way, that is, whether that consequence is part of the descriptive content of an expression, the concept applied, or stems rather from the force of using the expression, from applying the concept. A famous example is expressivist theories of evaluative terms such as 'good'. In their most extreme form, they claim that these terms have no descriptive content. *All* their consequences stem from what one is doing in using them: commending, endorsing, or approving. In his lapidary article "Ascriptivism,"[10] Peter Geach asks what the rules governing this move are. He offers the archaic term 'macarize', meaning to characterize someone as happy. Should we say that in apparently describing someone as happy we are not really describing anyone, but rather performing the distinctive speech act of macarizing? But why not then discern a distinctive speech act for *any* apparently descriptive term?

What is wanted is a criterion for distinguishing semantic from prag-

---

9. One might think that a similar distinction could be made concerning a parrot that merely reliably responsively discriminated red things by squawking "That's red." For when he does that, one might infer that there was something red there (since he is reliable), and one might also infer that the light was good and his line of sight unobstructed. So both sorts of inference seem possible in this case. But it would be a mistake to describe the situation in these terms. The squawk is a label, not a description. We infer from the parrot's producing it that there is something red, because the two sorts of events are reliably correlated, just as we would from the activation of a photocell tuned to detect the right electromagnetic frequencies. By contrast, John offers *testimony.* What he says is usable as a premise in our own inferences, not just the fact that his saying it is reliably correlated with the situation he (but not the parrot) reports (though they both respond to it).

10. *Philosophical Review* 69, no. 2 (1960): 221–225.

matic consequences, those that stem from the content of the concept being applied from those that stem from what we are doing in applying that
concept (using an expression to perform a speech act). Geach finds one in
Frege, who in turn was developing a point made already by Kant.[11] The
logical tradition Kant inherited was built around the classificatory theory
of consciousness we began by considering. Judgment was understood as
classification or predication: paradigmatically, *of* something particular *as*
something general. But we have put ourselves in a position to ask: is this
intended as a model of how judgeable contents are constructed, or of
what one is doing in judging? Kant saw, as Frege would see after him, that
the phenomenon of *compound* judgments shows that it can*not* play both
roles. For consider the hypothetical or conditional judgment

> [3]   If Frege is correct, then conceptual content
>        depends on inferential consequences.

In asserting this sentence (endorsing its content), have I predicated correctness of Frege (classified him as correct)? Have I described him as correct? Have I applied the concept of correctness? If so, then predicating or
classifying (or describing) is not judging. For in asserting the conditional
I have *not* judged or asserted that Frege is correct. I have at most built up
a judgeable content, the antecedent of the conditional, by predication.
For embedding a declarative descriptive sentence as an unasserted component in a compound asserted sentence strips off the pragmatic force its
freestanding, unembedded occurrence would otherwise have had. It now
contributes *only* its *content* to the *content* of the compound sentence, to
which alone the pragmatic force of a speech act is attached.[12]

This means that embedding simpler sentences as components of compound sentences—paradigmatically, embedding them as antecedents of
conditionals—is the way to discriminate consequences that derive from
the *content* of a sentence from consequences that derive from the *act* of
asserting or endorsing it. We can tell that 'happy' *does* express descriptive

---

11. I discuss this point further in Chapter One.
12. This point is further expounded and exploited in Chapter One.

content, and is *not* simply an indicator that some utterance has the pragmatic force or significance of macarizing, because we *can* say things like

[4]   If she is happy, then John should be glad.

For in asserting that, one does *not* macarize anyone. So the consequence, that John should be glad, must be due to the descriptive content of the antecedent, not to its force.

Similarly, Geach argues that the fact that we can say things like

[5]   If being trustworthy is good, then you have reason to be trustworthy

shows that 'good' *does* have descriptive content.[13] Notice that this same test appropriately discriminates the different descriptive contents of the claims

[6]   Labeling is not describing

and

[7]   I believe that labeling is not describing.

For the two do not behave the same way as antecedents of conditionals. The stuttering inference

[8]   If labeling is not describing, then labeling is not describing

is as solid an inference as one could ask for. The corresponding conditional,

[9]   If I believe that labeling is not describing, then labeling is not describing,

13. Of course, contemporary expressivists such as Gibbard and Blackburn (who are distinguished from emotivist predecessors such as C. L. Stevenson precisely by their appreciation of the force of the Frege-Geach argument) argue that it need not follow that the right way to understand that descriptive content is not by tracing it back to the attitudes of endorsement or approval that *are* expressed by the use of the expression in freestanding, unembedded assertions.

requires a good deal more faith to endorse. And in the same way, the embedding test distinguishes [1] and [2] above. In each case it tells us, properly, that different descriptive contents are involved.

What all this means is that any user of descriptive concepts who can also form compound sentences, paradigmatically conditionals, is in a position to distinguish what pertains to the semantic *content* of those descriptive concepts from what pertains to the *act* or pragmatic *force* of describing by applying those concepts. This capacity is a new, higher, more sophisticated level of concept use. It can be achieved *only* by looking at compound sentences in which other descriptive sentences can occur as unasserted components. For instance, it is only in such a context that one can distinguish *denial* (a kind of speech act or attitude) from *negation* (a kind of content). One who asserts [6] has *both* denied that labeling is describing *and* negated a description. But one who asserts conditionals such as [8] and [9] has negated descriptions, but has *not* denied anything.

The modern philosophical tradition up to Frege took it for granted that there was a special attitude one could adopt toward a descriptive conceptual content, a kind of minimal force one could invest it with, that must be possible independently of and antecedently to being able to endorse that content in a judgment. This is the attitude of merely *entertaining* the description. The picture (for instance, in Descartes) was that *first* one entertained a descriptive thought (judgeable), and *then*, by an in-principle subsequent act of will, accepted or rejected it. Frege rejects this picture. The principal—and in principle fundamental—pragmatic attitude (and hence speech act) is judging or endorsing.[14] The capacity merely to entertain a proposition (judgeable content, description) is a latecoming capacity—one that is parasitic on the capacity to endorse such contents. In fact, for Frege, the capacity to entertain (without endorsement) the proposition that $p$ is just the capacity to endorse *conditionals* in which that proposition occurs as antecedent or consequent. For that is to explore its descriptive content, its inferential circumstances and consequences of application, what it follows from and what follows from it, what would make it true and what would be true if it were true, without

---

14. In Chapter One I discuss the line of thought that led Kant to give pride of place to judgment and judging.

endorsing it. This is a new kind of distanced attitude toward one's concepts and their contents—one that becomes possible only in virtue of the capacity to form compound sentences of the kind of which conditionals are the paradigm. It is a new level of cognitive achievement—not in the sense of a new kind of empirical knowledge (though conditionals can indeed codify new empirical discoveries), but of a new kind of semantic self-consciousness.

Conditionals make possible a new sort of hypothetical thought. (Supposing that postulating a distinct attitude of supposing would enable one to do *this* work, the work of conditionals, would be making the same mistake as thinking that denial can do the work of negation.) Descriptive concepts bring empirical properties into view. Embedding those concepts in conditionals brings the contents of those concepts into view. Creatures that can do that are functioning at a higher cognitive and conceptual level than those who can only apply descriptive concepts, just as those who can do that are functioning at a higher cognitive and conceptual level than those who can only classify things by reliable responsive discrimination (that is, labeling). That fact sets a question for the different branches of cognitive science I mentioned in my introduction. Can chimps, or African gray parrots, or other non-human animals, not just use concepts to describe things, but also semantically discriminate the contents of those concepts from the force of applying them, by using them not just in describing, but in conditionals, in which their contents are merely entertained and explored? At what age, and along with what other capacities, do human children learn to do so? What is required for a computer to demonstrate this level of cognitive functioning?

*Conditionals* are special, because they make *inferences* explicit—that is, put them into endorsable, judgeable, assertible, which is to say propositional form. And it is their role in inferences, we saw, that distinguishes descriptive concepts from mere classifying labels. But conditionals are an instance of a more general phenomenon. For we can think of them as operators, which apply to sentences to yield further sentences. As such, they bring into view a new notion of conceptual content: a new principle of assimilation, hence classification, of such contents. For we begin with the idea of sameness of content that derives from sameness of pragmatic force, attitude, or speech act. But the Frege-Geach argument shows that we can also individuate conceptual contents more finely, not just in terms of their role in freestanding utterances, but also accordingly as substituting one for another as arguments of operators (paradigmatically the conditional) does or does not yield compound sentences with the same freestanding pragmatic significance or force. Dummett calls these notions "freestanding" and "ingredient" content (or sense), respectively. Thus we might think that

[10]    It is nice here

and

[11]    It is nice where I am

express the same attitude, perform the same speech act, have the same pragmatic force or significance. They have not only the same circumstances of application, but the same consequences of application (and hence role as antecedents of conditionals). But we can see that they have different *ingredient* contents by seeing that they behave differently as arguments when we apply another operator to them. To use an example of Dummett's,

[12]    It is *always* nice here

and

[13]    It is *always* nice where I am

have very different circumstances and consequences of application, different pragmatic significances, and *do* behave differently as the antecedents of conditionals. But this difference in content, this sense of "different content" in which they patently do have different contents, is one that shows up *only* in the context of compounding operators, which apply to sentences and yield further sentences. The capacity to deploy such operators to form new conceptual (descriptive) contents from old ones accordingly ushers in a new level of cognitive and conceptual functioning.

Creatures that can not merely label but describe are *rational,* in the minimal sense that they are able to treat one classification as providing a *reason* for or against another. If they can use conditionals, they can distinguish inferences that depend on the *content* of the concept they are applying from those that depend on what they are *doing* in classifying something as falling under that concept. But the capacity to use conditionals gives them more than just that ability. For conditionals let them *say* what is a reason for what, say *that* an inference is a good one. And for anyone who can do that, the capacity not just to *deny* that a classification is appropriate, but to use a *negation* operator to form new classificatory contents brings with it the capacity to say that two classifications (classifiers, concepts) are incompatible: that one provides a reason to withhold the other. Creatures that can use this sort of sentential compounding operator are not just *rational,* but *logical* creatures. They are capable of a distinctive kind of *conceptual self-consciousness.* For they can describe the rational relations that make their classifications into descriptions in the first place, hence be conscious or aware of them in the sense in which descriptive concepts allow them to be aware of empirical features of their world.

4.     There is still a higher level of structural complexity of concepts and concept use. I have claimed that Frege should be credited with appreciating both of the points I have made so far: that descriptive conceptual classification beyond mere discriminative labeling depends on the inferential significance of the concepts, and that semantically distinguishing the inferential significance of the contents of concepts from that of the force of applying them depends on forming sentential compounds (paradigmatically conditionals) in which other sentences appear as components. In each of these insights Frege had predecessors. Leibniz (in his *New Essays on Human Understanding*) had already argued the first point, against Locke. (The move from thinking of concepts exclusively as reliably differentially elicited labels to thinking of them as having to stand in the sort of inferential relations to one another necessary for them to have genuine descriptive content is characteristic of the advance from empiricism to rationalism.) And Kant, we have seen, appreciated how attention to

compound sentences (including "hypotheticals") requires substantially amending the traditional classificatory theory of conceptual consciousness. The final distinction I will discuss, that between *simple* and *complex* predicates, and the corresponding kinds of concepts they express, is Frege's alone. No one before him (and embarrassingly few even of his admirers after him) grasped this idea.

Frege's most famous achievement is transforming traditional logic by giving us a systematic way to express and control the inferential roles of *quantificationally complex* sentences. Frege could, as the whole logical tradition from Aristotle down to his time (fixated as it was on syllogisms) could not, handle iterated quantifiers. So he could, for instance, explain why

[14]    If someone is loved by everyone, then everyone loves someone

is true (a conditional that codifies a correct inference), but

[15]    If everyone loves someone, then someone is loved by everyone

is not. What is less appreciated is that in order to specify the inferences involving arbitrarily nested quantifiers ('some' and 'every'), he needed to introduce a new kind of predicate, and hence discern a structurally new kind of *concept*.

Our first grip on the notion of a *predicate* is as a *component* of sentences. In artificial languages we combine, for instance, a two-place predicate '*P*' with two individual constants '*a*' and '*b*' to form the sentence '*Pab*'. Logically minded philosophers of language use this model to think about the corresponding sentences of natural languages, understanding

[16]    Kant admired Rousseau

as formed by applying the two-place predicate 'admired' to the singular terms 'Kant' and 'Rousseau'. The kind of inferences that are made explicit by *quantified conditionals,* though—inferences that essentially depend on the contents of the predicates involved—require us also to distinguish a one-place predicate, related to but distinct from this two-place one, that is exhibited by

[17]  Rousseau admired Rousseau

and

[18]  Kant admired Kant

but *not* by [16].

[19]  Someone admired himself,

that is, something of the form $\exists x[Pxx]$, follows from [17] and [18], but not from [16]. The property of **being a self-admirer** differs from that of **being an admirer** and from that of **being admired** (even though it entails both).

But there is no *part* of the sentences [17] and [18] that they share with each other that they do *not* share also with [16]. Looking just at the subsentential expressions out of which the sentences are built does not reveal the respect of similarity that distinguishes self-admiration from admiration in general—a respect of similarity that is crucial to understanding why the conditional

[20]  If someone admires himself then someone admires someone, $(\exists x[Pxx] \rightarrow \exists x \exists y[Pxy])$, expresses a good inference,

while

[21]  If someone admires someone then someone admires himself, $(\exists x \exists y[Pxy] \rightarrow \exists x[Pxx])$, does not.

For what [17] and [18] share that distinguishes them from [16] is not a *component,* but a *pattern.* More specifically, it is a pattern of cross-identification of the singular terms that two-place predicate applies to.

The repeatable expression-kind 'admires' is a *simple* predicate. It occurs as a component in sentences built up by concatenating it appropriately with a pair of singular terms. '*X* admires *X*' is a *complex* predicate.[15] A number of different complex predicates are associated with any multi-place simple predicate. So the three-place simple predicate used to form the sentence

[22]   John enjoys music recorded by Mark and books recommended by Bob

generates not only a three-place complex predicate of the form *Rxyz*, but also two-place complex predicates of the forms *Rxxy, Rxyy,* and *Rxyx,* as well as the one-place complex predicate *Rxxx.* The complex predicates can be thought of as patterns that can be exhibited by sentences formed using the simple predicate, or as equivalence classes of such sentences. Thus the complex self-admiration predicate can be thought of either as the *pattern,* rather than the *part,* that is common to all the sentences {"Rousseau admired Rousseau," "Kant admired Kant," "Caesar admired Caesar," "Brutus admired Brutus," "Napoleon admired Napoleon" . . .}, or just as that set itself. Any member of such an equivalence class of sentences sharing a complex predicate can be turned into any other by a sequence of *substitutions* of all occurrences of one singular term by occurrences of another.

Substitution is a kind of *decomposition* of sentences (including compound ones formed using sentential operators such as conditionals). After sentences have been built up using simple components (singular terms, simple predicates, sentential operators), they can be assembled into equivalence classes (patterns can be discerned among them) by regarding some of the elements as systematically replaceable by others. This is the same procedure of noting invariance under substitution that we saw applies to the notion of *freestanding content* to give rise to that of *ingredient content,* when the operators apply only to whole sentences. Frege called what is invariant under substitution of some sentential components for others a '*function*'. A function can be applied to some arguments to yield a value, but it is not a *part* of the value it yields. (One can

---

15. This point, and the terminology of 'simple' and 'complex' predicates, is due to Dummett, in the second chapter of his monumental *Frege: Philosophy of Language.*

apply the function *capital of* to Sweden to yield the value Stockholm, but neither Sweden nor *capital of* is part of Stockholm.) He tied himself in some metaphysical knots trying to find a clear way of contrasting functions with *things* (objects). But two points emerge clearly. First, discerning the substitutional relations among different sentences sharing the same simple predicate is crucial for characterizing a wide range of inferential patterns. Second, those inferential patterns articulate the contents of a whole new class of concepts.

Sentential compounding already provided the means to build new simple concepts out of old ones. The Boolean connectives—conjunction, disjunction, negation, and the conditional definable in terms of them $(A{\rightarrow}B$ if and only if $\sim(A\&\sim B))$—permit the combination of simple predicates in all the ways representable by Venn diagrams, corresponding to the intersection, union, complementation, and inclusion of sets (concept extensions, represented by regions), and so the expression of new concepts formed from old ones by these operations. But there is a crucial class of new analytically *complex* concepts formable from the old ones that are *not* generable by such compounding procedures. One cannot, for instance, form the concept of a $C$ such that for every $A$ there is a $B$ that stands to that $C$ in the relation $R$. This is the complex one-place predicate logicians would represent as having the form $\{x{:}\ Cx\ \&\ \forall y{\in}A\exists z{\in}B[Rxz]\}$. As Frege says, such a concept cannot, as the Boolean ones can, be formed simply by putting together pieces of the boundaries of the concepts $A$, $B$, and $C$. The correlations of elements of these sets that concepts like these, those expressed by complex predicates, depend on, and so the inferences they are involved in, cannot be represented in Venn diagrams.

Frege showed further that it is just concepts like these that even the simplest mathematics works with. The concept of a <u>natural number</u> is the concept of a set every element of which has a successor. That is, for every number, there is another related to it as a successor $(\forall x\exists y[\text{Successor}(x,y)])$. The decisive advance that Frege's new quantificational logic made over traditional logic is a *semantic, expressive* advance. His logical notation can, as the traditional logic could not, form *complex* predicates, and so both express a vitally important kind of concept and logically codify the inferences that articulate its descriptive content.

Complex concepts can be thought of as formed by a four-stage process.

- First, put together simple predicates and singular terms, to form a set of sentences, say {*Rab, Sbc, Tacd*}.
- Then apply sentential operators to form compound sentences, say {*Rab→Sbc, Sbc&Tacd*}.
- Then substitute variables for some of the singular terms (individual constants), to form complex predicates, say {*Rax→Sxy, Sxy&Tayz*}.
- Finally, apply quantifiers to bind some of these variables, to form new complex predicates, for instance the one-place predicates (in *y* and *z*) {∃*x*[*Rax→Sxy*], ∀*x*∃*y*[*Sxy&Tayz*]}.

If one likes, this process can now be repeated, with the complex predicates just formed playing the role that simple predicates originally played at the first stage, yielding the new sentences {∃*x*[*Rax→Sxd*], ∀*x*∃*y*[*Sxy&Taya*]}. They can then be conjoined, and the individual constant *a* substituted for to yield the further one-place complex predicate (in *z*) ∃*x*[*Rzx→Sxd*]&∀*x*∃*y*[*Sxy&Tzyz*]. We can use these procedures to build to the sky, repeating these stages of concept construction as often as we like. Frege's rules tell us how to compute the inferential roles of the concepts formed at each stage, on the basis of the inferential roles of the raw materials, and the operations applied at that stage. This is the heaven of complex concept formation he opened up for us.

**5.** The result of all these considerations, which have been in play since the dawn of analytic philosophy, well over a century ago, is a four-stage *semantic* hierarchy of ever more demanding senses of 'concept' and 'concept use'. At the bottom are concepts as reliably differentially applied, possibly learned, *labels* or classifications. Crudely behaviorist psychological theories (such as B. F. Skinner's) attempted to do all their explanatory work with responsive discriminations of this sort. At the next level, concepts as *descriptions* emerge when merely classifying concepts come to stand in *inferential, evidential, justificatory* relations to one another—

when the propriety of one sort of classification has the practical signifi-cance of making others appropriate or inappropriate, in the sense of serv-ing as *reasons* for and against them. Concepts of this sort may still all have observational uses, even though they are distinguished from labels by also having inferential ones.[16] Already at this level, the possibility exists of em-pirical descriptive concepts that can *only* be properly applied as the result of inferences from the applicability of others. These are *theoretical* con-cepts: a particularly sophisticated species of the genus of descriptive con-cepts.

At this second level, conceptual content first takes a distinctive *propo-sitional* form; applications of this sort of concept are accordingly appro-priately expressed using *declarative sentences.* For the propositional contents such sentences express just are whatever can play the role of premise and conclusion in *inferences.* And it is precisely being able to play those roles that distinguishes applications of descriptive concepts from applications of merely classificatory ones. Building on the capacity to use inferentially articulated descriptive concepts to make proposition-ally contentful judgments or claims, the capacity to form sentential *com-pounds*—paradigmatically *conditionals,* which make endorsements of material inferences relating descriptive concept applications proposition-ally explicit, and *negations,* which make endorsements of material incom-patibilities relating descriptive concept applications propositionally ex-plicit—brings with it the capacity to deploy a further, more sophisticated kind of conceptual content: *ingredient* (as opposed to freestanding) con-tent. Conceptual content of this sort is to be understood in terms of the contribution it makes to the content of *compound* judgments in which it occurs, and only thereby, indirectly, to the force or pragmatic significance of endorsing that content.

Ingredient conceptual content, then, is what can be *negated,* or *condi-tionalized.* The distinctive sort of definiteness and determinateness char-acteristic of this sort of conceptual content becomes vivid when it is con-

---

16. A key part of the higher *inferential* grade of conceptuality (which includes the former, but transforms it) is that it is *multi-premise material* inferences that one learns to draw as con-clusions (=responses) now to Boolean combinations of the relatively enduring states that re-sult from one's own responses.

trasted with contents that cannot appear in such sentential compounds, such as that expressed by pictures. My young son once complained about a park sign consisting of the silhouette of what looked like a Scottish terrier, surrounded by a red circle, with a slash through it. Familiar with the force of prohibition associated with signs of this general form, he wanted to know: "Does this mean 'No Scotties allowed'? Or 'No dogs allowed'? Or 'No animals allowed'? Or 'No pets allowed'?" Indeed. With pictures one has no way of indicating the degree of generality intended. A creature that can understand a claim like "If the red light is on, then there is a biscuit in the drawer" without disagreeing when the light is not on and no biscuit is present, or immediately looking for the biscuit regardless of how it is with the light, has learned to distinguish between the content of descriptive concepts and the force of applying them, and as a result can entertain and explore those concepts and their connections with each other without necessarily applying them in the sense of endorsing their applicability to anything present. The capacity in this way to free oneself from the bonds of the here-and-now is a distinctive kind of conceptual achievement

The first step was from merely *discriminating* classification to *rational* classification ('rational' because inferentially articulated, according to which classifications provide reasons for others). The second step is to *synthetic logical* concept formation, in which concepts are formed by logical compounding operators, paradigmatically conditionals and negation. The final step is to *analytical* concept formation, in which the sentential compounds formed at the third stage are *decomposed* by noting invariants under substitution. This is actually the same method that gave us the notion of *ingredient content* at the third stage of concept formation. For that metaconcept arises when we realize that two sentences that have the same pragmatic potential as freestanding, force-bearing rational classifications can nonetheless make different contributions to the content (and hence the force) of compound sentences in which they occur as unendorsed components—that is, when we notice that substituting one for the other may change the freestanding significance of asserting the compound sentence containing them. To form *complex* concepts, we must apply the same methodology to sub-sentential expressions, paradigmatically singular terms, that have multiple occurrences in those same logically *compound* sentences. Systematically assimilating sentences into various equivalence classes accordingly as they can be regarded as substitutional variants of one another is a distinctive kind of *analysis* of those compound sentences, as involving the application of concepts that were not *components* out of which they were originally constructed. Concepts formed by this sort of analysis are substantially and in principle more expressively powerful than those available at earlier stages in the hierarchy of conceptual complexity. (They are, for instance, indispensable for even the simplest mathematics.)

This hierarchy is not a *psychological* one, but a *logical* and *semantic* one. Concepts at the higher levels of complexity presuppose those at lower levels, not because creatures of a certain kind cannot in practice, as a matter of fact, deploy the more complex kinds unless they can deploy the simpler ones, but because in principle it is structurally impossible to do so. Nothing could count as grasping or deploying the kinds of concepts that populate the upper reaches of the hierarchy without also grasping or deploying those drawn from its lower levels. The dependencies involved are not empirical, but (meta)conceptual and normative. The Fregean considerations that enforce the distinctions between and sequential arrangement of concept-kinds do not arise from studying how concept users actually work, but from investigation of what concept use fundamentally is. They concern not how the trick (of concept use) is done, but what could in principle count as doing it—a normative rather than an empirical issue. That is why it is philosophers who first came across this semantic hierarchical metaconceptual structure of concept-kinds.

But cognitive scientists need to know about it. For it is part of the job of the disciplines that cognitive science comprises to examine—each from its own distinctive point of view—all four grades of conceptual activity: the use of more complex and sophisticated kinds of concepts, no less than that of the simpler and less articulated sorts. The move from merely classificatory to genuinely descriptive concepts, for instance, marks a giant step forward in the phylogenetic development of sapience. I do not think we yet know what non-human creatures are capable of taking that step. Human children clearly do cross that boundary, but when, by what means, at what age or stage of development? Can non-human primates learn to use conditionals? Has anyone ever tried to teach them? The only reason to focus on that capacity, out of all the many linguistic constructions one might investigate empirically in this regard, is an appreciation of the kind of semantic self-consciousness about the rational relations among classifications (which marks the move from classification to rational description) that they make possible. Computer scientists have, to be sure, expended some significant effort in thinking about varieties of possible implementation of sentential compounding—for instance in exploring what connectionist or parallel distributed processing systems can do. But they have not in the same way appreciated the significance of the question of whether, to what extent, and how such "vehicleless" representational architectures can capture the full range of concepts expressed by complex predicates. (Those systems' lack of syntactically compositional explicit symbolic representations prohibits the standard way of expressing these concepts, for that way proceeds precisely by substitutional *de*composition of such explicit symbolic representations.) These are merely examples of potentially important questions raised by the hierarchy of conceptual complexity that cognitive scientists have by and large not been moved so much as to ask.

Why not? I think it is pretty clear that the answer is *ignorance*. Specifically, it is ignorance of the considerations, put forward already by Frege, that draw the bright semantic metaconceptual lines between different grades of concepts, and arrange them in a strict presuppositional semantic hierarchy. Any adequately trained cognitive scientist—even those working in disciplines far removed from computational linguistics—can be presumed to have at least passing familiarity with the similarly four-membered Chomsky hierarchy that lines up kinds of grammar, automaton, and *syntactic* complexity of languages in an array from most basic (finite state automata computing regular languages specifiable by the simplest sort of grammatical rules) to most sophisticated (two-stack pushdown automata computing recursively enumerable languages specifiable by unrestricted grammatical rules). But the at least equally significant *semantic* distinctions I have been retailing have not similarly become a part of the common wisdom and theoretical toolbox of cognitive science—even though they have been available for a half-century longer.

The cost of that ignorance, in questions not asked, theoretical constraints not appreciated, promising avenues of empirical research not pursued, is great. Failure to appreciate the distinctions and relations among fundamentally different kinds of concepts has led, I think, to a standing tendency systematically to overestimate the extent to which one has constructed (in AI) or discerned in development (whether by human children or by non-human primates) or reverse-engineered (in psychology) what *we* users of the fanciest sorts of concepts do. That underlying ignorance is culpable. But it is not the cognitive scientists themselves who are culpable for their ignorance. The ideas in question are those that originally launched the whole enterprise of analytic philosophy. I think it is fair to say that as we philosophers have explored these ideas, we have gotten clearer about them in many respects. For one reason or another, though, we have not shared the insights we have achieved. We are guilty of having kept this treasure trove to ourselves. It is high time to be more generous in sharing these ideas.

Name Index

Subject Index

# Name Index

# Subject Index